NORTH KOREA

NORTH KOREA
ANOTHER COUNTRY

BRUCE CUMINGS

THE NEW PRESS

NEW YORK
LONDON

Published in the United States by The New Press, New York, 2003
Distributed by W. W. Norton & Company, Inc., New York

ISBN 1–56584–873–X (hc.)
ISBN 1–56584–940–X (pbk.)
CIP data available

The New Press was established in 1990 as a not-for-profit alternative to the
large, commercial publishing houses currently dominating the book publishing
industry. The New Press operates in the public interest rather than for private
gain, and is committed to publishing, in innovative ways, works of educational,
cultural, and community value that are often deemed insufficiently profitable.

The New Press
38 Greene Street, 4th floor
New York, NY 10013
www.thenewpress.com

In the United Kingdom:
6 Salem Road
London W2 4BU

Composition by Westchester Book Group

Printed in the United States of America

2 4 6 8 10 9 7 5 3 1

CONTENTS

	Preface	viii
	Acknowledgments	xiv
1	War Is a Stern Teacher	1
2	The Nuclear Crisis: First Act and Sequel	43
3	The Legend of Kim Il Sung	103
4	Daily Life in North Korea	128
5	The World's First Postmodern Dictator	155
6	Beyond Good and Evil	177
	Recommended Reading	208
	Notes	210

Vivaldo dreamed that he was running, running, running, through a country he had always known, but could not now remember, a rocky country. . . . He was both fleeing and seeking, and, in his dream, the time was running out. There was a high wall ahead of him, a high, stone wall . . . as he ran or as he was propelled, he was weighed down and made sick by the certainty that he had forgotten—forgotten— what? some secret, some duty, that would save him. . . . And now he knew that his enemy was upon him. Salt burned his eyes. He dared not turn; in terror he pressed himself against the rough, wet wall, as though a wall could melt or could be entered. He had forgotten—what? how to escape or how to defeat his enemy.

James Baldwin, *Another Country*

PREFACE

JUDGING FROM OUR media, North Korea is the country every American loves to hate—beginning with President George W. Bush, who made it a charter member of his "axis of evil" and hoped to "topple" it. CNN never fails to introduce a story on the North using film clips of soldiers goose-stepping through Pyongyang.¹ It is led by Kim Jong Il, diagnosed by the well-known expert Greta van Sustern to be "insane or diabolical." The Central Intelligence Agency (CIA) says it possesses one or two nuclear weapons, along with chemical and biological "weapons of mass destruction" (WMD) and long-range missiles capable of delivering anything from atomic bombs to the smallpox virus along the American West Coast. "What we don't know is even worse," or so we are told. A mimetic American commentary unites diverse opinion on one point: this place is a rogue-terrorist-communist-Stalinist-totalitarian-Oriental nightmare, America's most loathed and feared "Other." The real mark of our continuous crises with the North, however, is the deafening absence of any contrary argument; the one remaining self-proclaimed top-to-bottom alternative to neoliberalism and globalization is anathema to everyone, progressives as well. Americans wish Kim Jong Il's socialism-in-one-family would just go away, the sooner the better.

North Korea has been around for a long time, however, and contrary to media punditry, we know a lot about it—and so does our government. An internal CIA study² almost grudgingly acknowledged various achievements of this regime: compassionate care for children in general and war orphans in particular; "radical change" in the position of women; genuinely free housing, free health care, and preventive medicine; and infant mortality and life expectancy rates comparable to the most advanced countries until the recent famine. A number of other recent books, based on captured North Korean documents or secret materials from the former Soviet Union and China, make this a knowable country, as fascinating as it is repellent, as formidable as it is unique and idiosyncratic.

North Korea does not exist alone, in a vacuum, even if the regime's inveterate solipsism would make you think otherwise. It cannot be understood apart from a terrible fratricidal war that has never ended, the guerrilla struggle against Japanese imperialism in the 1930s, its initial emergence as a state in 1945, its fraught relationship with the South, its brittle and defensive reaction to the end of the Cold War and the collapse of the Soviet Union, and its interminable daily struggle with the United States of America. On September 8, 1945, U.S. combat troops first occupied Korea; three months later the commander of the Occupation, Gen. John Reed Hodge, "declared war" on the communist party (the one in the southern zone), and in the spring of 1946, he issued his first warning to Washington of an impending North Korean invasion. If our postwar occupation of Iraq follows Korea's pattern, the country will be divided (probably into three parts, not two), five years later a civil war will erupt and millions will die but nothing will be solved, and in the 2060s, nearly 40,000 American troops will still be there, holding the line against the evil enemy (whoever he might be), with a new war possible at any moment. We have been locked in a dangerous, unending, but ultimately futile and failed embrace with North Korea since Dean Rusk consulted a map around midnight on the day after we obliterated Nagasaki with an atomic bomb, and etched a border no one had ever noticed before at the 38th parallel.

In our time, more than a decade of dangerous cat-and-mouse diplomacy has now passed between the United States and North Korea, with Pyongyang playing the hole card of its nuclear program and its missiles, and successive American presidents stumbling about to react and respond. In the new century the North doesn't want the United States out of Korea, in spite of regime propaganda, but wants us to stay involved, to deal with a new and threatening strategic environment since the collapse of the Soviet Union (which abruptly abandoned the North in 1991[3]), to help the country through its current difficult transition, and to keep the South from swallowing it. Sooner or later an American president will come to understand this, the crisis will end, embassies will be exchanged, and Americans will begin to enjoy touring this beautiful Hermit Kingdom and meeting its unknown but warm, proud, and dignified people.

In this slim volume I have tried to write for the reader who wishes to learn about our eternal Korean enemy. The experience of recent years, however, makes me wonder if Americans can ever transcend their own experience and join a world of profound difference. When all your truths are self-evident and when the fondest hope of foreigners from Azerbaijan to Zimbabwe is to become a citizen of your country, it is difficult to understand that not everyone in the world wants to be an American. Our history is one of launching out on missions to transform the world—in the contemporary case, "to rid the world of evil"—followed by inevitably chastened returns to a continental homeland that is fundamentally sufficient unto itself. The commanding interpretation of this back-and-forth phenomenon is Louis Hartz's classic, *The Liberal Tradition in America*. At the end of the book he hoped—it was only a hope—that Americans would find that "spark of philosophy" enabling them to live comfortably with a world very different from American imaginings.

My interest in North Korea succeeded my long involvement with South Korea, which I first got to know in the Peace Corps many moons ago. I have no sympathy for the North, which is the author of most of its own troubles, specializes in self-defeating behavior, treats like children the masses of its own population unlucky enough to be excluded from the elite, and indulges in such stereotypical hero worship, grandiose exaggeration, and wretched excess as to make even a scholar of East Asia reach for dusty old tomes with titles like "Oriental Despotism." But on my infrequent visits to the country, I have been happy—in trying to fathom an undeniable difference, in getting to know ordinary people who say and do the same things ordinary people do in the South, in meeting highly skilled officials who have taken the measure of our leaders more than once, and in not hearing my Calvinist conscience tell me it's all my fault. *It is their country*, for better or worse—another country. I don't feel a responsibility for what goes on there, except perhaps the significant responsibility that all Americans share for the garrison state that emerged on the ashes of our truly terrible destruction of the North half a century ago (it is our fault?).

New work by excellent younger scholars has enabled me to go beyond my previous publications that have dealt with the North. Indeed, so much new work and new information has spilled out that I cannot avoid citing it, in succinct footnotes that also refer to a short list of suggestions for further reading. One of the virtues of getting older is being around a long time, as Yogi Berra might say, and so it is the rare book on North Korea that has escaped my attention. The ones I list at the end are, in my opinion, reliable and grounded studies, most of them quite recent. A growing periodical literature on the North has also appeared in mainstream publications such as *The New Yorker, The New York*

Review of Books, and *Vanity Fair,* and magazines such as *Newsweek, Time, The Economist,* and *U.S. News and World Report.* With the occasional exception, most of it is uninformative, unreliable, often sensationalized, and generally fails to educate instead of deceive the public. Given the mimetic nature of our media, the same stories circulate endlessly; often they are contemporary variations on the same old tales that have been around since North Korea became our enemy sixty years ago: they're about to attack the South, their leader is nuts, their people are brainwashed, the regime will implode or explode. Literally for half a century, the South Korean intelligence services have bamboozled one American reporter after another by parading their defectors (real and fake), grinding the Pyongyang rumor mill, or parlaying fibs that even a moment's investigation in a good library would expose.

The canard I liked best was Kim Il Sung's brain tumor, because you could see it right there on the back of his neck, a round boil that began as a golf ball and mestasticized to a baseball, eating away at the very gray matter designated by North Korean scribes as "the supreme brain of the nation." Thirty years ago amusement parks in Seoul would have Kim Il Sung stick figures to throw baseballs at, with the biggest prize given for hitting the boil; cartoonists liked to draw flies buzzing around it. One year he was in Bucharest for brain surgery, the next he was in Budapest for radiation treatment, but alas, nothing could stop the tumor from eating away at his demented mind. This boil was a calcium deposit that Koreans call a *hok,* usually the result of childhood malnutrition. It wasn't very becoming to the Great Leader, so North Korean photographers always shot him from the left, while communist photographers elsewhere enjoyed taking a bead on it on it from the right. Kim Il Sung died of natural causes at the age of 82.[4]

If sympathy is impossible to extend to the North, how about empathy? Probably not, most readers may say; they don't deserve it. Perhaps they're right. But empathy for the underdog is something I can't help, being a lifelong fan of the Cleveland Indians. In *Dispatches*, Michael Herr has Victor Charlie up there in the mountains, strapped to his artillery gun as he fires off his shots, then disappearing back deep into the cave, the gun mounted on rails; the beleaguered Americans at Khe San call in airpower, artillery, napalm; they try to jam a few thousand tons of ordnance down the mouth of that cave. Then they wait, and wait, and finally Victor Charlie roars up to the demolished aperture and fires off his last shot—and the Marines shout and applaud. That's what I feel when the North Koreans refuse to collapse and go away, and tell us where to get off for the umpteenth time: we may not need it, but we do deserve it.

In human rights circles, the easiest thing has always been to look one way and condemn the communists, while ignoring the reprehensible behavior of our allies, that is, U.S. support for dictators who make Kim Jong Il look enlightened (the Saudis, for example). It is much harder to weigh a diverse and complicated world that will ultimately never respond to our ministrations and be what we want it to be, and learn instead to live in it—and with it—nevertheless.

ACKNOWLEDGMENTS

Andre Schiffrin first suggested this book to me and I thank him for that, and for his superb editorial guidance. Jonathan Shainin of the New Press offered friendly direction and expertise. Andrew Hudak and his colleagues at Westchester Book Services provided excellent copy-editing. Prof. Jun Yoo of the University of Hawaii gave me help with sources, and Dr. Balazs Szalontai was a rich source of new information on the Democratic People's Republic of Korea (DPRK). Prof. Andrei Lankov was kind enough to send me his new book just as I began writing. Former students of mine, Prof. Michael Shin of Cornell and Prof. Charles Armstrong of Columbia, and a current doctoral student, Suzy Kim, have taught me much about North Korea. In 2002–2003 Selig Harrison and I co-organized a Task Force on U.S. Korea Policy, involving many scholars and former government officials. I learned much from our discussions, and thank all of the participants. I would like to thank *The Nation, The Bulletin of Atomic Scientists, Current History,* and *Le Monde Diplomatique* for publishing articles of mine on North Korea over the past decade, some of which I draw upon in this book. Meredith Woo-Cumings made it possible for me to work long hours at the keyboard during an academic year that was very busy for both of us; our sons, Ian and Ben, always make both of our lives full and rich. All mistakes and errors, of course, are my responsibility.

I would like to dedicate this book to a lasting peace between Americans and the people of both Koreas.

Chapter One

WAR IS A STERN TEACHER

War is a stern teacher. So revolutions broke out in city after city. . . . What used to be described as a thoughtless act of aggression was now regarded as the courage one would expect to find in a party member; to think of the future and wait was merely another way of saying one was a coward; any idea of moderation was just an attempt to disguise one's unmanly character.

Thucydides, *History of the Peloponnesian War*

IN A CLASSIC article in 1941, Harold Lasswell defined "the Garrison State" as one in which "the specialists on violence are the most powerful group in society." North Korea has perfected Lasswell's idea: it is, above all else, the most astounding garrison state in the world. The DPRK Constitution calls for "arming all the populace [and] turning the entire country into a fortress." In a citizenry of 23 million, one million are in the military, six million in the reserves, and almost all adult men and women have had significant military experience. The CIA estimated in 1978 that 12 percent of males between 17 and 49 are in the regular armed service, "a level exceeded only by Israel,"[1] but the percentage of the population in the armed forces steadily increased from 1980 into the 1990s, moving from about 30 per 1,000 people (where it had been for much of the 1960s and 1970s) to 48 per 1,000 in 1991. Annual defense expenditures, however, moved up only incrementally in the 1980s, from about $1.3 billion in 1981 to $2 billion in 1990.[2] Military service is a compulsory eight years

for men at age 18; they are not allowed to go on home leave or
see their families until six years have passed. Only a few letters
to and from home are permitted each year. (Of course the
North's military often looks more like a vast construction brigade
than a state of the art military force; at any given time about half
a million soldiers are detailed to construction work, harvesting,
and the like.) The North has nearly 15,000 underground installations related to national security, including jet plane hangars,
tank revetments, and arms factories; it has burrowed deep into
the earth and the mountains to build hardened concrete shelters
to survive nuclear attack, and the government spends 30 cents of
every dollar in its budget to defend the country.

Huge numbers of women serve six-year terms in the military.
Paek Yi joined the KPA (Korean People's Party) when she was
seventeen, and she remained in the military for six years. During
that entire period she did not take a leave, go home, or speak
with her parents. She received and sent letters to her family. Her
day began at 5:00 A.M. when she washed up, did calisthenics, and
had inspections before breakfast, which was served at 7:30. Then
came political education for two hours, two hours of military
instruction, lunch, then various duties until dinner at seven
o'clock in the evening. After dinner the soldiers watched TV,
played musical instruments (the army issued guitars and violins
to everyone in her unit), and held singing competitions, before
lights out at 10:00 P.M. Her unit raised various vegetables and
made *kimch'i*, but the only meat available was pork. She left the
army when her six-year term expired and went home to get married.[3]

Why is it a garrison state? Primarily because of the holocaust
that the North experienced during the Korean War. The fiftieth
anniversary of the presumed end of that war came and went in
July 2003, but the war is still not over and appears unlikely to be
resolved anytime soon. We remain technically at war with North

Korea. The armistice signed on July 27, 1953, stilled the guns, but it brought no formal peace. Instead the Korean War is one of the longest-running conflicts remaining in the world, perhaps the longest in its yearly continuity—even if we have conflicts in the Middle East and the Balkans that have far more ancient roots. The longevity and insolubility of the Korean conflict makes it the best example in the world of how easy it is to get into a war and how hard it is to get out. American troops arrived in southern Korea in September 1945, and 37,000 of them are still there to-day, long after the Cold War ended and the Soviet Union collapsed. More daunting, war could come again, and very quickly. The North Korean population is constantly drilled to prepare for war, indeed for anything—including nuclear attack. It all goes back to the eruption of this war in June 1950.

The Korean War was clearly a war, but of what kind? A conventional war of aggression was the answer in the 1950s and again in the 1990s: "another Munich" according to Truman and "Stalin's war" according to researchers of Soviet documents unearthed after 1991. All blame goes to the Russians and the North Koreans. This point of agreement requires the war to begin on June 25, 1950, and only then; clearly there was an invasion of the South by the North (the whole world knew that on June 26, 1950). There you have it: an open-and-shut case of aggression. Beyond that Washington-forged consensus, the reigning trope consigns this war to oblivion: a forgotten war. The war's having vanished at home explains the experience of a North Korean official who came to New York on Olympic business in the 1980s, finding that people could barely recall when the Korean War occurred, that cab drivers thought communists ran South Korea (since human rights were so violated), and that Americans were friendly and innocent of the antagonism he expected to find. He rightly called it a form of amnesia but thought it might be useful in starting a new relationship.

Still, this is a way to think about the Korean War. By calling the Korean conflict a "forgotten war," we both name it, and we remember it—a paradox: What is it that we are remembering to forget? We do not remember history but particular verdicts, integral to and shaped by the raucous domestic politics of the 1950s, and especially McCarthyism. The war is forgotten and buried. But what is the epitaph on the American tombstone? The tombstone has two messages: for the Truman Cold War liberal, Korea was a success, "the limited war." For the MacArthur conservative, Korea was a failure: the first defeat in American history, more properly a stalemate, and in any case the result proved that there was "no substitute for victory." The problem for Gen. Douglas MacArthur's epitaph is that if MacArthur saw no substitute for victory, he likewise saw no limit on victory: each victory begged another war. The problem for the Truman liberal is that the limited war got rather unlimited in late 1950.

So we need another verdict: a split decision—the first Korean War, the war for the South in the summer of 1950, was a success. The second war, the war for the North, was a failure. In this manner Secretary of State Dean Acheson produced a schizophrenic epitaph: the decision to defend South Korea was the finest hour of the Truman presidency. The decision to march to the Yalu occasioned "an incalculable defeat to US foreign policy and destroyed the Truman administration," this was "the worst defeat . . . since Bull Run" (another interesting analogy). However, Acheson assumed that the latter happened not to him but to his *bête noire*. He squares the circle by blaming it all on MacArthur, and mainstream historiography has squared the circle in the same way. The Korean War happened during the height of the McCarthy period, and it was the handiwork of Dean Acheson and Harry Truman. Senator Joseph McCarthy attacked both, and so the experience of the war disappeared in the shaping of the Cold War consensus: Truman and Acheson were the good guys.

Cold War debate was almost always between the middle and the Right, the consensus anchored by the McCarthys on one end and the Achesons or Hubert Humphreys on the other. Furthermore the Korean War is no icon for the conservative or the liberal, it merely symbolized an absence, mostly a forgetting, but also a never-knowing. The result is a kind of hegemony of forgetting, in which almost everything to do with the war is buried history in the United States.

The forgetting perhaps has a deeper reason, one found in the pathological realm of amnesia: as the intimations of American decline multiplied in the 1980s and early 1990s, so did nostalgia for the 1950s. Reagan was the first two-term president since Eisenhower. His smiling persona drew on Ike's public mastery, and Reaganites made frank comparisons with that quintessentially Republican era. If this rerun had a B-movie and even a Brumairean first-time tragedy, second-time farce quality to it for Reagan's detractors, it clearly drew on a wellspring of mass nostalgia for a lost time when American was Number One. Subsequently Newt Gingrich nominated 1955 as the year when the American Dream hit its apogee. The Korean War is errant counterpoint to these rosy memories, and so it vanishes.

But there is still a nagging problem: unlike Saddam Hussein invading Kuwait, or Bush invading Iraq, Koreans invaded Korea. What do we make of that? In the midst of the terrible crisis in December 1950 that ineluctably followed upon the American decision to invade the North, another view surfaced: that of Richard Stokes, the British Minister of Works, who intuited this paradox. The 38th parallel decision in 1945, taken unilaterally by Americans, was "the invitation to such a conflict as has in fact arisen":

> In the American Civil War the Americans would never
> have tolerated for a single moment the setting up of

an imaginery [*sic*] line between the forces of North
and South, and there can be no doubt as to what
would have been their re-action if the British had intervened in force on behalf of the South. This parallel
is a close one because in America the conflict was not
merely between two groups of Americans, but was
between two conflicting economic systems as is the
case in Korea.[4]

Ever since 1950, this civil war analogy has been like a Rum-
plestiltskin for the official American view: say it and the logic
collapses, the interpretation loses its power. But Stokes carried
his argument one step further—not just a civil war, but a war
between two conflicting social and economic systems. It is precisely that Korean conflict which continues today, with the
United States using every resource at its command to support
the economic system of the South (even if in somewhat altered
form after the $70 billion bailout in late 1997, in return for re-
forms stage-managed by Treasury Secretary Robert Rubin), and
the North going it alone after 1991, with an utterly different economic conception—one of manifest and cruelly diminishing returns for the past twenty years, but nonetheless a stark alternative
to the South.

Stokes happened to have been right: the longevity of the conflict finds its reason in the essential nature of this war, the thing
we need to know first: it was a civil war, a war fought by Koreans, for Korean goals. Koreans know this war in their bones as
a fratricidal conflict. If Americans have trouble reflecting on this
"forgotten war" as a conflict primarily fought among Koreans,
for Korean goals, they should hearken to the great chroniclers of
their own civil war. That distant war was the last war to rage
back and forth across American territory. Six hundred thousand
Americans lost their lives in it, more than the total number of

American deaths in all the wars of the twentieth century, from World Wars I and II through Korea and Vietnam. The civil war pitted brother against brother, son against father, mother against herself. Memories of that war lasted so long that a bitter controversy about the flag of the Confederacy that flew over the South Carolina statehouse only ended in the year 2000. I first went to the South when I was twelve years old, to spend some time with relatives in Memphis, and my shock at seeing segregationist Jim Crow laws in action was only slightly greater than my shock at finding out I was a Yankee—almost a century after the war ended.

Consider this: in June 1950 the veteran industrialist Pak Hŭngsik showed up in Japan and gave an interview to *The Oriental Economist*, published the day before the war began. Described as an adviser to the Korean Economic Mission, he was also said to have "a circle of friends and acquaintances among the Japanese" (a bit of an understatement; Pak was widely thought to be the most notorious collaborator with the colonial regime, and his factories fueled the Japanese war effort). In the years after Liberation, a lot of anti-Japanese feeling had welled up in Korea, Pak said, owing to the return of "numerous revolutionists and nationalists." Today, however, "there is hardly any trace of it." Instead, the Republic of Korea (ROK) "is acting as a bulwark of peace" at the 38th parallel, and "the central figures in charge of national defense are mostly graduates of the former Military College of Japan." Korea and Japan "are destined to go hand in hand, to live and let live," and thus bad feelings should be "cast overboard."

The Japanese should buy Korean raw materials, he said, of which there was an "almost inexhaustible supply," including tungsten and graphite; the Koreans will then buy "as much as possible" of Japanese merchandise and machinery. They will also invite Japanese technical help with Korea's textile, glass, chemical, and machine industries. Pak himself owned a company that was an agent for Ford Motors: "[W]e are scheduled to start producing cars jointly in Korea before long." The problem today, Pak said, was the unfortunate one that "an economic unity is lacking whereas in prewar days Japan, Manchuria, Korea and Formosa [Taiwan] economically combined to make an organic whole." Pak Hŭng-sik was the embodiment of the Japanese colonial idea—having been born a Korean his only unfortunate, but not insurmountable, fate. Between him and Kim Il Sung, the only question was who killed whom.

It was the Vietnam War, of course, that Americans perceive as a civil war, and that got so deeply under the American skin. Ever since its conclusion in 1975, the party of forgetting, hoping "to put Vietnam behind us," has contended with the party of memory, a baby-boom generation seared to the core by a conflict that tore the body politic apart in the 1960s. But in the history of American foreign relations, the Korean War was far more important; Vietnam was a mere follow-on to the logic established in 1950. It was the Korean War, not Greece or Turkey or the Marshall Plan or Vietnam, that inaugurated historically unprecedented defense budgets (the budget quadrupled from June to December 1950, from $13 billion to $54 billion, or more than $500 billion in current dollars) and built the national security state at home and a far-flung archipelago of military base abroad, that transformed a limited containment doctrine into a global crusade, and that ignited McCarthyism just as it seemed to fizzle, thereby giving the Cold War its long run.

KNOW YOUR ENEMY

Americans died in Korea because their commanders had no idea who they were fighting. A disastrous misjudgment of Koreans began right at the top, the day the war began. "I can handle it with one arm tied behind my back," MacArthur said; the next day he remarked to John Foster Dulles that if he could only put the First Cavalry Division into Korea, "Why, heavens, you'd see these fellows scuddle up to the Manchurian border so quick, you would see no more of them." A few days later the generalissimo thought he would turn the KPA around at Suwŏn, just south of Seoul. On June 29 it now appeared that two full divisions would be required, and two weeks into the war he called for "the equivalent of not less than four to four and-a-half full strength infantry divisions." By mid-July he had developed some respect for the Koreans:

> The North Korean soldier must not be underestimated. He is a tough opponent, well-led, combines the infiltration tactic of the Japanese with the tank tactics of the Russian of World War II. He is able to march and maneuver and to attack at night with cohesion which [MacArthur] has never been able to do. These are the troops who served in China . . . [the] tank work is extremely efficient and skillful.[5]

American GIs were told, and believed, that as soon as Korean soldiers saw the whites of Yankee eyes, they would turn tail and run. Press commentary from around the world expressed absolute shock that the KPA was still rolling in early August; *Times* columnist Arthur Krock found it difficult to believe that "the weakest of the satellites is licking hell out of us."[6] There was the added, troubling postulate that these were puppet troops, fighting Stalin's battles. A puzzled Dulles found the North Koreans "fighting and dying, and indeed ruining the whole country, to the end that Russia may achieve its Czarist ambitions." Dean Rusk thought it important to find out how the Russians get the satellites "to fight their actions" for them—"here was a technique which had been very effective and it was not obvious how the success had been achieved." There appeared to be a "nationalist impetus," too, so it would be well to figure out how the Russians "stimulate this enthusiasm."[7]

Then there was an even more troubling fact: our Koreans would not fight. By May 1951 the South Koreans had left ten divisions worth of equipment on the battlefield, according to Gen. Matthew Ridgway. A CIA agent on the scene later wrote that the entire South Korean establishment, beginning with the president and high officers in the military, ran away "like turpentined rats."[8] As late as 1969, Ridgway was still vexed by this conundrum, even though, as he said, "My acquaintance with Orientals goes back to the mid-1920s." (He might have added that his experience included chasing down Sandino in Nicaragua.)[9] The North Koreans were more "fanatical" fighters than the Chinese, he learned, yet the South Koreans were not good soldiers: "I couldn't help asking why. Why such a difference between the two when they were the same otherwise." He speculated that perhaps the KPA was using "dope," but never found evidence of it.[10]

In the summer of 1950, basic knowledge about the KPA and its leaders was treated as a revelation—for example, the majority of its soldiers had fought in the Chinese civil war. Three months into the war, the *New York Times* found big news in a biography of Ch'oe Yŏng-gŏn released by MacArthur's headquarters: it discovered that he had fought with the Chinese communists, placing him in Yanan in 1931 (no mean feat, three years before the Long March). Also unearthed was the information that he was in overall command of the KPA, which appeared to suggest that international communism was allowing the locals to run things (he had been in command since 1948). Two days later the *Times* turned up the news that Mu Chŏng had also fought in China, and that most of the KPA's equipment had been *sold* to it by the

Russians in 1948. Ergo, "With its peculiar combination of fanat-
icism, politics and just plain rudimentary fighting qualities of Orientals . . . [the KPA] is a strange one. Some observers believe
that, in the absence of good pre-war intelligence, we have just
begun to learn about it."[11] Early on the *Times* had found a queer
tone in North Korean statements to the United Nations; they
"had a certain ring of passion" about them, as if they really believed what they were saying about American imperialism. The
Times's own rendering of the "imposter" Kim Il Sung read as
follows:

> The titular leader of the North Korean puppet regime
> and ostensible commander of the North Korean ar-
> mies is Kim Il Sung, a 38-year old giant from South
> Korea, where he is wanted as a fugitive from justice.
> His real name is supposed to be Kim Sung Chu, but
> he has renamed himself after a legendary Korean rev-
> olutionary hero . . . and many Koreans apparently still
> believe that it is their "original" hero and not an im-
> poster who rules in North Korea.[12]

The ordinary reader would believe that KPA soldiers were
trouncing Americans and dying by the thousands, all for a poseur
with a hyperactive pituitary, a John Dillinger on the lam from
august organs of justice in Seoul.

One thing that never seemed to give Americans pause, however, was the juxtaposition of a widely assumed Korean barbarism
against the KPA's superior morale and fighting skills. By the time
of the Vietnam War, blatant racism was mostly the province of
blowhards such as Curtis LeMay, who enjoyed giving vent to his
spleen about an Asia he could not control; in Korea it suffused
the political spectrum, from the the hard noses of the right wing
to the polite society of liberalism. Consider the judgment of the

military editor of the *Times*, Hanson Baldwin, three weeks into
the war:

> We are facing an army of barbarians in Korea, but
> they are barbarians as trained, as relentless, as reckless
> of life, and as skilled in the tactics of the kind of war
> they fight as the hordes of Genghis Khan . . . They
> have taken a leaf from the Nazi book of blitzkreig and
> are employing all the weapons of fear and terror.

Chinese communists were reported to have joined the fighting,
he erred in saying, and not far behind might be "Mongolians,
Soviet Asiatics and a variety of races" — some of "the most primitive of peoples." Elsewhere Baldwin likened the Koreans to invading locusts; he ended by recommending that Americans be
given "more realistic training to meet the barbarian discipline of
the armored horde."[13]
    A few days later Baldwin remarked that to the Korean, "[L]ife
is cheap. Behind him stand the hordes of Asia. Ahead of him lies
the hope of loot." What else "brings him shrieking on?"[14] Mongolians, Asiatics, Nazis, locusts, primitives, hordes, thieves — one
would think Baldwin exhausted his bag of analogies to capture a
people invading their homeland and defending it against the
world's most powerful army. But he came up with another for
dealing with "the problem of the convinced fanatic": "In their
extensive war against Russian partisans, the Germans found that
the only answer to guerrillas . . . was 'to win friends and influence
people' among the civilian population. The actual pacification of
the country means just that."
    Lest the reader think that I single out Baldwin, whose military
reporting on the war was often superb, listen to Telford Taylor,
chief counsel for war crimes at the Nuremberg Trials: "The
traditions and practices of warfare in the Orient are not identical

with those that have developed in the Occident . . . individual
lives are not valued so highly in Eastern mores. And it is totally
unrealistic of us to expect the individual Korean soldier . . . to
follow our most elevated precepts of warfare."[15] MacArthur
opined that "the Oriental dies stoically because he thinks of death
as the beginning of life" (utterly baseless in the secular Korean
context); "the Oriental when dying folds his arms as a dove does
its wings."[16]

Perhaps these are people with no experience in Korea. Edgar
Johnson, a former Marshall Plan administrator in Korea, lam-
basted the "wild, adolescent chauvinism" of the North Koreans
in their "shocking, shameful, criminal invasion" of June 25; these
were "half-crazed automatons" in the orbit of "a monolithic slave-
and-master world." An American who had worked in the occupation told the *Far Eastern Economic Review* that Koreans were "a
hard, fierce and cruel people," possessed of "a ferociousness and
wildness." Korea was a "hotbed of scoundrels, wildmen, semi-
barbarians." American missionaries (whom you might think
would know better), thought that too much inbreeding had led
to "an arrested mental development." British sources said that it
was precisely the foreigners living in Korea (meaning mainly
Americans) who "entertain the lowest opinion of Korean intelligence, mores, ability, and industry."[17] In Ian Fleming's *Goldfin-
ger*, written a decade later, a bull-necked Korean character named
Oddjob makes an appearance, famous for his ability to fling his
steel-ringed hat at someone's neck and take their head off. Koreans have "no regard for human life," Fleming wrote, and that's
why the Japanese employed them: to get the "cruelest, most ruthless people in the world."

This nauseating stew of racial stereotypes had the effect, for
Americans high and low, of stirring diverse peoples into what
Benedict Anderson calls "a nameless sludge," or accumulating
them under just one name ("gook"), as a way of "erasing nation-

ness"—and thus erasing a people from one's consciousness: "[N]ationalism thinks in terms of historical destinies, while racism dreams of eternal contaminations . . . outside history."[18] North Korea still remains "outside history" for Americans, even today.

In contrast to the war in Vietnam, barely a voice was raised against such racism. In the summer of 1950, I found but a single article that found virtue in Koreans (other than that the ROK was staunchly anticommunist, another mistaken stereotype if we speak of the majority) and vice in the ingrained racism of Americans in Korea and the "absolute contempt" in which most of them held Koreans.[19] Furthermore, the same American society that fought for freedom in Korea prohibited Koreans from entering the country in 1950 under existing racial quotas, and denied naturalization to 3,000 Koreans who came to the United States before 1924. Fifteen states prevented Korean-Caucasian marriages, eleven states refused to allow Koreans to buy or own land, and twenty-seven occupations in New York City were proscribed to Koreans.[20]

One hastens to "give the other side," to recite Korean virtues, to call up their long history, high achievement, and love of moral virtue, to mitigate the unrelieved crudity of it all. But any American who today drives a Hyundai Sonata, uses an LG computer, watches a Samsung 72" flat screen TV, shops at the ubiquitous fruit and vegetable stores in New York, the produce perfectly arranged and shined to brilliance, or watches a son or daughter lose out at Harvard to a Korean applicant, will presumably not need didactic aid. It was in fact the Americans quoted above, tabula rasa on everything Asian but sure they were right, who were the barbarians.

Such attitudes shaped the battle, pitting young American soldiers by the millions against an enemy that they were unprepared to fight, one that fought with rare courage, tenacity, and cunning.

And these attitudes shaped the behavior of the enemy, who commonly remarked that "the Americans do not recognize Koreans as human beings."[21]

BURNING MEMORIES

Almost always, media discussion of North Korea assumes that Washington is in a position of original innocence, and the North is assiduously trying to obtain and then to use "weapons of mass destruction"—the ubiquitous media trope for the arsenals of American enemies since the Cold War ended. Yet the American record in Northeast Asia since the 1940s is one of consistent use of, or threats to use, those same weapons. The United States is the only power ever to have used nuclear weapons in anger, at Hiroshima and Nagasaki, and for decades has consistently based its deterrence on threats to use them again in Korea.

"The Forgotten War" might better be called an *unknown* war. As an historian of that war, what is indelible is the extraordinary destructiveness of the American air campaigns again North Korea, ranging from the widespread and continuous use of firebombing (mainly with napalm), to threats to use nuclear and chemical weapons, and finally to the destruction of huge North Korean dams in the final stages of the war. Yet this episode is largely unknown even to historians, let alone to the average citizen, and it never gets mentioned in press analysis of the North Korean nuclear problem in the past decade. Korea is also assumed to have been a limited war, but its prosecution bore a strong resemblance to the air war against Imperial Japan in World War II, often directed by the same American military leaders. If the atomic attacks against Hiroshima and Nagasaki have been examined from many different perspectives, incendiary air attacks against Japanese and Korean cities have received much less attention. Meanwhile America's post–Korean War air power and nuclear strategy in Northeast Asia are even less well understood, yet these strategies have dramatically shaped North Korean choices and remain a key factor shaping its national security strategy today.

In 1968 I was walking through the streets of Taejŏn, a city south of Seoul. On a street corner stood a man (I think it was a man, or a woman with broad shoulders) who had a peculiar purple crust on every visible part of his skin—thick on his hands, thin on his arms, fully covering his entire head and face. He was bald, he had no ears or lips, and his eyes, lacking lids, were a grayish-white, with no pupils. He had a sandwich-sign with a story that went on at some length; at the time my Korean wasn't good enough to understand it. But judging by the dates on the sign, it clearly referred to some awful episode during the war. I did not know, until reading a recent book on the American air campaigns in Korea,[22] that this purplish crust resulted from a drenching with napalm, after which the untreated victim's body was left to somehow cure itself.

Napalm was invented at the end of World War II. It became a major issue during the Vietnam War, forwarded by horrific photos of little kids running down the road naked, their skin peeling off. By 1968 Dow Chemical Company, a major manufacturer of napalm, could not recruit employees on most college campuses; fifteen years later when the chairman of my department asked if I would object to an international studies grant from Dow Chemical, I said yes (and he accepted my objections). Far more napalm was dropped on Korea, however, with much more devastating effect, since the Democratic People's Republic of Korea (DPRK) had many more populous cities and urban industrial installations than did North Vietnam. Furthermore the U.S. Air Force loved it, as attested to by many articles in "trade" journals of the time: J. Townsend, "They Don't Like Hell Bombs," *Armed Forces Chemical Journal* (January 1951); "Napalm Jelly Bombs Prove a Blazing Success in Korea," *All Hands* (April 1951); also E. F. Bullene, "Wonder Weapon: Napalm," *Army Combat Forces Journal* (November 1952). In 2003 I participated in a conference with American veterans of the Korean War. During a discussion about napalm, a survivor of the Changjin (Japanese name, *Chosin*) Reservoir battle who lost an eye and part of a leg, said it was indeed a nasty weapon—but "it fell on the right people."

Ah yes, the right people, as in a "friendly fire" drop on a dozen American soldiers:

> Men all around me were burned. They lay rolling in the snow. Men I knew, marched and fought with begged me to shoot them. . . . It was terrible. Where the napalm had burned the skin to a crisp, it would be peeled back from the face, arms, legs . . . like fried potato chips.[23]

A bit later George Barrett of the *New York Times* found "a macabre tribute to the totality of modern war" in a village north of Anyang (in South Korea):

> The inhabitants throughout the village and in the fields were caught and killed and kept the exact postures they held when the napalm struck—a man about to get on his bicycle, fifty boys and girls playing in an orphanage, a housewife strangely unmarked, holding in her hand a page torn from a Sears-Roebuck catalogue crayoned at Mail Order No. 3,811,294 for a $2.98 "bewitching bed jacket—coral."

Dean Acheson wanted censorship authorities notified about this kind of "sensationalized reporting," so it could be stopped.[24]

One of the first orders to burn towns and villages that I found in the archives occurred in southeastern-most Korea, during heavy fighting along the Pusan Perimeter in early August 1950, when American soldiers were also bedeviled by thousands of guerrillas in their rear areas. On August 6, 1950, an American officer requested "to have the following towns obliterated" by the Air Force: Chŏngsŏng, Chinbo, and Kusu-dong. B-29 strategic bombers were also called in for tactical bombing. On August 16, five groups of B-29s hit a rectangular area near the front, full of towns and villages, creating an ocean of fire with hundreds of tons of napalm. Another such call went out on the August 20. On August 26 we find in this same source the single entry, "fired eleven villages."[25]

Reginald Thomson, a British journalist, provided an unforgettable account of the nature of this war in his much-neglected eyewitness account, *Cry Korea*. Thomson was sickened by the carnage of the American air war, with the latest machined military might used against "an almost unarmed enemy, unable to challenge the aircraft in the skies." In September 1950, he wrote, "[H]andfuls of peasants defied the immense weight of modern arms with a few rifles and carbines and a hopeless courage . . . and brought down upon themselves and all the inhabitants the appalling horror of jellied petrol bombs." Every shot fired at the enemy, he said, "released a deluge of destruction. Every village and township in the path of war was blotted out." In such warfare, "the slayer needs merely touch a button, and death is on the wing, blindly blotting out the remote, the unknown people, holocausts of death, veritable mass productions of death, spreading an abysmal desolation over whole communities."

Pilots were told to bomb targets that they could see to avoid hitting civilians, but they frequently bombed major population centers by radar, or dumped off huge amounts of napalm on

secondary targets when the primary one was unavailable. In a
major strike on the industrial city of Hŭngnam on July 31, 1950,
500 tons of ordinance was delivered through clouds by radar; the
flames rose two or three hundred feet into the air. The Air Force
dropped 625 tons of bombs over North Korea on August 12, a
tonnage that would have required a fleet of 250 B-17s in the Second World War. By late August, B-29 formations were dropping
800 tons a day on the North.[26] Much of the tonnage was pure
napalm. From June to late October 1950, B-29s unloaded 866,914
gallons of napalm. Air Force sources took delight in the virtues
of this relatively new weapon, introduced at the end of the previous war, joking about communist protests and misleading the
press about their "precision bombing." They also liked to point
out that civilians were warned of the approaching bombers by
leaflet, when all pilots knew these were ineffective.[27] This was
mere prelude to the obliteration of most North Korean towns
and cities after China entered the war.

The Chinese entry into the war caused an immediate escalation
of the air campaign. From early November 1950 onward, Mac-
Arthur ordered that a wasteland be created between the fighting
front and the Chinese border, destroying from the air every "installation, factory, city, and village" over thousands of square
miles of North Korean territory. As a well-informed British at-
taché to MacArthur's headquarters observed, except for Najin
near the Soviet border and the Yalu dams (both spared so as not
to provoke Moscow or Beijing), MacArthur's orders were "to
destroy every means of communication and every installation and
factories and cities and villages. This destruction is to start at the
Manchurian border and to progress south." On November 8,
1950, seventy-nine B-29s dropped 550 tons of incendiary bombs
on Sinŭiju, "removing [it] from off the map"; a week later Hoer-
yŏng was hit with napalm "to burn out the place." By November

25, "a large part of [the] North West area between Yalu River and southwards to enemy lines . . . is more or less burning"; soon the area would be a "wilderness of scorched earth."[28]

This was all before the major Sino-Korean offensive that cleared northern Korea of UN forces. When that began, the Air Force on December 14–15 hit Pyongyang with seven hundred 500-pound bombs, napalm dropped from Mustang fighters, and 175 tons of delayed-fuse demolition bombs, which land with a thud and then blow up at odd moments, when people are trying to rescue the dead from the napalm fires. At the beginning of January, Ridgway again ordered the Air Force to hit the capital, Pyongyang, "with the goal of burning the city to the ground with incendiary bombs" (this occurred in two strikes on January 3 and 5). As Americans retreated below the parallel, the scorched-earth policy of "torching" continued, burning Ŭijŏngbu, Wŏnju, and other small cities in the South as the enemy drew near them.[29]

The Air Force also tried to decapitate the North Korean leadership. During the war on Iraq in March 2003, the world learned about the "MOAB" bomb, nicknamed the "Mother of All Bombs," weighing in at 21,500 pounds with an explosive force of 18,000 pounds of TNT. *Newsweek* put the bomb on its cover, under the title, "Why America Scares the World."[30] In the desperate winter of 1950–51, Kim Il Sung and his closest allies were back where they started in the 1930s, holed up in deep bunkers in Kanggye, near the Manchurian border. After failing to find them for three months after the Inch'ŏn landing (an intelligence failure that included a carpet-bombing campaign along the old Sino-Korean tributary route extending north from Pyongyang to the border, on the assumption that they would flee to China), B-29s dropped "Tarzon" bombs on Kanggye; this was an enormous new 12,000-pound bomb never deployed before.[31] But it was a mere firecracker compared to the ultimate fire weapons,[32] atomic bombs.

On July 9, 1950 — a mere two weeks into the war, it is worth remembering — General MacArthur sent General Ridgway a "hot message" which prompted the Joint Chiefs of Staff (JCS) "to consider whether or not A-bombs should be made available to MacArthur." Gen. Charles Bolte, Chief of Operations, was asked to talk to MacArthur about using atomic bombs "in direct support [of] ground combat." Some ten to twenty bombs could be spared for the Korean theater, Bolte thought, without "unduly" jeopardizing American global war capabilities. Bolte got back from MacArthur an early suggestion for the tactical use of atomic weapons, and an indication of MacArthur's extraordinary ambitions for the war, which included occupying the North and handling potential Chinese — or Soviet — intervention as follows:

> I would cut them off in North Korea. In Korea I visualize a cul-de-sac. The only passages leading from Manchuria and Vladivostok have many tunnels and bridges. I see here a unique use for the atomic bomb — to strike a blocking blow — which would require a six months repair job. Sweeten up my B-29 force.

At this point in the war, however, the JCS rejected use of the bomb because targets sufficiently large to require atomic weapons were lacking, because of concerns about world opinion five years after Hiroshima, and because the JCS expected the tide of battle to be reversed by conventional military means.[33] That calculus changed, however, when large numbers of Chinese troops entered the war in October and November 1950.

At a famous news conference on November 30, President Truman rattled the atomic bomb, saying the United States might use any weapon in its arsenal.[34] The threat was based on contingency planning to use the bomb, rather than the faux pas so many

assumed it to be. On this same day, Air Force General Stratemeyer sent an order to Gen. Hoyt Vandenberg that the Strategic
Air Command should be put on warning, "to be prepared to
dispatch without delay medium bomb groups to the Far East . . .
this augmentation should include atomic capabilities." Air Force
Gen. Curtis LeMay remembered correctly that the JCS had earlier
concluded that atomic weapons would probably not be useful in
Korea, except as part of "an overall atomic campaign against Red
China." But, if these orders were now being changed because of
the entry of Chinese forces into the war, LeMay wanted the job;
he told Stratemeyer that his headquarters was the only one with
the experience, technical training, and "intimate knowledge" of
delivery methods. The man who directed the firebombing of
Tokyo in March 1945 was again ready to proceed to the Far
East to direct the attacks.[35] There was little worry at the time
that the Russians would respond with atomic weapons, because
the United States possessed at least 450 bombs and the Soviets
only 25.

A short while later (on December 9), MacArthur said that he
wanted commander's discretion to use atomic weapons in the
Korean theater, and on December 24 he submitted "a list of re-
tardation targets" for which he said that he required twenty-six
atomic bombs. He also wanted four to drop on the 'invasion
forces" and four more for "critical concentrations of enemy air
power." In interviews published posthumously, MacArthur said
he had a plan that would have won the war in ten days: "I would
have dropped between 30 and 50 atomic bombs . . . strung across
the neck of Manchuria"; then he would have introduced half a
million Chinese Nationalist troops at the Yalu, and then, "spread
behind us—from the Sea of Japan to the Yellow Sea—a belt of
radioactive cobalt . . . it has an active life of between 60 and 120
years. For at least 60 years there could have been no land invasion
of Korea from the North." He expressed certainty that the Rus-

sians would have done nothing about this extreme strategy: "my plan was a cinch."[36]

Cobalt 60 has 320 times the radioactivity of radium. One 400-ton cobalt H-bomb, historian Carroll Quigley wrote, could wipe out all animal life on earth. MacArthur sounds like a warmongering lunatic in these interviews, but if so, he was not alone. Before the Sino-Korean offensive, a committee of the JCS had said that atomic bombs might be the "decisive factor" in cutting off a Chinese advance into Korea; initially they could be useful in "a 'cordon sanitaire' [that] might be established by the U.N. in a strip in Manchuria immediately north of the Manchurian border." A few months later Congressman Albert Gore (2000 Democratic candidate Al Gore's father, and subsequently a strong opponent of the Vietnam War) complained that "Korea has become a meat grinder of American manhood" and suggested "something cataclysmic" to end the war, that is, a radiation belt dividing the Korean peninsula permanently into two. Although General Ridgway said nothing about a cobalt bomb, after replacing MacArthur as the U.S. commander in Korea, in May 1951 he renewed MacArthur's request of December 24, this time for thirty-eight atomic bombs.[37] The request was not approved.

The United States came closest to using atomic weapons in early April 1951, precisely at the time when Truman removed MacArthur. Although much related to this episode is still highly classified, it is now clear that Truman did not remove MacArthur simply because of his repeated insubordination, but because he wanted a reliable commander on the scene should Washington decide to use nuclear weapons; that is, Truman traded MacArthur for his atomic policies. On March 10, 1951, MacArthur asked for a " 'D' Day atomic capability" to retain air superiority in the Korean theater, after the Chinese massed huge new forces near the Korean border and after the Soviets and put 200 bombers into airbases in Manchuria (from which they could strike not just

Korea but American bases in Japan).[38] On March 14, General Vandenberg wrote, "Finletter and Lovett alerted on atomic discussions. Believe everything is set." At the end of March, Stratemeyer reported that atomic bomb loading pits at Kadena Air Base on Okinawa were once again operational; the bombs were carried there unassembled, and put together at the base, lacking only the essential nuclear cores. On April 5 the JCS ordered immediate atomic retaliation against Manchurian bases if large numbers of new troops came into the fighting, or, it appears, if bombers were launched against American assets from there. On that same day, Gordon Dean, chairman of the Atomic Energy Commission, began arrangements for transferring nine Mark IV nuclear capsules to the Air Force's 9th Bomb Group, the designated carrier for atomic weapons.

The main atomic capsule or core[39] available to the United States in early 1951 was the Mark IV, which had first been tested at the Pacific isle called Eniwetok in 1948, and which went into manufacture in March 1949; some 550 Mark IVs were built by the time the production line ended in May 1951. The United States also had some 120 Mark IIIs, produced between 1947 and 1949 and retired over the period March–December 1950. The Mark IV was considered a big improvement over these weapons; it could be fitted with one of three nuclear cores, yielding a blast range equivalent to 20 to 40 kilotons of TNT, depending on which core was used. In other words the Mark IV in its smallest version was the equivalent of the Hiroshima bomb. The fully assembled Mark IV atomic bomb weighed some 11,000 pounds, but could still be carried both by B-29s and by the Navy's AJ-1 attack bomber.[40]

Gen. Omar Bradley (the JCS chairman) got Truman's approval to transfer the Mark IVs "from AEC [Atomic Energy Commission] to military custody" on April 6, and the president signed an order to use them against Chinese and North Korean targets. The 9th Air Force Group deployed out to Guam. "In the confusion attendant upon General MacArthur's removal," however, Truman's order was never sent. Why was Truman's order never implemented? There were two reasons: Truman had used this extraordinary crisis to get the JCS to agree to MacArthur's removal (something Truman announced on April 11), and the Chinese did not significantly escalate the war. So the bombs were not used. The nine Mark IVs did not go back to the AEC, however, but remained in Air Force custody after their transfer on April 11. The 9th Bomb Group remained on Guam, but did not move on to the loading pits at Kadena AFB in Okinawa.[41]

The Joint Chiefs again considered the use of nuclear weapons in June 1951, this time in tactical battlefield circumstances,[42] and there were many more such suggestions as the war continued to 1953. Robert Oppenheimer, former director of the Manhattan Project, was involved in "Project Vista," designed to gauge the feasibility of the tactical use of atomic weapons. In early 1951 a young man named Samuel Cohen, on a secret assignment for the Defense Department, observed the battles for the second recapture of Seoul, and thought there should be a way to destroy the enemy without destroying the city. He became the father of the neutron bomb.[44]

Perhaps the most daunting and terrible nuclear project that the United States ran in Korea, however, was Operation Hudson Harbor. It appears to have been part of a larger project involving "overt exploitation in Korea by the Department of Defense and covert exploitation by the Central Intelligence Agency of the possible use of novel weapons" (a euphemism for what are now called "weapons of mass destruction"). Operation Hudson Harbor sought to establish the capability to use atomic weapons on the battlefield, and in pursuit of this goal, lone B-29 bombers were lifted from Okinawa in September and October 1951 (while being controlled from an American air base in Japan) and sent over North Korea on simulated atomic bombing runs, dropping "dummy" A-bombs or very heavy TNT bombs. The project called for "actual functioning of all activities which would be involved in an atomic strike, including weapons assembly and testing, leading, ground control of bomb aiming," and the like. The results indicated that the bombs were probably not useful, for purely technical reasons: "timely identification of large masses of enemy troops was extremely rare."[44]

One may imagine the steel nerves required of the DPRK's leaders, sitting in their deep bunker under Moran Hill in Pyongyang observing a lone B-29 simulating the attack lines that had resulted in the devastation of Hiroshima and Nagasaki just five years earlier, each time unsure of whether the bomb was real or a dummy. But then, they survived the kill-all, burn-all, loot-all campaigns launched under General Tōjō's command in the 1930s. Successive American administrations have foolishly underestimated this leadership and have paid the cost for it in American lives. "War is a stern teacher," Thucydides memorably wrote; indeed, it is the supreme teacher of one's memory. As Nietzsche put the point in discussing human "*mnemotechnics*," the oldest psychology on earth is that which must be "burned" in: "only that which never ceases to *hurt* stays in the memory."[45]

The declassified record shows that American commanders also considered the massive use of chemical weapons against Sino-North Korean forces. In penciled diary notes written on December 16, 1950, Ridgway referred cryptically to a subcommittee on "clandestine introduction [of] wea[pon]s of mass destruction and unconventional warfare." I know nothing more about this item, but it may refer to Ridgway's request to MacArthur that chemical weapons be used in Korea. The original of Ridgway's telegram is unavailable; one author claims that this was merely a request for tear gas,[46] but that would not explain MacArthur's reply on

January 7, 1951, which alluded to the laws of war, and read as follows: "I do not believe there is any chance of using chemicals on the enemy in case [American] evacuation is ordered. As you know, U.S. inhibitions on such use are complete and drastic." The next day, in a conference with General Almond and others, the transcript says, "If we use gas we will lay ourselves open to retaliation. This question has been taken up with General Mac-Arthur for decision. We have requested sufficient quantities to be shipped immediately in the event use of gas is approved."[47]

Without the use of "novel weapons"—although napalm was very new at the time—the air war nonetheless leveled North Korea and killed millions of civilians before the war ended. North Koreans will tell you that for three years they faced a daily threat of being burned with napalm; "you couldn't escape it," one told me in 1981. By 1952 just about everything in northern and central Korea was completely leveled. What was left of the population survived in caves. The North Koreans created an entire life underground, in complexes of dwellings, schools, hospitals, and factories. The Japanese built many tunnels and caves on the peninsula during World War II, for defense and storage of ammunition and equipment in anticipation of a ground campaign across the mainland against the home islands. During the Korean War, Korean and Chinese forces built massive underground installations because they had lost control of the air and because of well-grounded fears of nuclear attack. Commanding General Peng Dehuai's memoirs estimated that 1,250 kilometers of tunnels and 6,000 kilometers of trenches were dug just along the war front itself, in and behind the current DMZ. After Eisenhower won the 1952 election and issued veiled threats of ending the war through drastic escalation, thousands of workers blasted out new and deeper tunnels. A Chinese civil defense booklet from 1952 stated,

If an atomic bomb is dropped on a group of infantry
units occupying, say, 302 separate positions, then perhaps this could kill 2000 troops, but it would not be
able to injure soldiers hidden in underground tunnels
and concrete bunkers . . . [although because of] radiation effects, for several hours attackers would be unable to advance.[48]

In spite of World War II bombing studies showing that such
attacks against civilian populations only stiffened enemy resistance, American officials sought to use aerial bombing as a type
of psychological and social warfare. As Wise Man Robert Lovett
later put it, "If we keep on tearing the place apart, we can make
it a most unpopular affair for the North Koreans. We ought to
go right ahead."[49] The Americans did go right ahead and, in the
final act of this barbaric air war, hit huge irrigation dams that
provided water for 75 percent of the North's food production.
These attacks got almost no attention at the time.

On June 20, 1953, the *New York Times* announced in banner
headlines the execution of alleged Soviet spies Julius and Ethel
Rosenberg at Sing Sing Prison. In the fine print of daily war
coverage in the *Times*, the U.S. Air Force reported that its planes
had bombed dams at Kusŏng and Tŏksan in North Korea—and
in even finer print the North Korean radio acknowledged "great
damage" to these large reservoirs. By that time agriculture was
the only major element of the Korean economy still functioning;
the attacks came just after the laborious, backbreaking work of
rice transplantation had been done in the spring of 1953. The Air
Force was proud of the destruction it created:

The subsequent flash flood scooped clean 27 miles of
valley below, and the plunging flood waters wiped out
[supply routes, etc.]. . . . The Westerner can little con-

ceive the awesome meaning which the loss of [rice]
has for the Asian — starvation and slow death.

Many villages were inundated, "washed downstream," and even
Pyongyang, some twenty-seven miles south of one dam, was
badly flooded. According to the official Air Force history, when
the high containing wall of the Tŏksan Reservoir collapsed, the
onrushing flood destroyed six miles of railway, five bridges, two
miles of highway, and five square miles of rice paddies. After the
war it took 200,000 man-days of labor to reconstruct the reservoir; still, the Air Force marveled at how fast they were back up
and running. The Pujŏn River dam was also hit; built in 1932, it
was designed to hold 670 million meters of water, with a pressure
gradient of 999 meters; the dam station generated 200,000 kil-
owatts of electrical capacity from the collected water, which then
flowed down into rice paddies for irrigation.[50]

There is no record of how many peasants perished in the assault on this and several other dams, but the Air Force assumed
they were "loyal" to the enemy, providing "direct support to the
Communist armed forces." (That is, they were feeding the northern population.) The "lessons" adduced from this experience
"gave the enemy a sample of the totality of war . . . embracing
the whole of a nation's economy and people."[51] In fact this was
a war crime, recognized as such by international law, and especially after 1949 conventions designed to outlaw some of the
worst aspects of World War II. (In the latter stages of the war,
American leaders had declined to bomb agriculture dams and
dikes in Holland, precisely because they knew it to be a war
crime, yet they were much smaller than the huge dams in the
DPRK.)

Hungarian Tibor Meray had been a correspondent in North
Korea during the war; he left Budapest for Paris after his participation in the 1956 rebellion against communism. When a Lon-

don television team interviewed him in 1986, he said that
however brutal Koreans on either side might have been in this
war, "I saw destruction and horrible things committed by the
American forces": "Everything which moved in North Korea was
a military target, peasants in the fields often were machine
gunned by pilots who I, this was my impression, amused themselves to shoot the targets which moved." Meray had crossed the
Yalu in August 1951 and witnessed "a complete devastation between the Yalu River and the capital," Pyongyang. There were
simply "no more cities in North Korea." The incessant, indis-
criminate bombing forced his party always to drive by night:

> We traveled in moonlight, so my impression was that
> I am traveling on the moon, because there was only
> devastation . . . every city was a collection of chim-
> neys. I don't know why houses collapsed and chim-
> neys did not, but I went through a city of 200,000
> inhabitants and I saw thousands of chimneys and
> that—that was all.[52]

Over the course of the war, Conrad Crane wrote, the American Air Force "had wreaked terrible destruction all across North
Korea. Bomb damage assessment at the armistice revealed that
eighteen of twenty-two major cities had been at least half obliterated." A table he provided showed that the big industrial cities
of Hamhŭng and Hŭngnam were 80–85 percent destroyed; Sar-
iwŏn, 95 percent; Sinanju, 100 percent; the port of Chinnamp'o,
80 percent; and Pyongyang, 75 percent. A British reporter described one of the thousands of obliterated villages as "a low,
wide mound of violet ashes." Gen. William Dean, who was captured after the battle of Taejŏn in July 1950 and taken to the
North, later said that most of the towns and villages he saw were
just "rubble or snowy open spaces." Just about every Korean he

met, General Dean wrote, had some relative killed in a bombing raid.[53] Even Winston Churchill, late in the war, was moved to tell Washington that when napalm was invented in the latter stages of World War II, no one contemplated that it would be "splashed" all over a civilian population.[54]

This was Korea, "the limited war." We may leave as an epitaph for this unrestrained air war the views of its architect, Gen. Curtis LeMay. After the war started, he said,

> We slipped a note kind of under the door into the Pentagon and said, "Look, let us go up there . . . and burn down five of the biggest towns in North Korea—and they're not very big—and that ought to stop it." Well, the answer to that was four or five screams—"You'll kill a lot of non-combatants," and "It's too horrible." Yet over a period of three years or so . . . we burned down *every* [sic] town in North Korea and South Korea, too. . . . Now, over a period of three years this is palatable, but to kill a few people to stop this from happening—a lot of people can't stomach it.[55]

AN ATROCIOUS OCCUPATION

The ROK occupied nearly all of North Korea in the fall of 1950, in the name of the United Nations. This occupation transpired under a governing American policy document (NSC81/1), which instructed the commander of United Nations forces, Gen. Douglas MacArthur, to forbid reprisals against the officials and the population of the DPRK "except in accordance with international law."[56] In the event the extant "national security law" of the ROK, which for fifty years after 1948 defined North Korea as an "antistate entity" and punished any hint of sympathy or support for it among its own citizens, provided the legal framework for administering justice to citizens of North Korea—under international auspices but not under anything that would resemble "international law."

To my knowledge, the late Callum MacDonald and I were the only Western historians ever to examine this occupation using primary evidence. Otherwise it is an occupation lost to history and memory, and specifically to many histories of the Korean War, which routinely blame all atrocities on North Korean or Chinese forces. Max Hastings, for example (as Macdonald pointed out), thought that communist atrocities were the only ones worthy of his close attention (even though he does not catalog or verify them in any detail), and that they gave to the UN cause in Korea "a moral legitimacy that has survived to this day."[57] Not so for North Korea. As the only communist country to have its territory occupied by anticommunist forces after World War II, this particular episode is alive and well, burned into the minds of several generations, and it governs North Korean interpretations of the South's intentions today.

One North Korean atrocity frequently cited in the war literature is the murder of thousands of political prisoners in Taejŏn, a city south of Seoul. The official American history of the early stages of the Korean War by Roy Appleman made no mention of any ROK atrocities, and instead alleged that the North Koreans carried out this massacre by perpetrating "one of the greatest mass killings" of the war, he wrote, with between 5,000 and 7,000 people slaughtered and placed in mass graves.[58] The Communist journalist Alan Winnington, however, published an article in the London *Daily Worker* in August 1950 hyperbolically titled "U.S. Belsen in Korea," alleging that ROK police under the supervision of American military advisors advisers had butchered 7,000 people in a village near Taejŏn, during the period July 2–6, 1950. Accompanying KPA troops as a war correspondent,

Winnington found twenty eyewitnesses who said that on July 2, truckloads of police arrived and made local people build six pits, each 200 yards long. Two days later political prisoners were trucked in and executed, both by bullets to the head and decapitation by sword, and then layered on top of each other in the pits "like sardines." The massacres continued for three days. The witnesses said that two Jeeps with American officers observed the killings.[59] North Korean sources said 4,000 had been killed (changing it some months later to 7,000), mostly imprisoned guerrillas from Chcju Island and the T'aebaek Mountain area captured in the 1948–49 fighting and those detained after the Yŏsu-Sunch'ŏn rebellion in 1948. They located the site differently than Winnington, however.[60]

The American Embassy in London called the Winnington story an "atrocity fabrication" and denied its contents. Evidence from the time suggests that Winnington was more truthful in 1950, during the heat of war, than Appleman was with the benefit of hindsight and classified documentation. Callum MacDonald wrote that a French priest witnessed South Korean killings at this time in Taejŏn and sought to intervene to stop them.[61] U.S. Army intelligence on July 2 rated as "probably true" a report that the Korean National Police (KNP) in Taejŏn were "arresting all Communists and executing them on the outskirts of the city." The CIA stated the next day that "unofficial reports indicated that Southern Korean police are executing Communist suspects in Suwŏn and Taejŏn, in an effort both to eliminate a potential 5th column and to take revenge for reported northern executions in Seoul." Neither report gave numbers, however.[62] British officials in Tokyo who talked to SCAP (Supreme Command, Allied Powers) officers said that "there may be an element of truth in [Winnington's] report," but SCAP thought it was a matter to be handled between London and Washington. Alvary Gascoigne, a British representative at MacArthur's headquarters, said that re-

liable journalists have "repeatedly" noted "the massacre of prisoners by South Korean troops," but one "J. Underwood," of the
U.S. prisoners of war mission, told British sources that he
doubted 7,000 prisoners could even have been assembled in Taejŏn, as not more than 2,000 were in the city's prisons.[63]

As it happened, the United States not only knew the truth
about what happened at Taejŏn, but had American photographers on the scene to record it. In 1999 an independent scholar
living in New York, Dr. Do-young Lee, succeeded in getting the
U.S. Archives to declassify many of these photographs, which
document the massacre of thousands of political prisoners in Taejŏn by South Korean authorities, with the total ranging upward
from a minimum of 2,000.[64] The same was true of the massacres
at Suwŏn, an ancient walled town just south of Seoul, as subsequently related by an American CIA agent who observed the systematic slaughter of 1,800 political prisoners:

> I stood by helplessly, witnessing the entire affair. Two
> big bull-dozers worked constantly. One made the
> ditch-type grave. Trucks loaded with the condemned
> arrived. Their hands were already tied behind them.
> They were hastily pushed into a big line along the
> edge of the newly opened grave. They were quickly
> shot in the head and pushed into the grave.[65]

As South Korean authorities swept back up the peninsula in
the wake of MacArthur's Inch'ŏn landing in mid-September 1950,
they now took vicious and deadly retribution against collaborators with the North. British sources cited "a medieval witchhunt"
by the police, and a Korean from the South later likened it to
"the killing fields" in Cambodia. An American Marine chaplain
described South Korean officers forcing some one hundred alleged collaborators, including children, pregnant women, and old

men, to dig their own graves before being massacred — "This kind of thing happened all over the front."[66] Other sources witnessed many truckloads of "political" cases arriving at Seoul's West Gate prison; of the 4,000 people that the prison held, 1,200 were women, some with infants. Each ten-foot square cell held 24 people.

Western reporters witnessed the arrest of 5,000 political suspects within five days of the first recapture of Seoul. "Street courts were organized by the [rightwing] youth leagues and leftists were lynched."[67] A secret account by North Korean authorities, for internal consumption, detailed South Korean atrocities committed in Seoul: nearly 29,000 people were said to have been "shot" by ROK authorities, with 21,000 executions occurring in prisons and the rest perpetrated by police and "reactionary" organizations. Entire families of people's committee leaders were slaughtered, it said. The document accused the ROK and the United States of "slave labor" treatment of those collaborators with North Korea (and their families) who were not executed. They were not allowed to carry ROK citizenship cards, and were used for various corveé labor projects. The report detailed gruesome tortures, and alleged that 300 female communists and collaborators were placed in brothels where they were raped continuously ("day and night") by South Korean and American soldiers. This report may be false, but then why would DPRK officials lie to their superiors in secret internal materials?[68]

As ROK forces entered into the North, State Department officials sought some mechanism for supervision of the political aspects of the occupation, "to insure that a 'bloodbath' would not result. In other words . . . the Korean forces should be kept under control."[69] The British, however, quickly obtained evidence that the ROK as a matter of official policy sought to "hunt out and destroy communists and collaborators"; the facts confirmed "what is now becoming pretty notorious, namely that the re-

stored civil administration in [North] Korea bids fair to become
an international scandal of a major kind." The Foreign Office
urged that immediate representations be made in Washington,
D.C., because this was "a war for men's minds" in which the
political counted almost as much as the military. The British ambassador accordingly brought the matter up with Dean Rusk on
October 30, getting this response: "Rusk agrees that there have
regrettably been many cases of atrocities" by the ROK authorities, and promised to have American military officers seek to
control the situation.[70] Internal American documents show full
awareness of ROK atrocities; for example, U.S. military advisers
said the entire North might be put off limits to ROK authorities
if they continue the killings, and in one documented instance, in
the town of Sunch'ŏn, the United States replaced marauding
South Korean forces with American First Cavalry elements.[71]

The British representative in northern Korea said that many
more executions occurred when KNP officials sought to move
some 3,000 political prisoners to the South, after the Chinese
entered the war:

> As threat to Seoul developed, and owing to the de-
> struction of the death-house, the authorities resorted
> to these hurried mass executions by shooting in order
> to avoid the transfer of condemned prisoners South,
> or leaving them behind to be liberated by the Com-
> munists. However deplorable their methods one can
> readily grasp the problem.[72]

Americans were also involved in political murders in the
North. As we have seen, they stood idly by while South Korean
authorities killed their enemies without investigation or trial, including women and children. Americans also issued orders that
sanctioned such murders. We find chilling American instructions

to political affairs officers and counterintelligence personnel attached to the Tenth Corps in the eastern sector: they were ordered to "liquidate the North Korean Labor Party and North
Korean intelligence agencies," and to forbid any political organizations that might constitute "a security threat to X Corps." "The
destruction of the North Korean labor Party and the government" was to be accomplished by the arrest and internment of
the following categories of people: all police, all security service
personnel, all officials of government, and all current and former
members of the Korean Workers Party. The compilation of
"black lists" would follow, the purpose of which was unstated.
These orders are repeated in other X Corps documents, with the
added authorization that agents were to suspend all types of civilian communications, impound all radio transmitters, even to
destroy "[carrier] pigeon lofts and their contents."[73] The Korean
Workers Party was a mass party which had as much as 14 percent
of the entire population on its rolls; such instructions implied the
arrest and internment of upward of one-third of North Korean
adults. Perhaps for this reason the Americans found that virtually
all DPRK officials, down to local government, had fled before
the onrushing troops.[74]

Callum MacDonald documented numerous atrocities in the
Western sector as well. American Counter-Intelligence Corps
teams, working with Korean police and youth groups, rounded
up individuals found on KWP membership lists. A war diary of
the U.S. 441st Counter-Intelligence Corps team shows how that
unit actively sought out members of the KWP and, presumably,
turned them over to South Korean justice.[75] After they reoccu-
pied Pyongyang, North Korean sources claimed that 15,000 people had been massacred in that city alone, and some 2,000 were
said to have been murdered under American orders in a prison
courtyard on December 4. Thousands more bodies were piled in
twenty-six air raid shelters.[76] Dr. MacDonald found corroborat-

ing evidence of the prison-yard incident and the American role in it from one eyewitness, a British soldier named Julian Tunstall.[77] Another eyewitness in Pyongyang (an American) recalled,

> We drove into a schoolyard. Sitting on the ground were well over 1000 North Korean POWs. They sat in rows of about fifty with their hands clasped behind their heads. In front of the mob, South Korean officers sat at field tables. It looked like a kangaroo court in session. . . . To one side several North Koreans hung like rag dolls from stout posts driven into the ground. These men had been executed and left to hang in the sun. The message to the prisoners sitting on the ground was obvious.[78]

Meanwhile Americans perpetrated their own murders of North Korean civilians around this time: one GI admitted to slitting the throats of eight civilians near Pyongyang, but nothing was done about it. Finally someone was punished, however, when two GIs were sentenced to twenty years' hard labor for having raped a Korean woman and killed a man associated with her—probably because he was a South Korean policeman. Unfortunately that episode did not create a pattern for subsequent military discipline, according to Macdonald. Similar incidents occurred in 1951. In perhaps the worst episode, ROK authorities removed tens of thousands of young men of military age from Pyongyang and nearby towns when they retreated, forming them into a "National Defense Corps." In the terrible winter of 1950–51, somewhere between 50,000 and 90,000 of them died of beatings, torture, and neglect while in ROK hands.[79] The North Koreans, of course, also carried out massacres during the war. Not surprising—after all, they're communists. What surprises is this—

the South was much worse, and the United States covered up the crimes of its ally for fifty years.

Perhaps the official American logic for the past several decades has been this: Koreans invaded Korea in June 1950. The United States responded to this outrageous breach of the peace. And ever since 1950, this act of aggression has justified whatever weapon the United States may wish to use in Korea and however much the United States may wish to terrorize North Korea. It is important to note that just war doctrines have always emphasized rules of proportionality: if militarist Japan was a clear threat to world peace, a North Korea that wanted to unify the Korean peninsula in 1950 was at best no threat to any other country and at worst a threat to regional stability. The proper response to the North's aggression, most analysts believe, was to reestablish the 38th parallel and claim a victory for the containment doctrine.

Had that been done and the war concluded in September 1950, the violence would have claimed 111,000 South Koreans killed, 106,000 wounded, and 57,000 missing, and 314,000 homes were destroyed and 244,000 damaged. American casualties totaled 2,954 dead, 13,659 wounded, and 3,877 missing in action. North Korean casualty figures are unknown, but combat losses alone ran to perhaps 70,000.[80] Instead, as the dog days of August drew to a close in Washington, President Truman and his secretary of state decided to transform their undeclared war into a campaign to liberate North Korea. Just as victory for the containment thesis glimmered over the horizon of the bloody Pusan Perimeter, Cold War liberals reached beyond to its antithesis, liberation (or "roll-back" in the terms of the operative document, NSC 81). From that unnoticed point, the momentum of the battlefield and of American politics gathered a strength that carried the administration quickly onward toward the worst foreign policy crisis between World War II and Cuba in 1962, creating an irreversible watershed in American anticommunist strategy. We carried the battle to the North, thinking an easy victory was at hand, whereupon China entered the battle, and soon the world stood at the brink of general war. No other president would again send American armies to liberate an established state until George W. Bush invaded Iraq in 2003.

If extreme measures and threats may have been justified in the dark winter of 1950–51, they were not justified after the battle stabilized in the spring of 1951, essentially along the DMZ that exists today. Yet for the next two years the United States rained destruction on North Korea. Upward of three million North Koreans died, along with another one million South Koreans, and nearly a million Chinese. Fifty-two thousand more American soldiers died. And the war ended where it began. Anatole Rapaport once wrote that the exterminism acquiesced to by all the powers in World War II became the reigning doctrine during the long years of the Soviet-American "balance of terror":

> It is doubtful whether Clausewitz ever envisaged "civilized war" as a slaughter of civilian populations. Even in his "absolute war" he saw slaughter confined to the battlefield. . . . The modern advocates of "total war," e.g. the Nazis and some partisans of "total victory" in the United States, explicitly included (and now include) civilian populations as military targets. For example, the U.S. Air Force ROTC manual, *Fundamentals of Aerospace Weapons Systems* defines a "military target," as follows: "Any person, thing, idea, entity, or location selected for destruction, inactivation, or rendering non-usable with weapons which will reduce or destroy the will or ability of the enemy to resist."[81]

In the most influential American book on justice in war, Michael Walzer argues that wars are always judged twice: first as to the justice of going to war and second as to how the war is fought. People can use bad means to fight just wars, and vice versa. He defends the Truman administration's logic of intervention with the following argument: the U.S. response to North Korean aggression was correct because Truman took the problem to the United Nations, which was the legitimate organ of world opinion, and thus of global justice ("it was the crime of the aggressor to challenge individual and communal rights"), and the UN acted correctly in backing American involvement in the war. In justifying the American invasion of North Korea, however, the U.S. ambassador to the UN called the 38th parallel "an imaginary line." Walzer then comments, "I will leave aside the odd notion that the 38th parallel was an imaginary line (how then did we recognize the initial aggression?)." Walzer leaves this mouthful without further thought, because it is the essence of his argument that Truman was right to defend the 38th parallel as an international boundary—this was the "initial aggression."[82]

The counterlogic implied by saying "Koreans invade Korea" disrupts the received wisdom or renders a logical reconstruction of the official American position impossible, even for a political theorist with the rhetorical skills of Michael Walzer. Kim Il Sung crossed the five-year-old 38th parallel, not an international boundary like that between Iraq and Kuwait, or Germany and Poland; instead it bisected a nation that had a rare and well-recognized unitary existence going back to antiquity, and was a line no Korean, North or South, respected. It is also often forgotten that until the rupture of the Tet Offensive in 1968, the same original sin also marked North Vietnam, through the 1964 attack on American ships in the Tonkin Gulf, or the "indirect invasion" which it sponsored via the Vietcong insurgency in the South. The

United States had committed no sins in Vietnam, it was the innocent party along with South Vietnam, and with its allies was engaged in a collective-security response to aggression. Few in the media questioned the legitimacy of the Cold War premise that American policy sought only to preserve an anticommunist South against aggression. Vietnam was fought not as "a new kind of war" but as another Korea, with success defined as a permanently divided Vietnam—as the Pentagon's film *Why Vietnam?* stated in 1965.[83] When Walzer comes to the *way* in which Americans fought the Korean War, however, he is unequivocally damning: the air war was not restrained by the dictates of *jus in bello* (justice in war-fighting), and therefore, in his view, constituted a long series of war crimes.

American strategy toward North Korea during and after the hot war concluded in 1953 is not a question of whether North Korea has been governed by people we like or respect, or by people who are better than American leaders: That is clearly not the case. The question is whether we have lived up to our ideals. North Korea has always posed the same question that Nazi Germany and militarist Japan did, namely, that morality in warfare always requires the separation of the enemy leadership from the innocence of the people whom they lead—whether in the 1950s, or today when 23 million human beings live in North Korea's garrison state. In that, we have consistently failed.

Chapter Two

THE NUCLEAR CRISIS:
FIRST ACT AND SEQUEL

There is a real crisis brewing in a place the cameras don't go. [It is] the single most dangerous problem, the impending nuclearization of North Korea. . . . None will sleep well with nukes in the hands of the most belligerent and paranoid regime on earth. The North Korean bomb would be controlled by . . . Dear Leader Kim Jong Il . . . unpredictable, possibly psychotic, [he] would be the closest thing to Dr. Strangelove the nuclear age has seen.[1]

One of the world's most menacing powers [is now] bereft of its cold-war allies and on the defensive about a nuclear-weapons project that ranks among the biggest threats in Asia. . . . "North Korea could explode or implode," said General Robert Riscassi, the commander of the 40,000 US troops who remain here. As the Stalinist Government of Kim Il Sung is driven into a corner, its economy shrinking and its people running short of food, General Riscassi contends, "it is a debateable matter" whether the country will change peacefully or lash out as it once did before. . . . One senior Bush Administration official said last week that North Korea already had enough plutonium to build a crude nuclear weapon . . . this has helped fuel . . . fear that the country that has bombed airliners and tried to kill

the South Korean cabinet would make one last lunge
for survival.[2]

Experts monitoring North Korea say they are increasingly concerned that the country may be preparing to
use 50 tons of uranium now fueling a large reactor as
raw material for nuclear weapons . . . the 50 tons
would be enough to produce two or three nuclear
bombs. . . . General Robert Riscassi . . . said he was
"increasingly concerned that North Korea could slide
into an attack as an uncontrollable consequence of
total desperation or internal instability."[3]

It is one of the scariest scenarios the post-cold-war
world has produced: an economically-desperate North
Korea, its leadership as isolated as ever, rejects every
effort the West makes to persuade it to abandon its
steadfast pursuit of a nuclear bomb. Instead, it issues
warnings about the possibility of war, which are
promptly echoed by a high-ranking U.S. Defense Department official visiting Seoul. North Korea's troops,
70 percent of which are gathered within sprinting distance of the Korean peninsula's tripwire demilitarized
zone, go on combat alert and Communist Party officials gather at a hurriedly called meeting in Pyongyang, the North Korean capital. Last week in Korea,
the nightmares all seemed to be coming true.[4]

THESE EXTRACTS FROM the two newspapers that come closest to
being America's papers of record and the leading newsweekly are
typical of the American commentary on North Korea early in the
new century. A desperate rogue regime run by a paranoid dictator
now threatening the world with nuclear attack: these were the

tropes, and they reappear time and again. The problem is, the first quote is from Charles Krauthammer in 1993, the second from David Sanger in 1992, the third from Sanger again in 1993, and the fourth from *Newsweek*—more than a decade ago in each case.

Let's review the issues in the recent crisis over the North's nuclear program. George Bush doesn't want to buy out the North's program; that would be "responding to blackmail." North Korea should get back inside the Non-Proliferation Treaty (NPT), but to pay them to do so would be like "buying the same horse twice." North Korea engages in bluff and brinkmanship: "they are skirting right to the edge of the red line," an administration official said. Maybe the North ought to take a lesson from the attack on Iraq: "if they missed [it], this is a chance to catch a rerun." How about a preemptive strike on the Yŏngbyŏn facility, another Osirak (Saddam Hussein's nuclear reactor that the Israelis destroyed in 1981)? The ROK defense minister endorsed such a strike in a highly secret meeting with Dick Cheney. But such an attack might be a problem given CIA estimates that the North has one or two atomic bombs. Critics, including many South Korean physicists, responded that this was impossible; they couldn't make the implosion devices, and couldn't know if they had a bomb until they tested one, which they never did. But then the North Koreans themselves dropped hints during meetings with American diplomats that "maybe they had nuclear weapons" already.

So much bureaucratic infighting between hawks and doves goes on that U.S. strategy might best be described as "one of drift punctuated by spasms of zigzagging," in the words of a State Department official who favored negotiations with the North. Maybe China could help us out, by putting pressure on the North? But critics said this would never happen, China wants the North to stay in power: it's "a case of looking for love in all the wrong places." Meanwhile "unilateralists on the right wing

of the Republican Party" loathed both cooperation with China
and "the very thought of accommodation with a hateful communist regime." Right-wingers pine for the collapse of the regime
and say it could happen any day, while the North says it is not
East Germany: "We are not going to collapse. You cannot stran-
gle us." Wait a minute, say the critics, don't you understand, the
North wants to make "a package deal" with us, it will barter away
its entire nuclear complex, and actually prefers that we continue
to station our troops in the South. Another concern high in the
minds of advisers to the president was the possibility that a North
Korean SCUD missile with a nuclear warhead could be launched
against Israel from Iran or Syria. Pyongyang sold SCUD-C missiles to Syria, a rocket big enough to carry a one-ton nuclear
warhead 400 kilometers; indeed one DPRK ship full of missiles
turned around and went home when it looked like it might be
intercepted. Why not develop a program to interdict their ships
and "quarantine" their ports, so they can't ship missiles or bring
cash in from their friends in Japan? It all sounds quite difficult
and frightening, doesn't it?

Every single reference in the preceding two paragraphs is more
than a decade old.[5] What we saw in the sequel in 2002–3 was, at
least from the North Korean side and in our journalism, a rerun
of the previous nuclear crisis, shifted to fast-forward. Way back
when, Kim Jong Il was the same Mad Dog he is said to be today:
a drunk, a womanizer, a playboy, Stalinist fanatic, state terrorist,
unstable, psychotic, another David Koresh, Jim Jones, or Charles
Manson—"Public Enemy Number One," running a country always making "one last lunge for survival." When the father died,
the American media dredged up all these things, but *Newsweek*
perhaps outdid them with its racist cover article: "Korea after
Kim: The Headless Beast" (July 18, 1994). According to "one
U.S. diplomat," the son was "irrational, far more dangerous than
his father. . . . No one in his right mind wants to see Kim Jong

Il in charge of a nuclear-armed North Korea." South Korean "experts" told the magazine that the end of the regime was nigh; "great turmoil is on the way." As for the deceased father, *Newsweek*'s intrepid researchers had uncovered what no one else ever did: Kim's presence with "Stalin's military" in the Soviet Far East in the 1930s. But "whether he actually fought against the Japanese is a matter of debate."[6]

Then, six years later, top American officials actually met the Dear Leader, when Secretary of State Madeleine Albright visited Pyongyang in preparation for President Bill Clinton's (aborted-by-Bush) summit with the younger Kim: "He is amazingly well-informed and extremely well-read," an American who met him related to a reporter, "He is practical, thoughtful, listened very hard. He was making notes. He has a sense of humor. He's not the madman a lot of people portrayed him as." A State Department official said, "He can talk about almost any subject . . . market economics, the Internet, coming technologies."[7] Madame Albright presented him with an NBA basketball signed by his basketball hero, Michael Jordan; Jong Il immediately wanted to take the ball out and dribble it around.

THE FIRST CRISIS, 1991–94

Predicting the behavior of crazy people is by definition impossible, and American officials constantly harp on Pyongyang's unpredictability. I would argue, to the contrary, that North Korean behavior has been quite predictable and that an irresponsible American media, almost bereft of good investigative reporters, often (but by no means always) egged on by government officials, obscures the real nature of the United States–Korean conflict. The media has had the wrong stories in the wrong place at the wrong time; the absurd result is that often one has to read North Korea's tightly controlled press to figure out what is actually going on between Washington and Pyongyang. Because of this severe and often state-induced media bias, it is exceedingly difficult to figure out the real stakes in this conflict.

Two logics clashed in the crisis — back then, and again a decade later: the first, a rationality of historically informed, trial-and-error, theory-and-practice *learned* behavior growing out of the Korean civil conflict going back to 1945, yielding intransigent bargaining strategies and extreme conceptions of national sovereignty; and the second, an instrumental reason of superordinate power surveilling and seeking to control the recalcitrant, the heterodox, the enemy, the evildoer, without any real necessity to *know* that enemy. North Korea's stake in this confrontation, its position, was to use its nuclear program to fashion a new relationship with the United States; its hole card was the possibility that it might already possess one or two atomic bombs. In pursuing a shrewd diplomacy of survival, Pyongyang used bluff, sham, and brinkmanship to get what it wanted. The American goal was to stabilize an unruly post–Cold War world, one that had already produced a major war in the Gulf. Given an American public that often seemed to think the world's problems were over with the end of the Cold War and the collapse of the Soviet Union, successive American administrations constantly exaggerated threats to gain public support in policing intractable nations. The 1990s dealt North Korean leaders a very bad hand, but they played it with surprising skill; the 1990s dealt the United States the best hand imaginable, and it very nearly plunged into another major war in June 1994, three years after the Gulf War ended.

Where did the CIA mantra about "one or two bombs" come from? It was included in a National Intelligence Estimate in November 1993, and was arrived at by gathering all the government experts on North Korea together and asking for a show of hands as to how many thought the North had made atomic bombs. A bit over half raised their hands; they assumed both that the North had reprocessed every last bit of the fuel it removed prior to 1994 and that they had done the arduous work of fashioning an implosion device. Yet three years later, nuclear experts at the Livermore and Hanford labs reduced their estimate of how much fuel the North possessed to less than that needed for a single bomb; they thought the North could only have 7 or 8 kilograms of fuel, yet "it takes ten kilograms of weapons-grade plutonium to fabricate a first bomb," and 8 or 9 kilograms for subsequent ones. Another leading expert, David Albright, also concluded independently that "the most credible worst-case estimate," is that the North may have 6.3 to 8.5 kilograms of reprocessed plutonium.[8] The CIA estimate is incorrect, in other words. Less noticed, however, was its role in strengthening the North's hand at the bargaining table.

MAD DOGS AND AMERICANS

At a critical point in March 1994 when the United States thought its diplomatic effort vis-à-vis North Korea was collapsing, *New York Times* reporter David Sanger began an article this way: "Say this about North Korea's leaders: They may be Stalinist fanatics, they may be terrorists, they may be building nuclear bombs, but they are not without subtlety. They have mastered the art of dangling Washington on a string.

He went on to refer to North Korea as "a country with a mad-dog reputation."[9]

Prominent Americans lose any sense of embarrassment or self-consciousness about the intricate and knotty problems of racial difference and Otherness when it comes to North Korea and its leaders. Recently Greta van Sustern introduced a Fox News segment on Kim Jong Il as follows: "Is he insane or simply diabolical?"[10] This trope merges the Beltway discourse of the 1990s, when Kim came to power and was widely said to be nuts. A decade earlier, on ABC's *Nightline*, correspondent Chris Bury described Kim Jong Il as "a 51-year-old son about whom little is known other than his fondness for fast cars and state terrorism." As for the country he runs, "North Korea may be growing desperate. Its economy is in shambles. . . . Yet North Korea maintains a huge army, more than a million soldiers on a permanent war footing, nearly 70 percent of them within 60 miles of Seoul." Chris Bury, like all other mainstream reporters, did not say how many South Korean soldiers are between Seoul and the DMZ, and thus 60 miles from Pyongyang: roughly 540,000, that is, 90 percent.[11] Of course he did not say, because he would not know that threats of a northern invasion began in March 1946 and have never ceased since.[12] Take this quotation: "There's signs of a big buildup. . . . The [North Koreans] could be in Seoul in four hours if they threw in everything they have." James Wade got this from an American engineer working for the U.S. Army—in 1960.[13] South Korean security services and their American allies are the authors of this one-sided chiaroscuro; they have succeeded for decades in getting Americans to stare blankly at one side of the Korean civil conflict, like a pigeon with nystagmus such that its head turns only toward the left.

Examining the history of the Korean conflict or the perpetual special pleadings of the two sides, or flashing some light into the shadows they hope no one will notice, takes time. Far easier, then, to take the word of an American official. On the same *Nightline* segment, Richard Solomon, Nixon/Bush China expert, said this: "Not a bad way to look at it is to think of the Waco, Texas crisis, where you have a small ideological, highly armed and isolated community."[14] Mad dog Kim Il Sung becomes David Koresh in this rendering, and it was perfectly believable. If you are dealing with insanity, anything is possible. North Korea is an American blank slate, and anything written upon it has currency—so long as the words are negative. North Korea ended up thrice-cursed, a Rorschach inkblot absorbing anticommunist, Orientalist, and rogue-state imagery, but then that was its original image—Harry Truman called his 1950 intervention a "police action" to catch North Korean criminals.

AMERICAN NUCLEAR THREATS

The incessant intensity of the confrontation along the Korean demilitarized zone is something the Pyongyang leadership deals with every day, as against the handful of witting Americans who know this quotidian conflict from the other side and the mass of Americans always surprised to learn that 40,000 American troops are still in Korea (so was Donald Rumsfeld, according to two eyewitnesses, when he arrived at the Pentagon in 2001). Pyongyang's media drum war stories into the brain so frequently that one might think the Korean War just ended; meanwhile that same war, never understood at the time and forgotten quickly after its conclusion, yields an American tabula rasa.

It was therefore a simple matter to superimpose all the media tropes by which Americans were led to understand the 1990–91 Gulf War onto North Korea: North Korea was not our daily enemy of forty years' standing, but a new "renegade state." This transference began in the immediate aftermath of the four-day ground war that defeated Iraq. Leslie Gelb editorialized in the *New York Times* that North Korea was "the next renegade state," a country "run by a vicious dictator" with SCUD missiles, "a million men under arms," and likely to possess nuclear weapons "in a few years." Another Iraq, in short.[15] I was amazed by Gelb's editorial when it appeared and the mimetic commentary that followed on its heels; it made me understand that my professional knowledge was akin to paleontology or some other arcane and remote discipline and that the Korean War existed in the American mind under "ancient history"—if not "never happened."

The essence of the first nuclear crisis rested upon the American desire to get Pyongyang to commit to the inspection regime of the NPT, administered by the International Atomic Energy Agency in Vienna (IAEA), and Pyongyang's desire to get out from under a nuclear threat that had been palpable since the 1950s and that gave it rights of self-defense under the NPT. This is still the basic nub of the problem today. If we assume that Pyongyang's real goal was to build weapons, it had solid justifications for going nuclear. After all, it could argue that it is merely engaged in deterrence, that is, the classic argument that once both sides have nuclear weapons, the resulting Mexican standoff negates the possibility of use. Moreover, the DPRK was the target of periodic nuclear threats and extended nuclear deterrence from the United States for decades, yet until now has possessed no such weapons itself. To my knowledge no mainstream reporter in the United States examined this history during the crisis with North Korea.[16] But Pyongyang would truly be crazy not to take this history with total seriousness.

After the Korean War ended, the United States introduced nuclear weapons into South Korea, in spite of the 1953 armistice agreement that prohibited the introduction of qualitatively new weaponry. How did this come about? The United States took this drastic step primarily to stabilize the volatile civil war. Syngman Rhee had been meeting with his military commanders, with Americans thinking he was preparing to attack the North. Even though Dulles clearly understood that the introduction of such weapons would be a violation of the Armistice (article 13d in particular), he was more worried about a new war in Korea.[17] Pursuing the civil war deterrent that Secretary of State Dean Acheson had applied to Korea before the war, he wanted to restrain both sides. Hotheads such as Rhee and Kim Il Sung would think twice before starting a war that would rain nuclear destruction on the peninsula. But Dulles's nukes would be kept under exclusive American control and would only be used in the event of a massive and uncontainable North Korean invasion.

In January 1958 the United States positioned 280 mm nuclear cannons and Honest John nuclear-tipped missiles in South Korea, and a year later the Air Force "permanently stationed a squadron of nuclear-tipped Matador cruise missiles in Korea." With a range of 1,100 kilometers, the Matadors were aimed at China and the USSR, as well as North Korea.[18] By the mid-1960s Korean defense strategy was pinned on routine plans to use nuclear weapons very early in any new war. As a 1967 Pentagon war game script put it, "the twelve ROKA and two US divisions in South Korea had . . . keyed their defense plans almost entirely to the early use of nuclear weapons." In January 1968 the North Koreans seized the American spy ship *Pueblo,* capturing the crew and keeping it in prison for eleven months. The initial reaction of decision makers was to drop a nuclear weapon on Pyongyang; "the fact that all the US F-4 fighter planes held on constant alert on Korean airfields were loaded only with nuclear weapons did not help the leaders to think clearly."[19]

Later on, atomic demolition mines (ADM) were installed, defensive weapons designed to be used in South Korea, "to contaminate an advance area and to stop an armored attack," as one ADM engineer put it. ADMs weighed only 60 pounds and yet had a 20 kiloton explosive force (same as Hiroshima); "you could get two weeks worth of contamination out of it so that an area was impassable."[20] The ADMs were moved around in Jeeps and placed by special teams who carried them in backpacks; meanwhile U.S. helicopters routinely flew nuclear weapons near the DMZ. That one of them might stray across the DMZ during a training exercise (as a small reconnaissance helicopter did in December 1994) and give Pyongyang an atomic bomb was a constant possibility. Meanwhile forward deployment of nuclear weapons bred a mentality of "use 'em or lose 'em;" even a small

North Korean attack might be cause enough to use them, lest they fall into enemy hands.[21]

For decades, in other words, the United States planned to use tactical and battlefield nuclear weapons in the very early stages of a new Korean conflict, the usual scenario being nukes at "H + 1," or within one hour of the outbreak of war, if large masses of North Korean troops were attacking south of the DMZ. Established strategy in Europe was to delay, delay, and then delay some more, an invasion with conventional weapons—and then use nuclear weapons only if absolutely necessary to turn back the assault. The logic was that we dared not use nuclear weapons in Europe except in the greatest extremity because the other side had them, but we can use them in Korea because it doesn't. South Korean commanders quickly got used to the idea that the United States would use nuclear weapons at an early point in a war with North Korea. The "AirLand Battle" strategy developed in the mid-1970s added an element of preemption: it called for quick, deep strikes into enemy territory, again with the likely use of nuclear weapons, especially against hardened underground facilities (of which there are many in North Korea). These plans envisioned an initial containment of a North Korean attack, followed by thrusts into the North, ultimately to seize and hold Pyongyang and topple the regime.

North Korean forces both expanded and redeployed in the late 1970s as a response to the AirLand Battle doctrine. The redeployment led to the stationing of nearly 80 percent of their ground forces near the DMZ. American and South Korean sources routinely cite this expansion and redeployment as evidence of North Korean aggressive intent; in fact it was done so that as many soldiers as possible could get into the South (regardless of how a war started) to mingle with ROK Army forces and civilians before nuclear weapons would be used, thus making their use less likely.

The Gulf War, however, caused a reevaluation of the role of nuclear weapons. With "smart" bombs that reliably reach their targets, high-yield conventional weapons were more useful than the messy and uncontrollable effects of using nuclear warheads. The Army wanted out of battlefield nuclear weapons as soon as possible. Thus American policy reached a point where its own interests dictated withdrawal of obsolescent nuclear weapons from Korea. On September 27, 1991, President Bush announced that he was withdrawing all tactical and battlefield nuclear weapons on a worldwide basis, destroying them or putting them into storage (the weapons removed included forty 203 mm and thirty 155 mm nuclear artillery shells, plus large numbers of ADMs). Although his spokesmen refused to confirm or deny the removal of about sixty air-dropped A-bombs used by F-16 bombers stationed in Kunsan, Bush issued a top secret directive to remove them as well. But one analyst called it "largely a gesture to the North because nuclear-armed submarines could come right up to the coast."[22] The AirLand Battle plans were updated in 1992, when Operations Plan 5027, the basic war plan for Korea, was reconfigured with new plans to land the U.S. Third Marine Division and the ROK's First Marine Division at the port of Wonsan on the west coast; they would march west toward Pyongyang, linking up with huge tank-led infantry divisions attacking across the DMZ, thus putting the capital in a pincer and overthrowing the regime.[23]

From the Korean War onward, North Korea responded to this nuclear blackmail by building enormous facilities underground or in mountain redoubts, from troop and materiel depots to munitions factories, even to subterranean warplane hangars. There are said to be as many as 15,000 underground facilities of a security nature in the North. In the mid-1970s Pyongyang faced more threats as the Park Chung Hee government sought to develop nuclear capabilities; Park ceased the activity only under

enormous American pressure, while retaining formidable poten-
tialities. The ROK continued on in the 1970s and 1980s with its
clandestine program to develop "indigenous ability to build ballistic missiles" capable of carrying nuclear warheads. Most of the
technologies for the South's missile program came from American firms, along with expertise garnered from the coproduction
of missiles. One of them, the NH-K, could travel 110 miles and
carry nuclear warheads, thus bringing Pyongyang into range. The
United States corralled Seoul by offering advanced technologies
in return for abandoning long-range missiles, but this, of course,
gave the South new capabilities. South Korea also garnered a
reputation as a "renegade" arms supplier toward pariah countries
such South Africa and Iran and Iraq during their war.[24] Much of
this reads as if it were written about North Korea, not South
Korea, and puts Pyongyang's activity into perspective: much of
it was responsive to U.S. pressure and ROK initiatives.

Washington never tires of accusing the North of terrorism,
assassination plots, and the like, but few understand that the
South also mounted hundreds if not thousands of terrorist attacks
on the North. Before the Korean War, they happened all the
time, with infiltrators burning down homes, killing party members and police, and sabotaging facilities. After the war as many
as 5,000 South Korean spies and infiltrators died in various attempts at terrorism and sabotage, including a major attempt to
assassinate Kim Il Sung in 1971, which is now the subject of a
forthcoming Sony-Columbia film.[25] Many of the anticommunist
organizations in the South openly called themselves *t'erodan*, or
terror organizations. In any case, if we understand North Korea
as "team green" rather than TEAM RED, its behavior has been
consistent with the logic of the Korean civil conflict and the nuclear confrontation since 1958.

With the withdrawal of American nukes, the stage was set for
the United States to begin pressuring North Korea about its nu-

clear reactor at Yŏngbyŏn. By now any viewer of American television news will have seen a stock film clip of the Yŏngbyŏn nuclear facility, but never have they been told the meaning of the ubiquitous slogan affixed to the roof: *charyŏk kaengsaeng* (regeneration through one's own efforts). Here was the North Korean justification for Yŏngbyŏn from the beginning—to substitute nuclear power in an energy regime dependent on domestic coal and hydroelectricity and on imported petroleum. Pyongyang sought to do what Japan and South Korea have been doing for decades, with the difference that since the big powers refused to ship them any potentially reprocessable nuclear fuel, they built a reactor that would utilize North Korea's substantial deposits of uranium. The problem was that such reactors produce plutonium from uranium, which, with a bit of refining, can become the high-grade fuel for nuclear weapons.

A decade ago North Korea's per capita energy use was still quite close to South Korea's, and for decades had been higher. Given that so much South Korean energy use goes to private automobiles and home consumption, the per capita energy use for industry and the military was much higher in the North. In an interview in 1978, Kim Il Sung told a delegation of the Japan Socialist Party that in the late 1960s some Korean scientists wanted to start up another petrochemical factory for refining petroleum (probably because Park Chung Hee had done the same). However, Kim said, "[O]ur country does not produce oil," and the United States influenced the world oil regime; therefore, "we are not yet in a position to depend on imports . . . [to do so] means allowing a stranglehold on our jugular."[26]

Both Seoul and Washington agree that Pyongyang is only 10 percent dependent on imported petroleum for its energy use, a major achievement by any comparison. In 1992–93, the North Korean energy profile looked like this (in units of 10^{15} *joules*): 226 for petroleum, 1,047 for coal, 176 for hydroelectric, and 38 for

"Other," yielding a total energy usage of 1,486 10^{15} *joules*. All petroleum was imported; 75.4 *joules* of coal was also imported (out of 1,047 total usage); that is, coking coal used in steel mills, coming almost exclusively from China now that the USSR is gone. These data do not count fuel wood, which is also in heavy use, and minor exports to China of hydroelectricity from the huge dams along the Yalu River.[27] This energy regime has been in crisis since 1991, because of the demise of the USSR and the collapse of trade partners in East Europe, leading to escalating costs for imported oil. One source estimated that in 1993 China provided 72 percent of North Korean food imports, 75 percent of oil imports, and 88 percent of its coking coal. The North's energy regime required 52 million metric tons of brown coal or anthracite to provide 84 percent of its energy needs at close to full capacity. In 1993 it produced only 29 million tons, however. North Korea has the capacity to refine 3.5 million metric tons of oil, but only imported 1.5 million tons in 1993.[28] All the more reason to go nuclear at home. (Those pundits who say the North's 30 megawatt reactor is too small to be useful in electric generation are trying to kid someone; this was an experimental reactor, to figure out how to run the 50- and 200-megawatt reactors also being built.[29]) In short, to figure out this crisis, you need to know Pyongyang's energy regime. But you also have to know how to build an atomic bomb.

The DPRK obtained a small nuclear reactor for research purposes of perhaps 4 megawatts capacity from the USSR in 1962, which was placed under IAEA safeguards in 1977. It then built the 30-megawatt facility. Construction probably began around 1979, and it went into operation in 1987 at Yŏngbyŏn. North Korea has lots of uranium 238, the radioactive element found in nature that has 92 protons and 146 neutrons. This atomic structure is intrinsically unstable; when bombarded with a neutron, the uranium atom will split, giving off two neutrons. Each of these can split an additional uranium atom, and thus a chain reaction is born—or was born in a crude graphite pile under Alonzo Stagg stadium at the University of Chicago during World War II. North Korea uses a magnox type reactor which is an improvement on Enrico Fermi's pile, but not by much. Natural uranium is made into pellets and stuffed into hollow metal rods of a magnesium oxide alloy called magnox; these tubes are placed in a welded steel vessel, with a graphite pile or core inside, cooled by CO^2 gas.

The size of the reactor's core is 14 meters wide and 8 meters high, it has a stack of six fuel elements, consisting of massive amounts of uranium metal—the total weight amounts to 112 tons of uranium. The chain reaction in the tubes generates heat, which is used to generate electricity and move turbines. As this heat is produced, so is plutonium: U-238 absorbs slow neutrons to become U-239, which can be reprocessed into fissile plutonium. All natural uranium reactors produce plutonium. Each fuel element had 1,691 fuel channels for a total of 10,146 fuel elements (or rods). Each ton of so-called Magnix fuel when irradiated for 1,000 megawatt days contained 998 kilograms of unconverted uranium and 0.8 kilograms of plutonium. When the process is finished, hot fuel rods are withdrawn and put in a cooling pond; they are then immersed in nitric acid, which separates the plutonium from the uranium. A Nagasaki-type bomb can be made from as little as 8–10 kilograms of such plutonium, but it must first be reprocessed into weapons-grade fuel.[30]

North Korea's reactor is very much like the British "Calder Hall" of the 1950s, which produced England's first atomic arsenal and which first the Soviets and then the North Koreans copied. The Calder Hall generated electricity as a by-product of plutonium production, generally rated at 50 *MWe* in its second-generation "Chapelcross" type. When used for making weapons instead of electricity, the British irradiated and removed the whole core about twice a year; when used for generating electricity, the rods are only removed every few years.[31] Although the North Korean version is similar to the Calder Hall, the Yŏngbyŏn reactor was clearly adapted to capture heat for making steam and generating electricity. The fuel load has only been removed twice: in 1989 and 1994. If Pyongyang had wanted to build a usable nuclear arsenal, it would have removed the fuel much more often than this.

Yŏngbyŏn, in short, began in pursuit of energy self-reliance, and ended as a bargaining chip to trade for a new relationship with the United States. No one paid much attention to it for several years, including an IAEA that Pyongyang asked to come have a look—only to be told that North Korea had missed that year's deadline and would have to reapply for IAEA inspections. Subsequently in 1989 American spy satellites monitored a 75- to 100-day shutdown of the reactor, while fuel rods were withdrawn and new fuel was added.[32] But nothing much happened until the end of the Gulf War enabled prominent American officials to bathe North Korea in a new and threatening light.

The success of George H. W. Bush's "television war" in the Gulf propelled strategic logic to a new conclusion: a war to end all (post–Cold War) wars inaugurated a "new world order" in which the whole Third World must behave and police itself or suffer the consequences from an omniscient, omnipresent, technologically omnipotent America. The cunning of history, however, had provided fewer and fewer enemies to watch in the 1990s. As Colin Powell put it, "I'm running out of demons. I'm running out of villains. I'm down to Castro and Kim Il Sung."[33] Furthermore the IAEA was now "post-Iraq," meaning that after the Gulf War it clearly had been unaware of important elements of Iraq's nuclear program. Donald Gregg put the result this way: "I compare the IAEA to being like a bunch of very eager proctologists asking the North Koreans to submit to all kinds of embarrassing investigations without really making it clear why it would be better for them."[34]

The showdown in the North over nuclear policy, according to Selig Harrison, came in a Central Committee meeting in December 1991, resulting in an "uneasy compromise" in which Kim Il Sung blessed IAEA inspections as a way to develop relations with the United States, while hardliners "ridiculed the idea that Pyongyang would get any help from Washington."[35] One of the earliest North Korean statements to the effect that U.S. troops can stay in Korea even after unification came from Kim Yong Sun in 1992, and Anthony Namkung has long argued that this idea was also approved at the highest level in 1990–91. He concluded that the North had made three crucial decisions in the aftermath of the collapse of the Soviet Union: first to normalize relations with the United States, second to seek peaceful coexistence with the South, and third to introduce market reforms.[36]

In any case the North responded well to the withdrawal of American nukes. Six regular IAEA inspections of its nuclear facilities ensued after May 1992. In fact Hans Blix got much more than he bargained for during the first round of inspections, with the North showing him facilities as yet unknown to the IAEA. Among them were "two cavernous underground shelters," access to which required "several minutes to descend by escalator." They were there, Blix was told, in case someone attacked the complex.[37] But hardliners in Washington were not inclined to give the North any credit; instead they pressed for much more intrusive inspections: reporters paraphrased unnamed officials traveling to Korea with George Bush in 1992 to the effect that they would require "a mandate to roam North Korea's heavily guarded military sites at will" before they could be sure of DPRK capabilities.[38] Defense Department officials wanted to find ways to eliminate the DPRK's "entire nuclear program;" but they also favored intrusive verification schemes "precisely because they appeared unobtainable."[39] Meanwhile every year various CIA directors told Congress that the DPRK was "the worst threat we face," "the critical major military threat for the next few years," and so on.[40]

Nayan Chanda was for many years one of the best reporters in Asia, writing for the *Far Eastern Economic Review*. In 1993 he prepared a major study of the nuclear crisis, which, for the first time in my reading, dwelled on the IAEA's use of American intelligence imaging to surveil North Korea.[41] On February 22, 1993, the IAEA unveiled for its board at their Vienna home office "a series of amazingly detailed photographs taken by US spy satellites in 1989," which showed North Koreans "working to hook up their plutonium reprocessing plant with a huge waste storage tank." Spy satellite photos from 1992, also displayed at the time, showed that "the entire area around the building had been filled with tonnes of earth gently sloping from the tank and had been landscaped with trees, a parking lot and a road. These extraordinary photographs suddenly threw a flood of light on the mystery of the missing nuclear waste." The waste tanks — which were the key sticking point a decade ago and remain so today — were said to be 8 meters underground, with a concrete slab on top and a building put aboveground on top of the slab.

The used fuel rods from a Calder Hall–style reactor are washed in nitric acid solutions to extract plutonium, and the resultant hot chemical waste is stored in stainless steel tanks. Access to such tanks would enable specialists to determine how much plutonium was extracted in 1989. The CIA estimated that the North pulled out 10 to 16 kilograms in 100 days in 1989, or 22–35 pounds; North Korea admitted to experimenting with reprocessing small amounts of plutonium from damaged fuel rods, telling the IAEA that it only separated out 98 grams (3.5 pounds) of plutonium.[42] Chanda wrote that the IAEA had been told that the "time signature" on the plutonium and waste samples that the North Koreans provided did not match: "[T]he isotopic content of reprocessed plutonium and its residue in the waste changes at a fixed rate. This allows scientists to determine the exact time when plutonium was processed."[43]

Who told them? This determination also came from U.S. intelligence, not from the IAEA; the latter had shipped the waste sample to the Department of Energy for analysis.[44] The IAEA's conclusion was that the North Koreans had obviously processed more plutonium than they had admitted. The Department of Energy estimated that North Korea had reprocessed plutonium on four separate occasions. When the IAEA wanted a better sense of how much plutonium the Koreans had reprocessed in these episodes, "the CIA then came up with the suggestion that the IAEA examine the waste sites"; to help it out, "the CIA supplied the IAEA with satellite photographs." Chanda quoted Hans Blix (director of the IAEA) as saying he didn't worry about North Korean charges that he had compromised the IAEA's impartiality by using American intelligence information: "Satellite imagery today belongs to the realm of conventional sources of information. I don't see any reason why anyone should object to that." What Blix did not say is that the resources of the U.S. National Reconnaissance Office (NRO — the agency that has produced and deployed spy satellites since 1960, the existence of which was only acknowledged publicly by the U.S. government in 1992[45]) are vastly superior to private-eye satellite imagery. When I mentioned this at a conference in Milwaukee in 1994, a man from the audience rose up and said such intelligence sharing "happens all the time," it's no big deal. He then shouted out, "They got caught cheating, that's all!" He turned out to be a nuclear physicist from Los Alamos; you would think he might be smart enough to wonder if perhaps the Koreans purposely provided this particular sample, as yet another ace in the hole of their (apparently quite ample) deck.

In a 1994 letter from one of Japan's most experienced nuclear proliferation experts, addressed to a friend of mine who showed it to me on a not-for-attribution basis, we read this: "There is a whole issue of the most delicate [nature, the] international problem of sharing of intelligence across national borders." Delicate in any context, such intelligence sharing was incendiary in the Korean context. North Korea has been the object of a kind of international proctology since before the Korean War when surveillance by airplanes began. Every day a variety of satellites scrutinize its territory, using equipment so sophisticated that it allegedly can record conversations in autos speeding through Pyongyang; even the old U-2 spy plane retains a function in the Korean theater. Bereft of technologies to control its own air space (and "space" space), over the decades North Korea built underground facilities and engaged in elaborate shell games to confound the eyes intruding from above.

The reevaluation of DPRK armed strength in 1978–79 that derailed Jimmy Carter's troop withdrawal strategy was based on reinterpreted reconnaissance photos: tanks and other weapons originally thought to be wooden mockups were redefined as the real thing. "I have always suspected that the facts were doctored" by the Defense Intelligence Agency and others, Carter later told a reporter, "but it was beyond the capability even of a president to prove this."[46] So, what do we make of this regime unveiling a waste site in 1989 and then camouflaging it by 1992? Do they go about their business unaware of this round-the-clock surveillance? Of course, it meant that they wanted the NRO to witness these events; it wanted to show its ace in the hole, and then put it back in the deck.[47] If they had truly wanted a nuclear arsenal hidden from the world, they would have chosen the Israeli option and built everything underground.

The last crisis over the North's nuclear program began for the American press on March 12, 1993, when North Korea announced that it would withdraw from the Nuclear Non-Proliferation Treaty. Once again Leslie Gelb (by then head of the Council of Foreign Relations) held forth, arguing that North Korea's nuclear activity will bring on "the next crisis," where another "bad guy" like Saddam may soon test the mettle of "the sane nation[s]."[48] For Congressman John Murtha (D-PA.), chairman of the House Appropriations subcommittee on defense, North Korea had become "America's greatest security threat." If it did not let its nuclear facilities be inspected, he said in March, the United States ought to knock them out with "smart weapons."[49] By this time it was routine for influential American analysts to argue that Kim Il Sung was evil or insane or both, that his regime ought to be overthrown, and that if necessary his nuclear facilities should be taken out by force.[50]

For North Korea, however, the crisis began on January 26, 1993, when newly inaugurated President Bill Clinton announced that he would go ahead with Team Spirit war games (the largest military exercises in the world), which George Bush had suspended a year earlier and then revived for 1993. Team Spirit "games" routinely included the introduction to Korea of nuclear-capable aircraft and naval ships of all types, back-pack nukes controlled by mobile units, practice with nuclear cannons, and so on, with many South Korean units working together with the Americans on various nuclear war scenarios.

In late February, Gen. Lee Butler, head of the new U.S. "Strategic Command," announced that the Pentagon was retargeting strategic nuclear weapons meant for the old USSR, on North Korea (among other places). At the same time new CIA chief James Woolsey testified that North Korea was "our most grave current concern."[51] By mid-March 1993, tens of thousands of American soldiers were carrying out war games in Korea again, and in came B1-B bombers and B-52s from Guam, several naval vessels carrying cruise missiles and the like, whereupon the North turned another hole card over on the table by announcing that it was pulling out of the NPT.

It is a basic principle of the nonproliferation regime that countries without nuclear weapons cannot be threatened by those that possess them,[52] and since the demise of the USSR, America games in Korea aimed only at the North. By threatening to leave the NPT, the DPRK played a strong card; implicitly it raised the specter of other near-nuclear powers doing the same, when the current NPT was due for a global renegotiation in 1995 and such major countries as Japan and India were unhappy about it. Yet if North Korea merely wanted nuclear weapons, it would have stayed outside the NPT regime in the first place—like Israel, India, and Pakistan. Once Team Spirit was finished, however, the North agreed to high-level talks with the United States and subsequently (on June 11, 1993) suspended its withdrawal from the NPT—putting that Joker back in the deck. That Team Spirit and other U.S. nuclear threats were what motivated the North could not be clearer from reading the North Korean press, which warned against resuming the games since the November 1992 American elections. Yet amid the usual frothy bombast against American imperialism, all during this period Pyongyang continued to call for good relations with the United States.

The other issue that energized Pyongyang in early 1993 was the IAEA's demand to carry out "special inspections" of undeclared sites in North Korea, including the one that the IAEA said was a nuclear waste dump. The IAEA had never before demanded such an inspection for any other country,[53] but it was under international pressure for not ferreting out several sites in Iraq, discovered after Baghdad was defeated. The North knew this to be a demand of hardliners in the Pentagon,[54] and so it resisted these inspections on two grounds. First, the IAEA needed to utilize American intelligence to ferret out new sites to

visit; since the United States was a belligerent in Korea, this violated the mandate of the IAEA. Second, if the IAEA has passed
the results of its inspections to the United States and if the DPRK
allowed this to continue, the United States would eventually
want to open up all DPRK military facilities to the IAEA.[55] The
United States became obsessed with getting the DPRK to comply
with the IAEA, and the DPRK voiced its perennial fear that the
United States simply wanted to obliterate its existence as a state.

So, here was the intricately raveled knot of the disagreement
in 1993–94, with the IAEA demanding inspection of an alleged
waste site and the North Koreans claiming that the waste site was
a military installation and therefore off limits, while lambasting
the IAEA for following the desiderata of the DPRK's sworn enemy, the United States, and for not demanding equal time to see
what the United States might be doing at its many installations
in South Korea. And as if someone had been trying to force-feed
North Korean paranoia and encourage them to summon even
more of the blank recalcitrance for which they are justly famous,
the *New York Times* featured an essay by a well-placed expert who
referred darkly to "faddish and misguided notions" in Washington's new strategic war plans—such as "forming a nuclear expeditionary force" aimed at Third World "rogue states."[56] Little
wonder that the DPRK worked assiduously on its medium-range
(600 miles) missile, the Nodong 1, launching it well into the
Japan Sea during a test in May 1993, banging the target precisely
at a distance of 300 miles—and making no bones about its purpose.[57] (Foreign experts were not sure whether the precise targeting of the missile was an accident or an indication of the
North's technological prowess.)

After Iran made a deal to buy 150 Nodong-1 missiles in 1993,
Israeli negotiators flew to Pyongyang and offered $1 billion in
investment and technical assistance with gold mines if they called
the sale off. Foreign Minister Shimon Peres was about to fly off

to Pyongyang to close the deal when the Clinton administration intervened and shut his trip down. But this is another precedent illustrating the North's willingness to be bought off; unlike Washington, Israel understood that it couldn't get something for nothing.

Every so often during this sixteen-month-long crisis, headlines would blare that a new Korean War was about to erupt. On the weekend of November 5–7, 1993, coinciding with Defense Secretary Les Aspin's visit to Seoul, from *CBS Evening News* to the Fox Channel and even to National Public Radio, wild charges circulated about crazed North Koreans readying an atomic bomb, forbidding access to international inspectors, and concentrating 80 percent of their army on the border with South Korea—the implication being that they might attack at any minute. On Sunday, November 7, President Clinton told *Meet the Press* that "any attack on South Korea is an attack on the U.S.,"[58] and on November 18, *CBS Evening News* again ran a scare story saying North Korean nukes are the single greatest threat to world peace today. Essentially these were stories scripted by the Pentagon or the White House; you had to read the North Korean press to figure out if anything really new was going on.

In March 1994, a year into this crisis, the United States began moving toward bringing sanctions to bear on the DPRK through the UN Security Council. The decision was said to have come hours after North Korean officials walked out of a meeting in Seoul "and threatened war if Washington and Seoul mounted a pressure campaign. 'Seoul will turn into a sea of fire.' "[59] This statement was actually taken far out of its context; it was a reference to what would happen if the United States attacked the North. Kim Il Sung personally and publicly disowned the "sea of fire" remark and later fired the official who made it. But this got hardly any attention in the American press. Instead "sea of fire" became another trope in media commentary thereafter.

The route to the October Framework Agreement began in
June–July 1993 when the North Korean side proposed that their
entire graphite reactor nuclear program be replaced by American-
supplied light-water reactors (LWRs), which are much less prone
to weapons proliferation and which would also require that
Pyongyang become dependent on external supplies of fuel
(mainly enriched uranium). This offer came as "a total shock" to
American negotiators at the time.[60] (North Korea had often
stated that it was forced to use graphite reactors and its own
uranium because no one would help it with nuclear energy.)
Pyongyang instantly toned down its anti-American rhetoric, even
as the anniversary of the Korean War passed. Nothing came of
the North Korean LWR proposal in the summer of 1993, how
ever.

The two delegations met again in November 1993, and on
November 11, North Korea tabled a "package deal" to resolve the
confrontation. It demanded an American statement assuring
against the threat and use of force against the DPRK, but also
included a plan for the general improvement of relations between
the United States and North Korea, suspension of Team Spirit,
IAEA continuity-of-safeguards inspections (but no more than
that), a termination of antagonism and especially American nuclear threats against the DPRK, and a fundamental resolution of
the nuclear problem through the provision of LWRs. The DPRK
declared its intention to renounce its entire graphite system (all
three reactors, plus a reprocessing plant) in return. Other sources
say the still-unpublished November initiative went even further
toward a general resolution of all the difficulties remaining between Pyongyang and Washington. Selig Harrison, who was the
private analyst most aware of the significance of the November
11 proposal, listed ten items in the package deal, including liaison
offices in each capital, a new peace treaty to replace the armistice,
mutual force reductions, removal of trade restrictions and Trad-

ing with the Enemy Act items, a consortium to provide the LWRs, American support for Japanese and South Korean aid and investment in the DPRK, the admission of North Korea to the Asia-Pacific Economic Cooperation (APEC) organization, combined with American encouragement of private sector investment, and an American willingness to discuss ground force withdrawals from South Korea (timed to North Korean redeployments away from the DMZ).[61] More than a decade later, this "package deal" is still the essence of what Pyongyang wants.

This was a diplomatic watershed in the history of United States–North Korean relations, but it was all mostly secret.[62] South Korea got wind of it, of course, and President Kim Young Sam went ballistic in a meeting with Clinton, fearing that somehow Pyongyang might damage Seoul's relations with the United States, or even isolate it.[63] Meanwhile, Pyongyang publicly played the game it plays best: saber-rattling. At the end of November 1993, Pyongyang said, "[W]hen we declared our decision to withdraw from the NPT, we had taken into account all possible consequences, and we are fully prepared to safeguard the sovereignty of the country even if the worst such as 'sanctions' or war is imposed on us."[64] In a key statement on February 1, 1994, the Foreign Ministry in Pyongyang stated, "[T]he United States has created a momentous crisis that is likely to develop into catastrophe, at this crucial juncture when prospects are in sight for saving the DPRK-USA talks from the current deadlock and striking a package solution to the nuclear issue." Pyongyang blamed the IAEA and "hardline" forces in the United States for creating the obstacles in the path to agreement (like the Pentagon's decision to deploy Patriot missiles in South Korea), rather than Clinton and his advisers. With the United States pushing its allies and DPRK ally China toward supporting UN sanctions, Pyongyang tabled another trump card: it announced that sanctions would be taken as "an act of war."

The Pentagon had war-gamed a new Korean War many times over the years, but *Newsweek* leaked two outcomes that showed the North Koreans winning: "Pentagon simulations . . . showed the South's defenses collapsing so fast the hair stood up on the back of our necks," one Pentagon source said. Every scenario showed a death toll of at least 50,000 Americans and hundreds of thousands to millions of Koreans.[65] The North's *Nodong* missiles also raised the specter of Japan being drawn into a new war, since it would be a major base for the American war effort.

China played a quietly active role in the spring of 1994, seeking to defuse tensions; it hinted to the United States that it might support UN Security Council sanctions, or abstain from a vote, but also urged the United States to give North Korea security guarantees. It said essentially the same thing to Pyongyang about UN sanctions, trying to pressure it. Twice it mobilized high-ranking Korean War veterans, Gen. Hong Huezi and Gen. Xu Xin, to journey to Pyongyang to discuss the nuclear issue.[66] When push came to shove in May 1994, however, it welcomed the North's top military leader to Beijing. Manchurian guerrilla Ch'oe Kwang met all the top leaders, and President Jiang Zemin gave him a very public bear hug—thus to quiet Americans who were saying China would never support the North in a new war.

The two sides continued high-level talks trying to get a diplomatic settlement. By mid-1994 there was still no agreement, however, so Pyongyang forced Clinton's hand by shutting down its reactor (in May) for the first time since 1989, withdrawing some 8,000 fuel rods and placing them in cooling ponds. This provocative and dangerous ploy called Washington's bluff and left administration officials with no apparent room for maneuver.[67] Leon Sigal correctly noted that the North had delayed getting the fuel out of the reactor for over a year when they finally dumped the rods. He called it provocative, but not much more, and noted that IAEA inspectors were still on the scene there to witness the defueling; the rods could stay in the cooling ponds for some time.[68]

Predictably this act also occasioned another irresponsible media blitz about a new Korean War. In this case, however, the alarms were warranted, unbeknown to the media. The United States and North Korea came much closer to war at this time than most people realize. On NBC's *Meet the Press* on April 3, 1994, Defense Secretary William Perry said, "[W]e do not want war and will not provoke a war over this or any other issue in Korea," but if U.S. sanctions "provoke the North Koreans into unleashing a war . . . that is a risk that we're taking."[69] Perry's formulation was not just careful and precise. He and Ashton Carter Jr. had been studying for some time whether a preemptive strike could be carried out against Yŏngbyŏn without starting the next Korean War. They concluded that it couldn't.

By mid-June the Clinton administration "had devised a plan laying out the first steps the US should take to prepare for war," which included the addition of 10,000 American troops in Korea, dispatching Apache attack helicopters, and moving in more Bradley Fighting Vehicles.[70] Furthermore, "to make sure Clinton understood both the human and the monetary costs of a war, the Joint Chiefs had summoned all the regional commanders and four star generals in the service to Washington in late May [1994] to discuss Korea and brief the President." According to U.S. commander in Korea Gen. Gary Luck's estimates, he would need as many as 80,000 to 100,000 body bags in the field for the American soldiers who would die in a new Korean war, and Korean troop casualties could reach the hundreds of thousands. Moreover, if the North struck Seoul as expected, "the number of civilian casualties would be staggering." The cost of such a war, Luck predicted, would be at least $500 million and could top $1 trillion, far higher than the almost $60 billion spent on Desert Storm, a sum largely borne by U.S. allies.[71]

One way of expressing what happened in May and June 1994 is that Clinton and his advisers looked down the barrel of the other side's guns and blinked. Another way is to say that Pyongyang did the same thing. It did not want war, either. But it did want to rub American noses in the realities of the Korean conflict, so they would pay attention and settle the crisis through diplomacy (i.e., diplomacy in the sense that both sides give up something, not that one side imposes its will on the other). Former President Jimmy Carter had been invited to visit Pyongyang some years before. Alarmed by what he had learned about the depth of the crisis from briefings by Clinton administration officials, he decided to fly off to Pyongyang in mid-June 1994 and meet with Kim Il Sung (the first such meeting between Kim and a current or former U.S. president). By a sleight-of-hand that depended on Cable News Network's simultaneous transmission (direct TV mediation that short-circuited the ongoing diplomacy), Carter broke the logjam.

During discussions with Kim Il Sung, Carter suggested that Pyongyang freeze its Yŏngbyŏn facility in return for light water reactors and a new relationship with the United States. After gaining Kim Il Sung's assent, Carter then held a quick new conference broadcast worldwide on CNN. President Clinton appeared in the White House press room soon thereafter and declared that if Pyongyang were to freeze its program (i.e., leave the 8,000 fuel rods in the cooling ponds and halt ongoing construction on new facilities), high-level talks would resume — which they did on July 8 in Geneva. This critical breakthrough made possible the accord that was consummated in October 1994.

The October Framework Agreement promised Pyongyang

that in return for freezing its graphite reactors and returning to full inspections under the Nuclear Non-Proliferation Treaty, a consortium of nations (including the United States, Japan, South Korea, and others) would supply light-water reactors to help solve the North's energy problems; the consortium also agreed to supply long-term loans and credits to enable Pyongyang to purchase the new reactors, valued at about $4 billion. In the meantime the United States would supply heating oil to tide over the DPRK's energy problems, and would begin a step-by-step upgrading of diplomatic relations. The agreement called for full normalization of relations, and most important, an American pledge not to threaten or target North Korea with nuclear weapons. Since these provisions are often misconstrued by critics, let's extract the language:

> Article II. The two sides will move toward full nor-
> malization of political and economic relations.
>
> 1) Within three months of the date of this Document,
>   both sides will reduce barriers to trade and invest-
>   ment, including restrictions on telecommunica-
>   tions services and financial transactions.
> 2) Each side will open a liaison office in the other's
>   capital following resolution of consular and other
>   technical issues through expert level discussions.
> 3) As progress is made on issues of concern to each
>   side, the U.S. and the DPRK will upgrade bilateral
>   relations to the Ambassadorial level. . . .
>
> III. 1) The U.S. will provide formal assurances to the
> DPRK against the threat or use of nuclear weapons
> by the U.S.[72]

The framework agreement was predicated on mutual mistrust, and therefore both sides had to verify compliance at each step toward completion of the agreement, which was supposed to come in 2003 (or later), since constructing the reactors and bringing them on line would take years. Once the reactor construction was completed, the North Koreans would dismantle their mothballed reactors, and (before the LWRs began operation) they would be finally required to open up the famous "waste site" to IAEA inspection, which would at last show whether they ever reprocessed enough plutonium for an atomic bomb.

The LWRs cost the United States next to nothing. Building the reactors will probably run over $5 billion if they are ever completed; we paid in about $30 million a year, with Congress balking all the way, while the South Koreans and Japanese footed most of the bill. By contrast, the estimated direct and indirect cost of maintaining 37,000 American troops in the South and myriad military bases runs from $17 billion to $42 billion annually, depending on how the costs are calculated.[73]

Here are some principles I would derive from this complicated episode. First, those who live a particular history know it in their bones, both because they have to, and because of the venerable argument that there is no theory without practice. Thereby the concentrated logic and action of the weak can trump the logic of the powerful, which must be abstract by virtue of the number of abstractions it has to deal with. Robert Manning, a State Department official in the Bush and Clinton administrations, remarked that "the North Koreans had a very weak hand, and they played it brilliantly."[74] But then they had done so in the fall of 1950 as well, when their country was occupied, and they got Chinese troops to bail their chestnuts out of a very hot fire. They continue to do so today. The leaders of North Korea are formidable people; they should not be underestimated. This is the story of the Vietnam War, too. I do not think, however, that it is a story that Americans have yet learned, or want to learn. A second point is that knowing the "rogue" enemy seems difficult, but it is not so hard because their mind is concentrated by the power asymmetries. Third, understanding American foreign policy and the policy process seems easy, but it is extraordinarily difficult because of any number of false or misleading presuppositions placed before the analyst, especially by the American media. Last, it is some kind of statement about the United States that one could not grasp what was going on with North Korea through the American media by itself, but had to read the "rogue" press carefully as well.

The point is not to say that North Korea "won" the political and diplomatic struggle with the Clinton administration, or that Pyongyang has a better media policy. Quite to the contrary, its policy for half a century has been to pile lie upon lie, exaggeration upon exaggeration, even when it would be more convenient and helpful to its cause to tell the truth. But that is what we have learned to expect from communist regimes. The DPRK is not a nice place, but it is an understandable place, an anticolonial and anti-imperial state growing out of a half-century of Japanese colonial rule and another half-century of continuous confrontation with a hegemonic United States and a more powerful South Korea, with all the predictable deformations (garrison state, total politics, utter recalcitrance to the outsider) and with extreme attention to infringements of its rights as a nation.

THE SUNSHINE POLICY

In 1998, on a warm, beautiful winter day that would not come again to Korea for many Februaries, long-time dissident Kim Dae Jung was inaugurated. He was the first president to reflect a genuine political transition from the elites who had ruled the ROK since 1948. In his inaugural address he unveiled his "sunshine policy," pledging to "actively pursue reconciliation and coopera- tion" with North Korea and declaring his support for Pyong- yang's attempts to better relations with Washington and Tokyo — in complete contrast with his predecessors, who chafed mightily at any hint of such rapprochement. He soon underlined his pledges by approving large shipments of food aid to the North, lifting limits on business deals between the North and southern firms, and calling for an end to the American economic embargo against the North (during a visit to Washington in June 1998). Kim explicitly rejected "unification by absorption" along German lines (which was the de facto policy of his predecessors), and in effect committed Seoul to a prolonged period of peaceful coex- istence and reconciliation, with reunification put off for twenty or thirty more years.

Both governments now committed themselves to a staged, slow process of reaching a confederated reunification. The North first tabled its confederal plan in 1960, and Kim Dae Jung's scheme called for a prolonged period of confederation, the first stage of which would involve "close, cooperative" relations while maintaining two different systems, states, militaries, and foreign policies. The two sides would manage relations between each other through various inter-Korean organizations, pending the second stage when, after a fairly long period of preparation, for- mal unification would occur under a federal system of one people, one nation, one political system, but two autonomous regional governments. (In his inaugural address Kim had cited a practical need to respect the pride of the North Koreans and the necessity to govern the North Korean region separately for a considerable time, under a regional autonomous government.) The federal government would run Korea's diplomacy, defense, and major domestic policies. The third stage would be real unification under a central government. All this would be done with the consent of the people through a democratic process.

North Korea waited a year to test Kim Dae Jung's resolve, and a couple of submarines and several dead infiltrators washed up on the South Korean coast—suggesting that hardliners tried to bait Kim or disrupt North-South relations. But by mid-1999 it was apparent that Pyongyang viewed President Kim's "sunshine policy" as a major change in South Korea's position. Its attitude toward Washington also began changing. Long determined to get the United States out of Korea, North Korean leaders now began to make clear to various interlocuters that if the United States were to become an "honest broker" on the peninsula, American troops might stay on the peninsula, to deal with changed international power relations (especially a strong Japan and a strong China) and to help Pyongyang through its current economic difficulties.[75] Former Secretary of Defense William Cohen seemed almost to echo such views in July 1998, when he declared that American troops would stay in Korea even after it was unified.

In late August 1998, a hailstorm of alarmist press reports claimed that North Korea was building nuclear weapons in an enormous underground redoubt, and had sent a long-range missile arcing through the stratosphere over Japan, leading to virtual panic in Tokyo—as if the missile had barely cleared the treetops. The story about the underground facility was based on a strategic intelligence leak to David Sanger, who reported that "[t]housands of North Korean workers are swarming around [this] new site, burrowing into the mountainside." Throughout the 1990s the North moved more and more assets underground, as a response to the increasing efficacy of American precision-guided weapons (by the end of the decade, according to the top U.S. Air Force officer in the ROK, "Virtually all DPRK army and air force assets

[were] now underground"[76]). After various negotiations, however, in the spring of 1999 the North surprised everyone and opened the site up to an unprecedented U.S. military inspection: All they found was a cavernous underground facility—completely empty. There was no evidence that any nuclear activity had taken place there.

The North's missiles are another matter. In August 1998 North Korea's press had spoken for weeks of little else but preparations for the celebration of the fiftieth anniversary of the regime on September 9, which would finally bring Kim Jong Il to full power after the long mourning period for his father. In late August, Pyongyang announced that it had launched a three-stage rocket that had put a satellite in orbit—its photo in DPRK-aligned newspapers in Japan looked just like the small satellite China had first put into orbit in 1970, whirring around the globe beeping out "The East Is Red." It was a clear case of *epatér le Chinoise*—albeit beeping out the "Song of Kim Il Sung," of course. The international media, however, treated this as a direct threat to Japan, and denied that it was a satellite throw. It took weeks for the U.S. intelligence groups to do retrospective analysis of radar tapes; finally they concluded that it was indeed a fireworks display probably meant to commemorate the fiftieth anniversary, but that the satellite had failed to reach orbit. In all the hoopla, it was conveniently forgotten that the North had not tested a missile from May 1993 to August 1998.

When the North Koreans blasted off their rocket, everyone seemed to assume that they violated Japanese sovereignty. Few asked in what other direction the North might fire off a rocket—over Russia? China? South Korea? Meanwhile, sovereignty only extends up to that which a nation can shoot down. When we sent U-2 spy planes over the USSR in the late 1950s, Soviet leaders naively assumed that "the traditional, geographically-based concept of sovereignty extended upwards into the atmosphere without limit," in the words of Geoffrey Klingsporn. But Secretary of State Christian Herter set the Russians straight after Senator Mike Mansfield asked him for the Eisenhower administration's "official interpretation of international law as regards the extension of national sovereignty skyward." Herter responded, "I don't think we have any. . . . there is no definition as to what is considered the atmosphere above the air." Essentially a nation's sovereignty extended only to what it was capable of shooting down; otherwise, as Quincy Wright of the University of Chicago put it, "beyond airspace is outer space which is not under the sovereignty of any state."[77]

North Korean missiles are good; indeed, they are the best available on the world market for countries not allied to the United States. The Scud-C had a range of about 500 kilometers, but the May 1993 test was of an enhanced Scud capable of 1,000 to 1,300 kilometer range with a one ton payload. It used a cluster of four Scud engines wrapped around the missile body.[78] In this, its only test, it flew down range 300 miles (or 500 kilometers) and banged the target right on the nose—thus making clear that the North could hit Japan. The North Koreans squeezed everything possible out of this technology to give the Scud such range, but to go beyond it, they developed the Taepodong-1, a long-range ballistic missile capable of 1,500–2,000 kilometers.

Like the early American rocket tests in the late 1940s, this was essentially one missile stacked on top of another—a Scud-C on top of a Nodong, with a small third-stage booster for the satellite. The Taepodong-2 has a different base rocket, resembling the Chinese DF-3 or CSS-2, with much greater thrust, capable of throwing a warhead 3,500 to 6,000 kilometers—thus theoretically bringing into range the northwest coast of the United States. (Alaska is about 5,000 kilometers from North Korea, but the closest point in the contiguous forty-eight states is about 8,000 kilometers.) However, it has never been tested, and independent experts believe the North has no rocket like the DF-3, or the much more powerful engines needed to power it. The only evidence that this rocket exists is a North Korean model, a mock-up that they allowed to be photographed in 1994.[79] It may be a rocket under development, but much more likely, it's another card pulled out of their deck, turned over briefly, and then put back in the deck.

Evil-doer Kim Jong Il's long-range missile quickly became Donald Rumsfeld's poster child for missile defense (Rumsfeld had chaired a task force on missile defense, issuing its report in the summer of 1998), but it needs a shot of Don's Viagra. It has insufficient lift capacity to carry a nuclear warhead because the North lacks the technology either to lighten missile throw-weight (by using aluminum alloys) or to manufacture a sufficiently small nuclear warhead (which would require high-speed X-ray cameras that the North does not have). Even if lighter chemical or biological warheads were installed, it is unclear that its first stage has the thrust to lift that payload fast enough and far enough to reach any part of the United States. Nor does North Korea appear to have heat-resistant technologies that would keep the warhead from burning up upon reentry into the atmosphere;[80] it would turn into a "charcoal briquette," which happens to be what Colin Powell wanted to turn North Korea into should it launch a missile at the United States—or so he said in 1995. The missile launching site is rudimentary, with no barracks for a crew; the missiles have to be trucked in, warmed up, and then fired off. In a crisis the United States would take them out before they got to the launch pad.

In retrospect, 1998 was also the year that the North began seriously to question Washington's real policies toward it. Selig Harrison has argued that the North lost patience with American unwillingness to fulfill its commitments under the Framework Agreement. The foreign minister told him in May 1998, "We are

losing patience. Our generals and atomic industry leaders insist
we must resume our nuclear program. . . . If you do not act in
good faith, there will be consequences." Good faith, to the foreign minister, means "showing us that you are serious about normalization."[81] Critical to the Clinton administration's failure to
implement the Framework Agreement was the "Gingrich Revolution" that swung the House firmly into the Republican column
in November 1994. For months it seemed that Gingrich had
more clout inside the Beltway than the president did, until the
Republicans stupidly shut down the government in the spring of
1995 and Clinton got a second wind that eventually put him back
in the White House in 1996. Republicans railed on against the
nuclear deal for months and years, beginning with a *Wall Street
Journal* editorial saying that Clinton will be remembered "for
pouring money into the Kim regime just as it should have been
allowed to crash"; why help out this "Orwellian state at its moment of maximum vulnerability"?[82]

Somehow the editors' Friedmanite rationality deserted them;
North Korea gives up its huge investment in the Yŏngbyŏn complex, up front, in return for reactors to be finished a decade later.
In August 2002 construction crews finally get around to pouring
concrete for the buildings that will house the LWRs, with delivery of the reactor cores estimated to begin in 2005.[83] So who
poured their money down a rathole?

Furthermore, American nuclear threats never stopped. Documents recently obtained by Hans M. Kristensen of the *Bulletin of
Atomic Scientists* show that in June 1998 the Pentagon staged simulated long-range nuclear attack drills on North Korea out of the
Seymour Johnson Air base in North Carolina. F-15E fighter-
bombers of the 4th Fighter Wing dropped dummy BDU-38 nuclear bombs on concrete emplacements arrayed like the hundreds
that protect Korean underground facilities. Such "stand-off" nuclear attacks replaced previous plans to utilize nukes based in the

South. Kristensen emphasized that this new strategy of targeting hardened underground facilities was to be used "as early in a crisis as possible."[84]

As if the North Koreans might not get the point, in October 1998 Marine Lt. Gen. Raymond P. Ayres spoke publicly (on a not-for-attribution basis) about plans for rolling back the DPRK, installing a South Korean occupation regime, and possibly beginning the whole thing preemptively if they had "unambiguous signs that North Korea is preparing to attack." He said that "the entire resources" of the U.S. Marines would be sent into the battle; they would "abolish North Korea as a state and . . . 'reorganize' it" under South Korean control. "We'll kill 'em all."[85] The North responded with a farrago of unusually bellicose statements. A retired American general who commanded the U.S.-ROK first Corps in Korea, Lt. Gen. John H. Cushman, said that if preemptive strikes were part of the American war plan, "it would be very dangerous and would represent a fundamental departure from the past. No commander wants to wait for the other side to strike first if he can see it coming. But there is a very delicate calculation on both sides and it's very important to give North Korea assurance that we will not be the first to attack."[86] The 1998 *Defense White Paper* issued by the Pentagon, however, once again suggested that a new war wouldn't be so easy: 640,000 American soldiers from all branches of the military would be needed to defeat North Korea.[87]

In the fall of 1998, the State Department (at odds with Pentagon hardliners then, just as it is now) had begun a months-long review of American policy toward Korea, led by Ambassador William Perry and Wendy Sherman. In May 1999 this group traveled to Pyongyang to meet with First Vice-Minister of Foreign Affairs Kang Sok-ju and officials close to Kim Jong Il. He and his entourage were afforded every courtesy, and the North seemed to have been quite satisfied with the visit.[88] In

June, however, a bad clash over crabbing grounds in the West sea left twenty North Koreans dead. In another augur of Pyongyang's mood, they took the deaths lying down, and after an investigation, Kim Jong Il issued a highly unusual apology.

Dr. Perry finally issued a public version of his report (and this policy review) in October 1999, the essence of which was a policy of "engagement" predicated on the coexistence of two Koreas for another considerable period of time, a progressive lifting of the fifty-year-old American embargo against the North, establishment of diplomatic relations between the two sides, and a substantial aid package for the North. The North, for its part, agreed to continue to observe the 1994 agreement, to put a moratorium on missile testing, and to continue talks with the United States about ending its missile program, including sales of missiles to the Middle East. All this was predicated on the recognition that the DPRK was not going away, would not collapse, and therefore had to be dealt with "as it is, not as we would like it to be," in the words of Ambassador Perry. This helped to set the stage for the June 2000 summit when Kim Jong Il welcomed Kim Dae Jung to Pyongyang.

Kim Dae Jung had said many times that North Korea did not oppose a continuing U.S. troop presence in Korea if Washington were to pursue engagement with Pyongyang rather than confrontation (U.S. troops would continue to be useful in policing the border, i.e., the DMZ, in assuring that the South's superior armed forces don't swallow the North, and in keeping Japan and China at bay). At the June summit, Kim Jong Il confirmed this view, telling Kim Dae Jung directly that he did not necessarily oppose the continuing stationing of U.S. troops in Korea. In this sense, Kim Dae Jung's policies constituted the first serious attempt in fifty years to achieve North-South reconciliation *within* the existing Northeast Asian security structure.

This summit, and the State Department's major review of policy, prepared the ground for a deal on North Korea's missiles that was deeply in the Korean, American, and world interest. North Korea was willing to forgo construction, deployment, and international sales of all missiles with a range of more than 300 miles. If President Clinton had been willing to do Kim Jong Il the favor of a summit in Pyongyang, American negotiators were convinced that Kim would also have agreed to enter the Missile Technology Control Regime (MTCR), which would limit all North Korean missiles to an upper range of 180 miles (and thus remove a threat felt deeply in nearby Japan). In return the United States would have provided $1 billion in food aid to the regime for several years.[89] In other words, getting North Korea into the MTCR would cost $1 billion annually and a summit meeting between the American president and Kim Jong Il. National missile defense—said by spokesmen of the Bush administration to be directed particularly at North Korea—had already cost $60 billion by that time.

Kim's missiles are commodities for sale, indeed they are the biggest earners of foreign exchange for the regime, and Bill Clinton rightly wanted to buy them out (again, you don't get something for nothing). In a fateful month, November 2000, everything was poised for a Clinton visit to Pyongyang. Clinton wanted to go to Pyongyang, and his negotiators had their bags packed for weeks in November—but as Sandy Berger later put it, it wasn't a good idea for the president to leave the country when they didn't know "whether there could be a major constitutional crisis."[90] After the Supreme Court stepped in to give the 2000 presidential election to George W. Bush, there was a touch-and-go moment when it looked like Clinton might still go. I met Kim Dae Jung along with some other scholars in Seoul on December 22, 2000, and he said he was waiting to hear from the White House if Clinton was on his way, that day or the next. Then I flew back to the United States in time to read morning

headlines saying he had decided against the trip. Later on it became clear that the Bush transition team didn't like the deal; even
if Clinton had signed off on it, they would have undone it, according to former officials in the Clinton administration.

The new administration was quickly at loggerheads over
whether there had been any real progress in Korea in the late
1990s. A day before President Kim Dae Jung showed up as the
first foreign leader to meet with Bush in the White House in
March 2001, Secretary of State Colin Powell told reporters that
he would pick up where the Clinton administration left off in
working toward a deal that would shut down North Korea's missiles. Soon he had to backtrack, caught up short by the president's
own hard line taken in his Oval Office meeting with Kim — a
meeting that was a diplomatic disaster by any standard. Kim Dae
Jung, fresh from winning the 2000 Nobel Peace Prize, was ex-
pecting to welcome the North Korean leader to Seoul in April
or May of 2001, with this meeting being the follow-on to the
previous summit. He returned home with his advisers publicly
calling the meeting embarrassing and privately cursing President
Bush.[91] Powell backed and filled and right-wing Republicans lam-
basted him for "appeasement," while President Kim's upcoming
summit and his "sunshine policy" were suddenly plunged into
deep trouble, with Pyongyang abruptly canceling a Cabinet-level
meeting with Southern negotiators.

Months after Kim Dae Jung's visit, President Bush appeared
to reverse himself when the administration announced that it
would be willing to talk with the North Koreans after all. This
period was punctuated by the terrorist attacks on the World
Trade Center, and Pyongyang's unprecedented official condo-
lences published within twenty-four hours of those terrible
events. Newspapers reported that a policy paper from former
Ambassador to Korea Donald Gregg to former President Bush
reached the Oval Office and turned the new president around on

talks with the North. It was clear during the Clinton administration that engagement with North Korea had backing from both Democrats and Republicans, and Republican Gregg was one of the vocal backers. It isn't clear, though, that Kim Dae Jung's assiduous courting of Republicans of both the middle and the right over the past few years (e.g., several conservatives in the Heritage Foundation) helped him much in the last two years of his term in office, particularly in regard to furthering reconciliation with North Korea. Bush administration and Republican Party affinities run in the direction of the old ruling group, the party of Generals Park, Chun, and Roh, which had hoped to make a comeback in the 2002 presidential elections. The backtracking on Korea since Bush assumed office is also an unfortunate example of the degree to which Washington still dominates the diplomacy of the Korean peninsula.

Under the 1994 Framework Agreement, the United States promised to give the DPRK "formal assurances" that it would not threaten it with nuclear weapons, but such assurances were never provided. This failure did not seem to be an insurmountable stumbling block to continued implementation of the agreement, however, and in October 2000 when Clinton met with Gen. Cho Myŏng-nok in the Oval Office, the joint communiqué stated that "neither government would have hostile intent toward the other." Both sides also again committed themselves to begin normalizing relations by opening liaison offices in both capitals, and to lift restrictions on trade and investment. Former Clinton administration officials says the North dragged its feet in opening a liaison office in Washington. Nothing prevented the United States from opening one in Pyongyang, however, but it didn't. In January 1995 the North lifted its trade and investment barriers, but the United States did nothing about the embargo it slapped on the North during the Korean War until June 2000, when some minor barriers were relaxed on buying American consumer goods and allowing people in the United States to transfer funds to the DPRK. (The embargo first began with a limited one in 1949, then the North came under the Trading with the Enemy Act in 1950, and in the 1970s and 1980s other bills were tacked on: the Trade Act of 1974; the Export Administration Act; the Arms Control Export Act; the Foreign Assistance Act, which prohibits World Bank or IMF loans; and finally the Anti-Terrorism Act of 1989, barring various transactions with any country on the State Department's list of "terrorist countries.")

While Bush's advisors continued to argue over whether to confront or to engage Pyongyang, Kim Dae Jung's leading adviser on the North, Lim Dong Won, traveled to the North in April 2002 to convey President Kim's judgment that "the global strategy of the United States has fundamentally changed" and that after the September 11 attacks, "the United States is prepared to resort to military means of counter-proliferation and that Chairman Kim must fully, and clearly, understand that North Korea itself is also included in the possible targets for such military efforts by the United States." (This was an early warning of the preemptive doctrine officially announced the following September.) The North responded with energetic diplomatic activity for the next several months, renewing high-level talks with the South, making a number of agreements on relinking railways and establishing new free export zones in the North, and culminating in Kim Jong Il's August meeting with President Putin and the unprecedented visit by Prime Minster Koizumi to Pyongyang in September 2002, with both sides appearing to think that a final normalization of relations was in the offing.

Koizumi's summit with Kim Jong Il was opposed by the Bush administration. A few days before it was announced, Undersecretary John Bolton (a protégé of Senator Jesse Helms) was in Seoul denouncing the North as armed to the teeth and thoroughly evil. In early September, Assistant Secretary of State

James Kelly traveled to Tokyo and tabled evidence that the North had a new nuclear program, this time to enrich uranium. Koizumi went ahead anyway, an act of independence unprecedented in United States–Japan relations going back to 1945. To avoid the appearance of a breach with Tokyo, however, U.S. diplomats publicly pretended that Washington agreed with the summit.

Koizumi was particularly interested in probing Kim Jong Il about mysterious disappearances of Japanese citizens along Japan's west coast. To everyone's amazement, Kim admitted that the regime had kidnapped a number of young Japanese, male and female, to use in its spying operations in Japan. For Kim Jong Il to admit to such acts was unprecedented in North Korean behavior. The regime always placed complete primacy on its own conceptions of national dignity; for the top leader to admit to these crimes was for his entire nation to lose its face. He also directly apologized to Koizumi, vowed that such things would never happen again, and said he had punished those responsible. This surprise completely reversed the expectation that Koizumi's visit would be about a Japanese apology for its colonial and wartime rule (the atrocities committed by Japanese forces in Korea went way beyond the kidnapping of a relatively small number of innocent people), followed by a large package of aid (as much as $10 billion) that the North Koreans would call "reparations." But the whole idea of normalizing relations between Tokyo and Pyongyang dissolved amid a media frenzy in Japan over the victims and their families.

NUCLEAR CRISIS: THE SEQUEL

In October 2002 a second nuclear crisis erupted, which was not simply "*déjà vu* all over again," in the words of the sage named Yogi Berra, but a virtual rerun of events that transpired a decade ago—played on fast-forward. The North Koreans pulled out their play book and began running a very predictable sequel, except they sped it up. What took them more than a year to do in 1993–94, they mostly accomplished in December 2002. The DPRK again kicked the IAEA inspectors out, took the seals off and re-opened their 30 megawatt reactor, and soon began loading new fuel rods. They again castigated the IAEA for being a tool of Washington, announced their withdrawal from the NPT, and said that any Security Council sanctions would be interpreted as "a declaration of war."[92] In the summer of 2003, they said they had reprocessed the 8,000 fuel rods that they recovered from the IAEA, but no one seemed clear on whether the rods were still encased in concrete casks or whether their reprocessing plant was up and running (the Bush team said yes, experts in Seoul and Washington said no[93]). Again the North played an elaborate game of braggadocio and bluff about whether they had nuclear weapons or not.

As if a Nietzschean genie indulging the "eternal recurrence of the same" were running the show, the Bush administration re-vived the stuttering, confused, and confounded policies of the early Clinton administration. This rerun began when Assistant Secretary of State James A. Kelly of the State Department went to Pyongyang in October 2002 and tabled evidence of renewed nuclear activity, this time involving enriched uranium. According to him the North Koreans at first denied it and then admitted it, not without a certain belligerent satisfaction. Sometime in 1998, Bush administration leaks had it, the North Koreans made a deal with America's long-time ally in Islamabad: their missiles for Pak-istan's uranium enrichment technology. Sometime in the summer of 2002, the same sources said, evidence that the North was man-ufacturing enriched uranium came to light.[94] Shortly after Kelly's return to Washington, a high American official told reporters that the 1994 Framework Agreement that froze the North's Yŏngbyŏn reactor was null and void, a self-fulfilling prophecy since Bush's advisers had declared it a dead letter soon after coming to power. (There is nothing in the agreement prohibiting uranium enrichment, Bush spokesmen to the contrary, but the North certainly violated the spirit of the agreement.)

The North Koreans later denied that they said anything about building "a program to enrich uranium for nuclear weapons"; rather they suggested that Kelly had misunderstood (or even fabricated) what First Vice-Minister for Foreign Affairs Kang Sok Ju had told him, which they rendered as follows: "the DPRK made itself very clear to the special envoy . . . that the DPRK was entitled to possess not only nuclear weapon [sic] but any type of weapon more powerful than that so as to defend its sovereignty and right to existence from the ever-growing nuclear threat by the U.S."[95]

Independent American experts say that the North's enrichment program is based on gas centrifuge technology, most likely using aluminum rotor tubes, an old design. Uranium in gaseous form is passed through the centrifuges many times and spun at high speed to separate fissionable U238 atoms from common uranium (U235); slowly the heavier atoms of U238 begin to collect along the outer wall through centrifugal force. The North "would need to operate about 5000 centrifuges connected together in cascades to make about 15 kilograms of weapons-grade plutonium, roughly enough for one fission implosion-type nuclear weapon." On the other hand, if the North has its hands on enough maraging steel, a lighter and stronger material than aluminum, it would have to build about 1,200 centrifuges to get the same result. (Pakistan has used both methods.)[96] Most experts think it would take them four or five years to begin turning out weapons-grade fuel from the centrifuges, but the Bush administration has said repeatedly that it may well be only a matter of months. Uranium enrichment can be done almost anywhere, above or underground; it doesn't require large amounts of electricity, and the task can be divided among centrifuges located in different places. Thus the program may serve as an even better hole card than Yŏngbyŏn, retaining ambiguity while not forcing the North to test a weapon and reveal whether its hole card is an ace or a deuce.

Since then, the sequel quickly emerged on the American side, amounting to an accumulation of pratfalls. Washington won't negotiate with the North Koreans, which would reward "nuclear blackmail." Wait a minute, we better talk to them or they'll just become a nuclear power—but we can't "reward" them. Hold on! The DPRK is getting out of line again: we better take the problem to the Security Council. Whoa, no we can't, because China won't go along. OK, our new policy is "tailored containment" (which literally lasted about a day; Condoleeza Rice announced it in December 2002, and Colin Powell quickly repudiated it). We better send a low-level or back-channel envoy to Pyongyang. Nothing doing, Pyongyang wants to talk with someone who actually makes decisions. We can't do that, though, because that would be like legitimating this regime. No, said Deputy Secretary Dick Armitage, we have to talk directly to them. Armitage's remarks made President Bush "off-the-wall angry," however, so it was again back to the drawing board. "[T]he result is that while North Korea is accelerating its nuclear programs, there is virtually no conversation under way. 'We're at the point,' said one official involved in the internal debate, 'where nothing is happening.' "[97] The internal splits in the Bush administration on what to do about North Korea were likened by Senate Foreign Relations Committee Chair Joseph Biden to "the San Andreas fault."[98] Obsessive concentration on the problem at hand in Pyongyang is met by inattention and confusion in Washington, and North Korea keeps winning. As Leon Sigal put it to me, "You don't want to get into a pissing match when the other guy has a full bladder." But Washington has done just that for more than a decade.

George W. Bush repeated over and over that the United States had no intention of "invading" the DPRK, while close readers pointed out that this does not mean he won't attack the North. Hardliners in the Pentagon revived Clinton's plans for a "surgical strike" against Yŏngbyŏn, and they all lamented Kim Jong Il's multiple interruptions of their march toward war against Iraq. But the extended dilation of the Iraq problem occasioned by Bush's decision in September 2002 to put the problem of Iraq's "weapons of mass destruction" in the hands of the UN Security Council and the IAEA was clearly the occasion for North Korea to fast-forward the current crisis. Bush had serial plans for "the axis of evil": first Saddam Hussein, then North Korea, and then Iran. Kim Jong Il was, understandably, a man in a hurry.

Only in April 2003 did we learn that the North's "talking points" for the October meetings included a trade-off of its nuclear programs *and* its missile exports in return for American aid and recognition of the DPRK—the November 1993 "package deal" again, with missiles thrown in for good measure.[99] In the aftermath of the October meeting, the Bush administration announced another new policy: the only thing worth talking to Pyongyang about was how it was going to dismantle its nuclear programs, and the only acceptable forum for such discussions was a multilateral one. In April 2003, however, the administration reversed itself yet again and agreed to meet in Beijing for what were, in effect, open-ended bilateral talks. Once again the North reported that it had tabled a "bold proposal" to settle all outstanding problems with the United States, but Kelly had ignored it.[100] Days later Powell was forced to admit that the North had indeed offered "to scrap" their nukes and missiles if the United States would normalize relations and provide basic security guarantees.[101] But Kelly again grabbed all the headlines by telling reporters that in a verbal aside, one of the North Koreans had told him that the North did, indeed, have a couple of bombs; furthermore they might sell them—or fissile material—on the world market, depending on Bush's strategy toward them.

Since 1991 the North cleverly kept their nuclear hole card concealed, but in Beijing they were artful: the negotiator spoke of having two unwieldy nuclear devices, which they did not know how to dismantle. (This is Bush's first demand: dismantle!) And they were recklessly bluffing; they know as well as anyone that sale of a bomb or fissile material to others would sooner or later be traced back to Pyongyang, and if that fissile material had been used to attack Americans, the DPRK would be destroyed. What appears to have happened in Beijing is that the North again turned a hole card over, and Kelly fell for it—immediately relaying the news to the world media, but without a plan for what to do about it. Meanwhile former Clinton administration officials say that back in 1993 North Korea related the same story about having a bomb, again in an unstructured verbal aside during negotiations, and they chose to ignore it. The Bush administration, to the contrary, leaks everything it hears.[102]

If the United States were to do what the North Koreans want, that would only return things to the unfulfilled promises Bill Clinton made as part of the "Framework Agreement" of October 1994, in which the United States pledged to normalize relations with the North and to refrain from threatening it. And it would return to the missile deal that Clinton successfully negotiated, just before leaving office, which Bush turned his back on. But Bush can't do any of this. Diplomacy with the North is anathema, because the Republican right won't allow it and because the same group that brought us an illegal war with Iraq wants to overthrow Kim Jong Il, too. According to Seymour Hersh, the best investigative reporter in Washington since 9/11, a participant in White House strategy meetings said of Kim Jong Il, "They want that guy's head on a platter. Don't be distracted by all this talk

about negotiations. There will be negotiations, but they have a
plan, and they are going to get this guy after Iraq. He's their
version of Hitler."[103]

This sequel has the same solution as the original: get North
Korea's nuclear program mothballed and its medium- and long-
range missiles decommissioned by buying them out, at the price
of American recognition of the DPRK, written promises not to
target the North with nuclear weapons, and indirect compensation in the form of aid and investment (i.e., the purchase-price
quid pro quo, instead of something for nothing). Indeed, William Perry was the point man for getting both jobs done in 1998–
2000 as Clinton's roving ambassador, moving toward mutual
diplomatic recognition and a full buy-out of Kim Jong Il's missiles, *in spite of* intelligence evidence that in 1998 North Korea had
begun to import aluminum centrifuge tubes and other technology relevant to a separate nuclear program to enrich uranium.

PREVENTIVE WAR

George W. Bush cannot yet star in the new sequel, however,
because of a host of ostensible foreign policy commitments laid
down since the day of his inauguration. In a display of partisan
foreign policy decision-making unlike any previous episode, Bush
determined first of all to be the anti-Clinton: Clinton wanted the
Kyoto Treaty? Bush didn't. Clinton loved multilateral confabs
and pressing the flesh with allied leaders? Bush would go uni-
lateral, and consult only with those allies who agreed with
him (mainly Britain's Tony Blair). Clinton froze the DPRK's reactors and was on the verge of buying out their missiles as well?
That was mere appeasement of a reprehensible "rogue state."
More deeply, Bush's advisers moved toward a general reversal of
previous American strategy. Instead of deterrence, we would
have what political scientist Thomas C. Schelling once called

compellence — marshaling America's overwhelming and unchallen-
ged military might to shape relations with allies and constrain
adversaries. Instead of nonproliferation, the overwhelming influence in Clinton's policies toward near-nuclear and "rogue"
nations, we would have *counter*proliferation, that is, using the
threat or reality of American military force to stop WMD development dead in its tracks.

Until recently the Cold War doctrine of containment was still
in place, however, formally against countries like the DPRK and
Iraq or Iran, informally against Chinese expansion or Russian
resurgence, and (as always since 1945) through hidden constraints
on allies like Japan and Germany provided by keeping a myriad
of U.S. military bases on their soil. Along came Osama Bin Laden
and friends, a force that could not be deterred or contained, and
a new strategy of preemptive attack came into place, which was
formally announced in September 2002. In the midst of this evolution of strategy, President Bush fatally conflated a group of
nations that could easily be contained and deterred, namely, Iraq,
Iran, and North Korea, with the diabolical and uncontrollable Al
Qaeda. Thus emerged the "axis of evil." These evil-doers were
not suicidal and had return addresses, but no matter: they might
give or sell their weapons to terrorists.

George Bush, a naïf in world affairs, brought into office with
him a highly experienced crew of Republican foreign policy
hands: Donald Rumsfeld often seems to be the main spokesman
for the administration's strategies, Dick Cheney has unprecedented weight in foreign policy for a vice president, and Colin
Powell seeks to carry on diplomacy in an administration that does
not believe in it. As often as not these three big egos would prefer
not to consult with each other, either, let alone with foreign leaders. The result has been a set of independent kingdoms presided
over by a weak and inattentive president, extraordinary divisions
and battles over policy, and the most incoherent foreign policy

in memory. But Bush has added insult to injury with continuous if utterly gratuitous outbursts against Kim Jong Il.

Nobel Peace Prize winner Kim Dae Jung came halfway around the world in March 2001 to meet Bush and be informed that the North Korean leader could not be trusted to keep any agreements (as if the 1994 deal had been based on trust rather than verification); the following October Bush traveled to Shanghai to meet various Asian leaders (including Kim Dae Jung again) and denounced Kim Jong Il as a "pygmy." Then, in a discussion with Bob Woodward, Bush blurted out, "I *loathe* Kim Jong Il!" shouting and "waving his finger in the air." In a less-noticed part of this outburst, Bush declared his preference for "toppling" the North Korean regime.[104] One gets the sense from these impromptu ad hominem eruptions that Bush's resentments might have something to do with the widespread perception that both leaders would not be where they are without Daddy's provenance.

* * *

After three years of an American foreign policy that often resembles amateur night at a halfway house in its ill-thought demarches, incessant internal clashes, and inevitable reversals, it was inevitable that one of the "axis" countries threatened with preemptive attack would preempt the center stage and call Bush's bluff. Kim Jong Il did that, but North Korea presents a far more difficult crisis for the Bush administration than Iraq did, not to mention another sharp diversion from what one would assume to be America's primary quarry: Osama Bin Laden and Al Qaeda.

Through its recent provocations, Pyongyang has dropped the fat into a fire fanned by an administration that listens to no one, but that lacks the wherewithal to fight major wars on more than one front. North Korea knows this, and therefore has pushed its advantage while Bush was fixated on Saddam Hussein. Furthermore, Bush completely dropped the ball on Bill Clinton's last-minute attempt to buy out North Korea's medium- and long-range missiles, while keeping its nuclear facilities frozen. How could a devastating new war possibly be justified when that option was left to slide into oblivion? Nonetheless, we again heard from William Perry and Ashton Carter, in a January 2003 editorial, that we must "make clear our determination to remove the nuclear threat even if it risks war."[105]

Even more damning, insiders say that the outgoing Clinton team fully briefed the Bush newcomers on the intelligence about the DPRK's imports of nuclear enrichment technology from Pakistan, but that the Bush people did nothing about it until July 2002, when they picked up evidence that the North might be beginning to build an enrichment facility.[106] Many knowledgeable experts, including former Clinton administration officials, believe that North Korea clearly cheated on its commitments by importing these technologies, but these same former officials also believe that whatever the North planned to do with them could have been shut down in the context of completing the missile deal and normalizing U.S.-DPRK relations. By ignoring this evidence, however, and then using it to confront the North Koreans in October 2002, the Bush people turned a soluble problem into a major crisis, leaving little room to back away on either side.

The acute danger, though, really derives from a combination of typical and predictable North Korean cheating and provocation, longstanding U.S. war plans to use nuclear weapons in the earliest stages of a new Korean War, and Bush's new preemptive doctrine. Bush's doctrine conflates existing plans for nuclear preemption in a crisis initiated by North Korea, which have been standard operating procedure for the U.S. military in Korea for decades, with the apparent determination to attack states such as

North Korea simply because they have or would like to have
nuclear weapons like those that the United States still amasses by
the thousands. As if to make this crystal clear, someone in the
White House leaked presidential decision directive 17 in September 2002, which listed North Korea as a target for preemption.

In September 2002 the National Security Council released a
new "Bush Doctrine" moving beyond the Cold War staples of
containment and deterrence toward preemptive attacks against
adversaries that might possess weapons of mass destruction. This
came out of Condoleeza Rice's shop, and, as she later explained
to reporters, preemption is "anticipatory self-defense," that is,
"the right of the United States to attack a country that *it thinks*
could attack it first [emphasis added]."[107] In the document itself
we read that other nations "should [not] use preemption as a
pretext for aggression." When actually implemented against Iraq,
it turned out to be a strategy of preventive war, with goals of
"regime change," liberation, and rollback.[108] Running through
this new doctrine is a messianic idealism proposing to "rid the
world of evil." We have come full circle a half-century later, as if
nothing was learned, back to the quiet American—"impregnably
armored by his good intentions and his ignorance."[109]

In the Korean theater, however, a new war could erupt over
something like the recent "June crab wars," which have occurred
frequently as North and South Korean fishermen compete for
lucrative catches in the Yellow Sea, and a vicious cycle of preemption and counterpreemption could immediately plunge the
Northeast Asian region into general war. Adding to the danger
is a new threat to the existing deterrent structure on the peninsula. According to a retired U.S. Army general with much experience in Korea,[110] American advances in precision-guided
munitions now make it feasible to take out the 10,000 artillery
tubes that the North has imbedded in mountains north of Seoul,
which were heretofore impregnable, and constituted the North's

basic guarantee against an attack from the South. To the extent
that this is true, in the absence of credible security guarantees any
general sitting in Pyongyang would now move to a more reliable
deterrent.

THE GREATER EVIL

All this is truly tragic, given the enormous progress toward reconciliation between North and South Korea, propelled mightily
by Kim Dae Jung's leadership since he took office in early 1998.
In December 2002 the South Korean people elected Kim's protégé, Roh Moo Hyun, a lawyer with a sterling record of courageous defense of labor leaders and human rights activists during
the darkest days of the military dictatorship in the 1980s. A bur-
geoning movement among younger Koreans against the seemingly endless American military presence in the South, conducted
in successive, truly massive, and dignified candlelight processions
along the grand boulevard in front of the American Embassy in
Seoul, united citizens who were educated on the raucous college
campuses of the 1980s while American diplomacy backed the dictatorship and its bloody suppression of the Kwangju uprising in
1980, with the Roh administration and a set of advisers well
aware of America's shared responsibility for the current crisis.

President Roh's inauguration in February 2003 was a much
less festive affair than Kim Dae Jung's five years before. A somber
mood prevailed because of the growing crisis with the North and
the rift between Seoul and Washington. The next day I met with
President Roh along with twelve other Americans for what was
supposed to be a brief congratulatory get-together. Instead three
prominent Americans gathered across the table from Roh and
began to lecture him on what was wrong with just about everything he had said about his position vis-à-vis the North. One of

them, a former ambassador to Japan, hulked menacingly over the table, his face red and seemingly angered, telling Roh that Americans would never understand his statement that he would "guarantee the security and survival of the North," since the American people found that regime "detestable." Roh responded gently by saying that in solving international problems it was not necessarily the best procedure to begin by name calling and casting all blame on one's adversary, and abruptly brought the meeting to a close. Thus Bush finds himself having to manage two very difficult relationships on the Korean peninsula, amid the mammoth task of occupying and stabilizing Iraq, and the failed search for Osama Bin Laden (and Saddam Hussein, for that matter).

Just as it did a decade ago, a supine American media fell in line with this administration's caricature of the crisis in Korea, instead of doing serious investigative reporting. The cover story of the January 13, 2003, issue of *Newsweek* carried a photo of Kim Jong Il, "North Korea's Dr. Evil." But where is the greater evil? The essential principle of the nonproliferation regime is that countries without nuclear weapons cannot be threatened by those that possess them. In order to obtain the requisite votes from nonnuclear states to get the NPT through the United Nations in 1968, the United States, United Kingdom, and USSR committed themselves to aid any "victim of an act or an object of a threat of aggression in which nuclear weapons are used" (see UN Security Council Resolution number 255, March 7, 1968).[111] In 1996 the International Court of Justice at the Hague stated that the use or threat of nuclear weapons should be outlawed as "the ultimate evil." It could not come to a decision, however, whether the use of nuclear weapons for self-defense was justified: "The Court cannot conclude definitively whether the threat or use of nuclear weapons would be lawful or unlawful in an extreme circumstance of self-defense, in which the very survival of a state would be at stake."[112] By this standard, North Korea is more justified in developing nuclear weapons than the United States is in threatening a nonnuclear North Korea with annihilation.

Once again the DPRK believes that its "very survival" is at stake.[113] Probably they are wrong, but in the current volatile conditions of world affairs, one can't expect them to take chances on a matter of such gravity. The only way to unravel this emergent calamity, short of war, is a quick return to the *status quo ante* 2001, to the compelling and still feasible dénouement to the original crisis fashioned by Kim Dae Jung, Bill Clinton, and Kim Jong Il—because no one will benefit from this sequel, except hardliners in both capitals who believe that true security lies only in the deployment and brandishing of nuclear weapons.

North Korea often says it prizes national sovereignty like life itself; this has been the leitmotiv of the regime since it was founded in the aftermath of decades of brutal Japanese colonialism, and all the more so after we tried to "liberate" it in 1950 at an appalling human cost, only to get into a war with China and ultimately fail. Bush, however, has run roughshod over essential principles of international relations and world peace. In place of respect for other's sovereignty, he puts assassination, decapitation, and "regime change." Our last foray into North Korea helped to bring about an armed-to-the-teeth garrison state, and fifty years later it is still with us. If North Korea does finally get the bomb, there's very little we can do about it. So let's just call it Bush's bomb.

Chapter Three

THE LEGEND OF KIM IL SUNG

> You may *think* you know what you're dealing with, but
> believe me, you don't.
>
> John Huston to Jack Nicholson in *"Chinatown"*

ON MY FIRST visit to the country in 1981, my North Korean
guides sat me down and asked me what I would like to see. Two
or three of your history museums, I responded, and then I would
like to visit a steel mill, since I had watched the North Korean
film *Steelworkers* (a classic of socialist realism) and had labored at
Republic Steel in Cleveland for three long summers in my youth.
They took me to the Folk Museum, a fascinating display of things
Korean from year one, punctuated by homilies from Kim Il
Sung: "Koreans can hardly be Korean if they don't eat *toenjang*"
(a pungent fermented bean paste). They took me a large pre-
twentieth-century history museum, where visitors can walk
through famous (to archeologists) tombs from the *Koguryŏ* kingdom (313–668 A.D.), and observe horse-rider murals that bear a
more-than-coincidental resemblance to horse-rider murals in the
tombs of the Japanese imperial line. They took me to the Korean
War museum, otherwise known as the Museum of the Victorious
Fatherland Liberation War, where visitors can contemplate vintage American Sabre jet fighters and M-16 tanks, betraying various bullet holes from North Korean guns. They never took me
to a steel mill.

What about modern history? I asked. Off we went to the Museum of the Revolution, where modernity begins on the day the

Titanic sank—April 15, 1912—but not because the tragedy of the *Titanic* put into question the conceits of modernity. No, that was the day Mother Kang Ban Sok gave birth to the Great Leader, who from the murals and artifacts there assembled would appear to have been in the van of every important event since touching off the March 1, 1919, Independence Movement against the Japanese at the tender age of seven. A major exhibit, full of detailed topographical maps and various bells and whistles, chronicled the greatest battle of World War II, when Kim Il Sung and his guerrilla band killed off some Japanese police in the town of Pojŏn in 1937. By the time I reached the last exhibit, consisting entirely of gifts given to the Great Leader by foreign dignitaries, I was at my wit's end. My guide, a young woman whose English was less than fluent, paused in front of a glass-encased chimpanzee, and began to instruct me in a sing-song voice that "the Gleat Reader" had received this taxidermic specimen from one Canaan Banana, vice president of Zimbabwe. I dissolved into hysterics and could not stop laughing as she continued to intone her mantra without dropping a single (mangled) syllable.

In 2002 I got a note from a leading scholar of my generation, who works on Japan. A graduate student in his seminar had insisted that Kim Il Sung was a rank imposter who had stolen the name of a famous guerrilla who fought the Japanese in Manchukuo, the puppet state created out of the Japanese seizure of China's northeast provinces in 1931—the invasion that began the Pacific War. The scholar believed this story to be untrue, but wanted my opinion. I responded that the student probably was from South Korea, where this myth had been spread since 1945, primarily by Koreans who led the southern army and had done the bidding of the Japanese—also in Manchukuo. This "big lie" then became the staple item invoked in the textbooks vetted centrally by the Ministry of Education (little reformed from the colonial ministry) that generations of South Korean students imbibed. The result was that as recently as 1998 a scholar wrote that the legend of Stalin handpicking the imposter Kim and then ordering him to attack the South in 1950 is for nearly all South Koreans "an unquestionable truth."[1]

Somewhere along the yawning chasm between the desperate lies of the South Korean Ministry of Education and the ceaseless hagiography of the North Korean Ministry of Education, there may be a truth (example: Zimbabwe *did* have a vice president named Canaan Banana). That truth begins on *Ma'an-shan* (Mount Ma'an) in northern Manchuria in 1935, and it ends with the creation in 1948 of what Japan's leading expert on the North, Prof. Wada Haruki, calls "the guerrilla state" of North Korea. Kim and his allies in the anti-Japanese partisan struggle occupied the commanding heights of the DPRK for the next half-century, and even today a visitor might be excused for thinking that the conflict with Japan ended only yesterday.

Kim Sŏng-ju, the boy born to Kang Pan-sŏk on the day the *Titanic* capsized who took the nom d'guerre Kim Il-sŏng, opened the frozen door of a log cabin on Mt. Ma'an in the winter of 1935 and found it full of desolate and desperate people in rags, who would not lift their eyes to look him in the face. They were the starving, sick, miserable, physically and psychologically demolished remnant of a witch-hunt that also got going at the founding of Manchukuo. A woman named Kim Hwak-sil, born into the family of slash-and-burn farmers in the Manchurian fastness, explained to Kim that these wretched people had done nothing wrong, but were victims of murderous campaigns carried out by Chinese communists and Japanese imperialists, in battles, purges, and betrayals that cut a large mass movement down to a few hundred remnants.[1] Shortly Kim Il Sung told one of the forsaken to take the "legal documents of the Purge Committee" outside and burn them. Soon there was a purgatory bonfire, as Kim wiped the slate clean and gave every one of them a new

beginning. Using this unlikely human material, Kim Il Sung organized the guerrilla units who carried out the Pojŏn (later
known as Poch'ŏn-bo) attack, which in turn brought Kim Il Sung
widespread fame throughout Korea and Japan.

Also huddled on the east side of this mountain (now sacred
to North Koreans and memorialized in the omnipresent film, *Sun
of the Nation*) were twenty to thirty children, most of them orphans of guerrilla parents, murdered in the purges and the monstrous counterinsurgency campaigns mounted by the Japanese,
or starved to death in Japanese wintertime blockades of the
mountains. These children were supervised by Kim Chŏng-suk,
a diminutive woman later to become the wife of Kim Il Sung.
Kim Il Sung brought these youngsters to sleep with him at night
(an ancient Korean custom, still practiced); every bedtime, they
fought over who got to be next. Among these children was Chu
To-il, subsequently a vice marshall of the armed forces of the
DPRK. One of his brothers died in a Japanese "pacification" campaign, two others died as guerrillas on the battlefield, and his
mother starved to death at a blockaded guerrilla base. Another
was Yi O-song, whose father also starved to death in a guerrilla
base, even thought he was in charge of food supplies. Yi's
brother-in-law was executed in the purges; his two sisters were
part of his guerrilla group, but both died of starvation. Extremely
malnourished himself, Yi never reached full adult growth.

In 1971 Yi O-song, by then a lieutenant-general in the North
Korean army, became headmaster at the Man'gyŏngdae Revolutionary School, successor to the School for the Offspring of Revolutionary Martyrs first established in 1947 for the hundreds of
orphans collected by then. As headmaster he followed in the foot-
steps of orphans Ch'oe In-dŏk, Kim Yong-yŏn, and O Chae-wŏn.
The devastation of the Korean War sent many more thousands
of children to this parentless haven and into the leadership. This
is "the core educational institution" for the North Korean power

elite and the symbolic crucible for molding the astonishing "family state" created out of the ashes of two devastating wars.

When North Korea frankly broke with Marxism-Leninism in the late 1960s to establish the nationalist philosophy "Juche" as the reigning state doctrine, the key ideologues were orphans from *Ma'an-shan*.[3] When Kim Jong Il (who also graduated from Man'gyŏngdae) needed a better birthplace than a Soviet camp in Khabarovsk, the orphans vouched for his birth on the slopes of Paekt'u-san (White Head Mountain, mythical source of the Korean people). When the 6th Party Congress in 1980 anointed him the designated successor to his father, the Man'gyŏngdae graduates promoted the familial succession. And when the great man died in 1994, they led the multitude who were weeping and the mourning that lasted three years.[4] As Charles Armstrong wrote, "[A] new state and society for Korea had been imagined at the interstices of colonial control and unregulated frontier."[5]

At the core of almost every grandiose, prideful, hyperventilating North Korean myth, fairy tale, implausible story, or unlikely miracle, there is a kernel of truth. Often it is a molehill from which mountains of propaganda are born, but one underestimates the hold of these stories at one's peril. Loyalty and filial piety form the deepest wellsprings of Korean virtue, nurtured over thousands of years, just as myriad Korean tales of the rare powers, magnificent ethics, and bottomless omniscience of the very long list of kings who presided over a millennium of dynasties form the subjective basis of the Korean identity and its love of exemplary leaders. As it happened, however, the story of Ma'an Mountain was not manufactured out of a molehill. The "purge" was a world-historical witch-hunt perpetrated against mostly innocent Koreans by Chinese nationalists and communists, amid a counterinsurgency campaign as vicious and brutal as any in modern history.

Kim Il Sung was born in a village close to Pyongyang, then a

growing center of commerce and American missionary education; his parents were part of the Christian, upwardly mobile,
budding middle class that originated in the rich alluvial rice paddies and growing urbanism of the Seoul-Kaesong-Pyongyang region in the early decades of the twentieth century, a class that
would quickly have led Korea into the modern era had the Japanese not snatched away its sovereignty in 1910.[6] Still, the 1919
uprisings forced the imperial overlords to make space for Koreans
interested in industry, commerce, new forms of education, ver-
nacular literature, and publishing. They would have inherited an
independent Korea had the Japanese made good on Premier Hara
Kei's 1919 pledge to make Korea independent "in due course."
By 1925 when Kim Il Sung's father took the family into exile in
Manchuria, American missionaries were already complaining of
"Roaring 20s" inroads on traditional Korean morals and virtues.[7]
But the depression hit in 1929, and the Japanese chose to respond
with more imperial expansion and, later, a forced-pace industri-
alization and militarization of their colonies.

Kim joined an underground Marxist group while still a high
school student in Jilin, leading to his arrest and imprisonment
for several months in 1929. After his release he joined up with a
guerrilla group, and kept on fighting until October 1940. He
changed his name from Kim Sŏng-ju to Kim Il Sung (Il-sŏng)
in the mid-1930s; by 1937 he was commander of the 6th Division
of the Northeast Anti-Japanese United Army (NEAJUA), a unit
usually known as "the division of Kim Il Sung." By 1940 he was
the commander of the second operational region of the First
Army of the NEAJUA, and was the most feared guerrilla leader
in Manchuria. He and his guerrillas were forced across the Amur
River thereafter, into the Sino-Russian border area near Khabarovsk where, for the most part, he remained until 1945.

Careful scholarship in recent years, made possible by the avail-

ability of new Korean, Chinese, Japanese, and Soviet documentation and by the hard labors and open minds of a younger
generation of historians, has now made clear that Koreans formed
the vast majority of resisters to the Japanese takeover of Manchuria, the native place for the rulers of the Qing Dynasty (1644–
1911). By the early 1930s, half a million Koreans lived in the
prefecture of Kando (Jiandao in Chinese) alone, long a Korean
immigrant community just across the border in China, and since
1949 an autonomous Korean region in the People's Republic of
China (PRC). After the establishment of Manchukuo around 80
percent of anti-Japanese guerrillas and upward of 90 percent of
the members of the "Chinese Communist Party" were Korean.
Most Koreans had moved to Kando in hopes of escaping Japanese oppression, although some previous emigrants had also gotten wealthy developing the fertile soils of Manchuria, yielding
tales that farming families could double or triple their income
there. By and large, though, these Koreans were very poor and
thoroughly recalcitrant in their hatred of the colonizers, and remained so in 1945 when U.S. intelligence estimated that 95 percent of the nearly two million Koreans in Manchuria were
anti-Japanese, and only 5 percent were sympathizers and collaborators.

Meanwhile, a contrasting organization known as *Minsaengdan*
(People's Livelihood Corps) emerged in the fall of 1931, made up
mostly of pro-Japanese Koreans (businessmen, landlords, and officers in various Japanese organizations, including the military)
who urged the Japanese Army to send troops to Kando to put
down "communists," and like the Kwantung Army, which pre-
cipitated the invasion of Manchuria, even staged violent incidents
that could be blamed on anti-Japanese insurgents.[8] The *Minsaengdan* political program, of course, downplayed their ties to the
Japanese, and called for Korean independence; several leaders had

been progressives in Korea in the 1920s, when the colonizers' "cultural policy" allowed some room for Korean initiative. All that had ended by 1931, however.

An organization like this aroused the fury of insurgents even more than did the Japanese, of course, and within months they decimated it; the settlers had tried to counter "red terror" with "white terror," but were no match. Japanese police sources estimated that 490 "civilians" were killed by "communists"⁹ in 1932, with the height of the violence coming in March 1932—the month when Manchukuo was born, on the first day of March, just to stick their 1919 independence movement, which shook Japanese imperialism to its roots, back in the Korean craw. Japanese officials encouraged Korean allies to think that if they helped colonize Manchuria, Korea itself might get closer to independence. But after the puppet state was created, they no longer needed these same Koreans.

The Japanese launched their first major antiguerrilla campaign in April 1932 in Kando, killing anyone said to be a "communist," or aiding communists; many victims were innocent peasants. Korean sources at the time said 25,000 died, perhaps an exaggeration, but it surely was an unholy slaughter. This experience became the *locus classicus* for the most famous North Korean opera, *Sea of Blood (P'ibada)*,¹⁰ and it came amid a drastic fall in peasant livelihoods, brought on by the Depression and the collapse of the world economy. By the end of 1934, after successive waves of attack, the number of Korean mass organizations linked to the insurgents had dropped from nearly 12,000 in 1933 to barely 1,000, and only the number of guerrillas had increased—but not by much (guerrilla bases held about 1,000 insurgents; 80 percent were still Koreans). A Japanese police chief remarked that "if you killed a hundred Koreans, there was bound to be at least one communist among them."¹¹

But Koreans got murdered from both sides; Chinese com-

munists and guerrillas had become convinced—because of the
Minsaengdan and other factors—that Koreans had not only aided
the Japanese takeover of Manchuria, but also continued to be
spies and collaborators, years after the organization itself had disappeared. Thus the Chinese Communist Party (CCP), which
should have been called the Korean Communist Party because of
the overwhelming majority (usually 80–90 percent) of Korean
members, began vast purges and slaughters against any Korean
remotely suspected of aiding the Japanese. More than 1,000 Koreans were arrested and expelled from the party as suspects, including Kim Il Sung, and somewhere between 500 and 2,000
ethnic Koreans were executed from 1933 to 1936. This was a classic
witch-hunt, turning friend on friend, brother against brother, all
in response to a catastrophe in which nearly all the insurgents
had lost loved ones at the hands of ruthless Japanese suppression.
As South Korean scholar Han Hong-koo wrote, "[T]heir resent-
ment against the Japanese and their Korean collaborators had
pierced their very marrow."[12]

   Kim Il Sung organized his first guerrilla unit in the spring of
1932, but did not make a name for himself until a battle at
Dongning in September 1933. Chinese leaders mounted an unusually large attack on this city, aided by two Korean guerrilla
companies led by Kim. The Chinese failed to take it over, beaten
back by a strong Japanese counterattack; soon they were surrounded. Kim's guerrillas broke through this siege and escaped,
rescuing a Chinese commander (Shi Zhongheng) in the process.
From then on Kim was a confidant of top Chinese leaders, which
saved him when he himself was arrested on suspicions of being
a hidden *Minsaengdan* member. Commander Shi declared that "a
great figure like Kim Il Sung" could not be "a Japanese running
dog," and said he would take his guerrillas and leave the CCP if
it convicted Kim.[13]

   A few months later Kim led 170 guerrillas north toward

Ning'an, another Manchurian location with significant numbers of Korean residents; they were chased and laid siege all the way by Japanese troops, and by January 1935 (with typical winter temperatures of 40 and 50 degrees below zero) only seventeen insurgents were left, and Kim had fallen into a coma brought on by "a severe chill"—perhaps pneumonia. An elderly slash-and-burn farmer nursed him back to health, telling Kim that the isolation of his family's existence, however terrible, was preferable because at least he could escape the Japanese; he likened his penurious conditions to "the paradise of *Yulttoguk*," referring to the utopia depicted in the struggles of Hong Kil-dong, a storied peasant rebel in the Koryŏ Dynasty. Soon the guerrillas headed back to the Kando region, fighting battles every day for a week to break the Japanese siege. By now the Japanese had elaborated a "collective hamlet" strategy to "drain the sea" of peasants that the guerrillas swam in, a technique later followed in Vietnam by the Americans.[14] Their draconian methods included forcing peasants at gunpoint from their lands into collective hamlets, wholesale burning of recalcitrant villages, "white cells" organized to counter red cells, so-called "Concordia Associations" (*hyŏpjohoe*) to organize and monitor the thoughts of "good" citizens, brutal torture of suspected guerrillas and sympathizers, and fiendishly intense methods of "thought reform" to create apostates and spies who could later be used against the insurgents. When Japan's bacteriological warfare criminals in Unit 731 in Harbin needed more "logs" (*murata*) to do live experiments on, they would call the local prison and say, "Send us more communists." Readers may be interested to learn that in the mid-1930s the head of the Central Control Committee of Police Affairs for Manchukuo and concurrent Provost Marshall of the Kwantung Army was Gen. Tōjō Hideki, in command when Japan attacked Pearl Harbor, and subsequently sentenced to death for his war crimes by the American occupation under Gen. Douglas MacArthur.

The majority of these penurious farmers had traded tenancy in Korea for a hardy but unimaginably difficult life in the woods and mountains; for reasons of contiguity, most of them came from the northernmost parts of the peninsula.[15] After the ravages of depression and war, Japanese sources put their total numbers in the early 1940s at 8 percent of all Korean farmers. They went running off to the hills, these *hwajŏnmin* (fire-field people), burning a clearing in the forest and farming it for a season or two. But they also kept displacing northward — into Manchuria and the Soviet Far East. They were major constituents of the growing Korean minority in Manchuria, which was nearly a million strong by 1931, and close to two million by 1945. The slash-and-burn farmers mingled with "squatters, wanderers, and outlaws," not to mention secret societies, rural bandits, and anti-Japanese guerrillas. Owen Lattimore wrote that Manchuria probably had more villages made up of outlaws than any other place in the world.[16]

Kim Il Sung situated himself among these sturdy people, becoming a classic Robin Hood figure. When he and his guerrillas stole across the Korean border, it was often to the Kapsan region, where the majority of peasants were self-employed farmers or slash-and-burn farmers, working dry fields or wooded uplands free of the lush rice-paddy agriculture that was for centuries the base of the Korean aristocracy. Lying on the lower slopes of White Head Mountain, Kapsan was one of the poorest places in Korea. Fire-field farmers dotted the hillsides, and starving beggars were familiar sights in town. Temperatures dipped to minus 40 degrees centigrade, yielding many frozen bodies in the dead of winter. Farmers also raised opium poppies there, however, which Kim's guerrillas apparently used to support their activities. One man born there in 1935 recalled that if you urinated in winter, it would freeze before it hit the ground; his mother, from a poor family, had no proper name before marriage, only a nickname: *kaettong* (dogshit). Siberian tigers and great gray wolves haunted the hills and valleys. The only roads were oxcart tracks. Most people had never seen a car, a train, or electric lights. Less than 10 percent of the residents were literate. During the dynastic period, it was a location for exiled criminals. Peasants only ate two meals a day, and a perennial "spring hunger" (*ch'un'gŭn*) of eating tree bark and wild roots was common.[17]

In the early 1930s, several small guerrilla base areas were organized in eastern Manchuria, having a total population of about 20,000 men, women, and children, with the largest bases perhaps holding 6,000, and most having 1,000 or 2,000 thousand people. In 1933 a Japanese punitive force numbering about 1,000 attacked several of these base areas, an attack beaten back after a battle lasting more than two weeks, and costing in one county alone (Yanji) some 150 Japanese lives and upward of 500 people in the bases. This and other battles enabled the bases to persist, until they were mostly eliminated by 1935. The raw human material for the guerrillas were *lumpen* and poverty-stricken elements in Manchurian society, poor Korean immigrants, and people made rootless by the global depression and Japanese marauding in Manchuria. Guerrillas took land from "evil" landlords and Japanese puppets, gave it to poor peasants, managed its cultivation through the "Soviet" or base camp, and eliminated remnants of "feudalism," especially discrimination against women. It was in these base areas that Kim Il Sung and his friends developed strategies that they would later use to build North Korea in the 1940s.[18]

Kim Il Sung took a leading role in trying to reconstitute Chinese-Korean cooperation in the Manchurian guerrilla struggle, in spite of the terrible losses suffered at the hands of Chinese racism; his fluency in Chinese and long association with Chinese guerrillas leaders certainly helped. He was not alone, though, working with other Korean guerrilla leaders such as Ch'oe Yonggŏn (Minister of Defense when the Korean War began), Kim

Ch'aek, and Ch'oi Hyŏn. By February 1936 a formidable army had emerged, with Kim Il Sung commanding the 3rd Division, with several Chinese regimental commanders under him. Koreans still were the largest ethnic force, constituting 80 percent of two regiments, 50 percent of another, and so on. By this time Kim was "the leader of Korean communists in eastern Manchuria with a great reputation and a high position."[19]

Kim's reputation was also plumped up by the Japanese, whose newspapers featured the conflict between him and the Korean Quislings whom the Japanese employed to track him down and kill him, like Col. Kim Sŏk-wŏn (who commanded ROK forces along the 38th parallel in 1949). Kim Sŏk-wŏn had taken the Japanese name Kaneyama Shakugen, and he reported to Gen. Nozoe Shotoku, commander of the "Special Kim Detachment" of the Imperial Army. Colonel Kim's greatest success came in February 1940, when he killed Yang Jingyu, a famous Chinese guerrilla and close comrade of Kim Il Sung. In April Nozoe's forces captured Kim Hye-sun, thought to be Kim's first wife; the Japanese tried in vain to use her to lure Kim out of hiding, and then murdered her.[20]

Soviet publicists also took note of Kim Il Sung, leading the State Department to think that some 35,000 Korean guerrillas might be at the beck and call of Moscow when World War II ended. If the figures were inflated, by 1945 Kim was known to the top Korean specialist in the department, George McCune of the Japan Affairs Division. He had the following text translated from a 1937 article in a Soviet journal:

> In the course of combat with Japanese imperialists great and talented leaders have had the opportunity to distinguish themselves. . . . Among them the detachment of Kim-Ni-Chen [Kim Il Sung] stands out, especially. The men in this detachment are very brave.

> All the most dangerous operations are carried out by
> this detachment. . . . The unsuccessful hunt for the
> detachment of Kim-Ni-Chen by the Japanese has al-
> ready been in progress for a year.[21]

During the Korean War, U.S. forces, beset by guerrillas,
sought out Japanese counterinsurgency specialists to advise them,
including two Japanese Kwantung Army colonels debriefed in
1951, officers who chased Kim in Manchuria and who provided
Americans with their experience and their racist judgments on
how to fight Korean guerrillas. They depicted Kim Il Sung as
"the most famous" of Korean guerrilla leaders in the late 1930s:
"Kim Il Sung was particularly popular among the Koreans in
Manchuria, it is said that there were many Koreans who praised
him as a Korean hero and gave him, secretly, both spiritual and
material support." Although Kim and other Korean guerrillas co-
operated with Chinese leaders, they were under no one else's effective command. "They did not care about the relation of their
command organ with the Soviet Army or the Chinese Communist [army]." They ran back and forth across the Russian border
to escape counterinsurgency units, but the Soviets provided no
weaponry or material aid; instead the guerrillas took weapons,
ammunition, and other supplies from the Japanese armies.
"When they were attacked by a subjugation unit, they had to
move like monkeys through the woodmen's paths in the dense
forest." They never established permanent positions and fought
in small units of fifty or one hundred, which they was termed
"natural" because larger groups would be much more liable to
attack and capture. Instead, they "always make [a] surprise attack
on the enemy with resourceful plans and tactics." Local police
"were at the complete mercy" of the guerrillas until 1939, they
indicated, when yet more extraordinary counterinsurgency campaigns ensued. Japanese forces sustained major losses in 1938–39:

"Not infrequently, units under the command of the Kwantung Army . . . were annihilated by bandit [guerrilla] ambush." Entire convoys and companies were destroyed in the spring of 1939.

The guerrillas got the aid of the local Korean population time and again. Kando, where the largest number of Koreans lived, was "a very safe place for Korean bandits." To these Japanese officers, the Korean population in Manchuria was "depraved, rebellious, and anti-Japanese." Only a few good people could be found amid this "rebellious, crafty and lazy . . . very discontented race." Their nasty habits included appearing "very gentle outwardly," while they nonetheless "harbored ill feeling against Japan." They gave up no information about the guerrillas to the Japanese, another index of their general depravity, one would assume.[22]

"Kim Il Sung fought all during 1938 and 1939," Dae-Sook Suh wrote, "mostly in southern and southeastern Manchuria." Maeda Takashi headed the Japanese Special Police unit, with many Koreans in it, that tracked Kim's guerrillas for months in early 1940. Maeda's forces finally caught up with Kim when he and his guerrillas attacked them on March 13, 1940. After both sides suffered casualties, Kim's group released POWs so they could move faster; Maeda pursued him for nearly two weeks, walking into another battle on March 25. Kim threw 250 guerrillas at 150 soldiers in Maeda's unit, defeating them and killing Maeda, 58 Japanese, 17 others attached to the force, and taking 13 prisoners and large quantities of weapons and ammunition. This single battle was much bigger and more significant than Fidel Castro's legendary attack on the Moncada Barracks, which later became a centerpiece of Cuban political folklore.

Kim Il Sung encouraged the captives to join his guerrilla group, which grew to 340 fighters by July 1940. This force, however, became the target of General Nozoe's expeditionary force; soon many of his comrades died, and Kim was forced into "small-unit" operations after August 1940.[23] In September 1939, the month when Hitler invaded Poland and started World War II, a "massive punitive expedition" combining Japanese forces from the Kwantung and Manchukuo armies, as well as paramilitary police, destroyed many cadres and units in the NEAJUA and forced the remnant forces ever northward, until Korean and Chinese guerrillas finally crossed the Soviet border a year later.[24] By the time of Pearl Harbor, the Korean insurgency was reduced to minor forays into Manchuria, and the Korean Left—a strong force everywhere in the Korean diaspora, including the United States—was nearly demolished by a combination of severe Japanese repression at home and in Manchukuo and the breathtaking perfidy of Stalin.

As Soviet dissident Roy Medvedev was among the first to point out, during the purges of the late 1930s Stalin executed every Korean agent of the Communist International he could get his hands on—after all, they might be Japanese spies. Plus Koreans looked like Japanese—who could tell them apart?—and so in 1937 Stalin deported 200,000 Koreans living in the Soviet Far East to Central Asia, primarily to Kazakhstan and Uzbekistan. For good measure the Russians also arrested Kim Il Sung and his guerrilla allies when they first encountered them in October 1940, accusing them of spying for Japan. Upon their release, Moscow demanded that Korean guerrillas stop their struggle against the Japanese, lest Tokyo be provoked into attacking Siberia (a lively possibility, of course, until Japan's "turn south" in July 1941).[25] This appalling Stalinist racism added insult to the vast injury inflicted by Chinese ethnic prejudice, which, in a final symbolic act, took even the life of the veteran Korean revolutionary Kim San, memorialized by Nym Wales's wonderful book, *Song of Ariran*. Kang Sheng (later to become Mao Zedong's chief of security) accused Kim San of being a Japanese spy and ordered his execution in 1938.[26] Is it any wonder that for a Communist arrested by both Chinese and Soviet "comrades," independence and self-reliance would later become Kim Il Sung's leitmotiv?

In the 1930s the Soviets were alone among the great powers willing to confront Japanese expansion directly, in skirmishes and major battles along the Korean and Mongolian borders in 1938 and 1939. But this was not much of a sacrifice, and anyway the Soviets needed to convince the Japanese to turn south rather than north. There is no evidence of substantial Soviet support to Korean and Chinese anti-Japanese guerrillas thereafter, yet they bore the brunt of the struggle to keep Japan from a northward instead of southward strategy. The late (and great) historian Ienaga Saburo wrote in *The Pacific War* that the Manchurian guerrilla quagmire constituted the longest battle of this war, which he dates from 1931, and was instrumental in the decision to give up trying to control the Chinese mainland and turn south, resulting in the attack on Pearl Harbor.[27] Furthermore, after Kim Il Sung, Kim Ch'aek, Ch'oe Yong-gŏn, Mu Jŏng (who was a commander with Mao's forces on the Long March), and other Korean guerrillas had been fighting the Japanese for a decade, the Soviets signed a neutrality pact with Japan, which they did not break until 1945. There were good reasons of state for this policy; they had their hands entirely full with Hitler's legions. But this meant that the Soviets were careful not to arm guerrillas against Japan, and restrained them when they could. Koreans who had long fought the Japanese awaited what everyone thought would be a prolonged struggle to throw Japanese power off the Asian mainland. Suddenly in August 1945 the war ended overnight, and the Soviets marched in first. Then, they stopped at the 38th parallel when the peninsula was theirs for the taking. The end of the war was, therefore, a mixed blessing for Korean guerrillas.

What fighting did the Soviets do in liberating Korea, precisely? According to a U.S. Army intelligence account, Soviet amphibious forces left Vladivostok and landed at Ŭnggi on August 9, taking this Korean port without a shot. On August 12, the Soviets lost thirty men in fighting for the port of Ch'ŏngjin; on August 13, Soviet units were "badly mauled," until Soviet marines landed that evening. The war ended the next day.[28] Even more interesting, recent work has demonstrated that Japanese leaders sought to draw the Russians into the peninsula, pulling their armed forces in Manchuria and Korea back or surrendering quickly, thus to bring the Red Army up against the United States, and perhaps achieve an outcome in Korea that would enable the Japanese someday to return (example: a divided Korea).[29]

By comparison, in August 1939 the Japanese mobilized six battalions of the Kwantung Army and 20,000 men of the Manchurian Army and police force in a six-month guerrilla suppression campaign, the main target being guerrillas led by Kim Il Sung and Ch'oe Hyŏn. In September 1940 an even larger force embarked on a counterinsurgency campaign against Chinese and Korean guerrillas:

> The punitive operation was conducted for one year and eight months until the end of March 1941, and the bandits, excluding those led by Kim Il Sung, were completely annihilated. The bandit leaders were shot to death or forced to submit.[30]

Thus massive counterinsurgency punctuated the last two years of this conflict, which lasted until the eve of the German onslaught against the Soviet Union. Thousands of guerrillas were wiped out, and could be added to the estimates of about 200,000 guerrillas, communists, secret society members, and bandits slaughtered by the Japanese going back to the Manchurian Incident in 1931. Kim Il Sung, Kim Ch'aek, Ch'oe Hyŏn, and about 200 other key Korean leaders were the fortunate survivors of pitiless campaigns that dyed the hills of Manchukuo with Korean blood. Still, the remnant of surviving guerrillas remained "a great menace to the Kwantung Army," the former Japanese officers indicated, "because the Army had planned an offensive operation against the Soviet Union, and especially [so] because the Army intended to fight the main decisive battle in East Manchuria." Without denigrating the Soviet war effort, it is not surprising that these guerrillas would believe that they helped the Soviet Union by preventing a Japanese northward advance and the opening of a two-front war in 1941 that might well have killed off the USSR (Hitler's *Barbarossa* from the West and Tōjō's invasion from the East), and thus would look askance at Soviet sacrifices in Manchuria and Korea in August 1945.

By the time Kim fought his way north across the Amur River and into Russia, he had only a dozen fighters left in his unit. Other Koreans who would later become prominent followed suit, including Kim Ch'aek, Kim Il, and Ch'oe Yong-gŏn, as did many top Chinese guerrilla leaders. The Soviets set up a training camp for them, while limiting their forays into Manchuria for fear of provoking the Japanese. They reorganized the NEAJUA survivors into the 88th Independent Brigade of the Soviet Red Army.[31] Much is made of these events, coming at the end of a courageous and incredibly bitter campaign against Japanese imperialism, as if Kim were a mere stooge of the Russians. South Korean sources love to depict him in his 88th Brigade Red Army uniform,[32] whereas photos of the many Koreans officers in the uniforms of their Japanese superiors were systematically suppressed — perhaps because Park Chung Hee (ROK president, 1961–79) was one of them, assigned to a unit to track down and kill guerrillas like Kim Il Sung, under the name Lt. Takagi Masao. (Park later denied that he ever tried to repress guerrillas led by Kim Il Sung, but experts believe he did.)

The 88th Independent Brigade totaled somewhere between 1,000 and 1,700 fighters, the majority of whom were Chinese, but the number also included 200–300 Soviet personnel, advisers, and political officers. It was divided into four battalions, one of which was commanded by Kim Il Sung; according to one Russian who knew him then, he did not fight in Manchuria after 1940, but his soldiers still made frequent raids across the border. Kim remained with his wife, who produced two boys: Kim Jong Il and a younger brother. After the war against Japan ended, the 88th Brigade disbanded, and its leaders were appointed aides and deputies to Soviet officers who occupied major cities in Manchuria and northern Korea. According to Soviet sources, "Stalin himself apparently vetoed the proposal to utilize the 88th Brigade troops in the liberation of Korea, preferring the more trustworthy 'Soviet-Koreans.' "[33] Kim Il Sung was appointed a deputy *kommendant* of Pyongyang in August 1945, and took off for Korea with members of his battalion. They arrived in the port city of Wonsan on September 19, aboard the steamship *Pugachev*: "It is probable that at the moment of Kim Il Sung's arrival in Pyongyang neither he nor those around him has any particular plans for his future."[34]

A central element in the received wisdom on the American role in Korea is that we came into Seoul without plans or intentions, whereas the Russians came into Pyongyang with full-blown schemes for Sovietization. Formerly secret documents demonstrated to me years ago that the first assumption was entirely untrue: the U.S. began planning for a postwar occupation of Korea within six months of Pearl Harbor, and the 38th parallel decision in August 1945 was a follow-on to three years of preparation in the State Department. It was impossible to know what the Soviets had in mind, however, in the absence of useful historical sources. But Andrei Lankov has now proved, based on Soviet internal materials, that Moscow had no "clear-cut plan or a predetermined course of action" when it occupied the North in August, and proceeded for many months to improvise and get by with daily ad hoc decisions taken on the ground, with little advice from Moscow. Kim Il Sung was not handpicked by the Russians but for a number of months was subordinate in Russian minds to the nationalist Cho Man-sik; Kim was going to be the defense minister under an interim regime headed by Cho. By February 1946, Kim was at the top of the power structure, "almost by accident" in Lankov's words.[35] It was the United States that acted first to build up an army, a national police force, and an interim government under Syngman Rhee, with all three elements thought by Americans on the scene to have been accomplished by the end of 1945.

After the guerrillas returned, they pushed Kim Il Sung forward as first among equals. In an important interview in 1946 with Kim's first biographer, an unnamed member of his guerrilla unit promoted a Kim Il Sung line that remains the official history today:

> This sort of person naturally has an extremely strong power of attraction to others. . . . And it goes without saying that a guerrilla organization with such a person at the center is incomparably strong. The sublime good fortune of our guerrilla detachment was to have at our center the Great Sun. Our general commander, great leader, sagacious teacher, and intimate friend was none other than General Kim Il Sung. Our unit was an unshakeable one, following General Kim and having General Kim as the nucleus. The General's embrace and love are like the Sun's, and when our fighters look up to and receive the General, their trust, self-sacrifice and devotion are such that they will gladly die for him.

The detachment's "philosophy of life" was their willingness to follow Kim's orders even to the death; "its strength is the strength deriving from uniting around Kim Il Sung . . . our guerrillas' historical tradition is precisely that of uniting around Kim as our only leader." Kim loved and cared for his followers, so they said, and they responded with an iron discipline for which "a spirit of obedience is needed, and what is needed for that is a spirit of respect":

> Above all, the spiritual foundation [of our discipline] was this spirit of respect. And the greatest respect was for General Kim Il Sung. Our discipline grew and became strong amid respect and obedience for him.

This officer recommended the guerrilla tradition as a good principle for party and mass organizations; he might have added that it would be the principle for the organization of the entire North Korean state.

It was within the military, more than any other institution, that Kim and his guerrilla comrades invoked the imagery of a maximum leader at the center, with concentric circles spreading outward to encompass the membership in an organic, personal relationship with Kim. Kim and the other Manchurian guerrillas were revolutionary warlords, uniting a hardy band of followers around one individual leader, with no clear hierarchy among the units and leaders. This both facilitated their survival, since large units would be discovered by Japanese forces, and coincided with the Korean preference for patron-client organizations linked by personal relationships.

At the founding of the Korean People's Army (KPA) on February 8, 1948, only Kim Il Sung's picture was displayed, instead of the usual tandem portraits with Stalin; the KPA was said to have emerged from the traditions of the Kim Il Sung guerrilla detachment. Kim's speech laid emphasis on the necessity for a self-reliant nation to have its own army: "At all times and in all places our Korean people must take their fate into their own hands and must make all plans and preparations for building a completely self-reliant, independent nation in which they alone are the masters, and a government unified by their own hands." The KPA, he said, grew out of the Manchurian guerrilla struggle, with a tradition of "100 battles and 100 victories." He made no reference to Soviet help in building the KPA.[36]

A year later at the first anniversary of the KPA, Kim was for the first time referred to as *"suryŏng,"* an ancient *Koguryŏ* term meaning supreme or maximum leader, which had been reserved for Stalin until that time. It became his title thereafter, down to his death. At the second anniversary in 1950, the emphasis on Kim as *suryŏng* was even more palpable, and day after day newspapers ran articles glorifying the Manchurian guerrillas. To call Kim by this title was a form of nationalist heresy to Soviet ideologues; their formula was Stalin as world leader of the revolution, and Dmitrov and Mao and Kim and all the rest as "national leaders." The Koreans had honored this until the Soviet troops left in December 1948, by calling Stalin the *suryŏng* of the world's working people and Kim the *chidoja* (leader) of the Korean people.

For weeks leading up to the second anniversary of the KPA in 1950, the party newspaper burnished the reputations of the Kim-aligned guerrillas by giving their biographies or publishing accounts of their exploits. These partisans dominated the central media. Kim Il, third in the leadership before his death in 1985 and a close confidant of Kim Il Sung since the 1930s, wrote that the KPA was "the newborn baby" of the Kim guerrilla detachment, which in turn formed the marrow of the new army. It had "blood relations" with the people, who "love and respect" it. The KPA, unlike most armies, had "lofty virtues," all of which derived from "the glorious victory achieved in the arduous armed struggle

of General Kim Il Sung, peerless patriot." The KPA inherited
and carried on the guerrilla tradition, having "the lofty patriotic
thought of boundless loyalty to one's own people and one's own
homeland."[37]

Kang Kŏn was born in 1918 in Sangju, N. Kyŏngsang; he went
with his poor peasant family to Manchuria to escape the Japanese
and joined Kim Il Sung in 1933. He wrote in February 1950 that
the Kim group was the backbone of the Manchurian resistance
and was now the center of the KPA. In the 1930s varieties of
mass organizations, youth volunteers, women's groups, and the
like "united around" the leader; the Kim partisans "fought against
the Japanese dwarfs for a longer period than any other [group],
making its military accomplishments known throughout the
world." (Of course, the world knew little or nothing about these
guerrillas, and vice versa; from Kim Il Sung on down, their entire
universe was circumscribed by Korea and Manchuria, with none
of the leavening of a young Ho Chi Minh in Paris.)

Ch'oe Hyŏn, another intimate of Kim's, said he joined the
anti-Japanese struggle at the age of 12, and worked with Kim
from 1932 onward; he emphasized the strong belief in themselves
possessed by the guerrillas. Pak Hun-il, who ran his own detachment in tandem with Kim, said the Japanese police "trembled at
the sound of Kim Il Sung's name." He and Wang Yŏn dwelt on
the tight unity of the Korean and Chinese guerrillas, but never
mentioned Soviet help. O Paek-ryŏng, another high leader in the
North, went with his family to Manchuria after his father was
oppressed for his participation in the March 1, 1919, movement.
Like the others, he lauded Sino-Korean cooperation against the
Japanese, and noted how Kim always set up "study groups"
whenever possible, making the guerrilla detachments into floating
schools.

Ch'oe Yong-gŏn, who led a detachment independent of Kim's,
nonetheless wrote on this second anniversary that the Kim de-

tachment was the center of the Manchurian resistance, and now of the KPA. The one writer who said least about the Kim guerrillas was none other than Mu Chŏng, Kim's greatest rival, who dwelt on his own struggle in South and North China. He noted that he began fighting in 1930 (i.e., two years before Kim), said his units were "victorious everywhere," and linked his armed following to Kim's presumed leadership of the anti-Japanese guerrillas in a perfunctory way. Apart from this article, the rest were either written by or about the Kim guerrillas, and clearly were meant to demonstrate who controlled the top levels of the KPA.[38]

In those early days, Kim Il Sung liked to call himself *changgun* or "general," using the same characters for Shogun; there was something of the warlord about him and his guerrilla friends, and something reminiscent of the founding of another dynasty half a millennium earlier. Yi Sŏng-gye was also a man on horseback, who founded the Chosŏn dynasty in 1392 at the point of a gun, and then created a new elite by doling out land grants and other emoluments to the soldiers who helped him win power. All in all, the Manchurian experience is the crucible of North Korean truth, storytelling, drama, myth, and hagiography ever since— "an epic tale of national loss, struggle, and ultimate redemption, a metaphor for Korea's colonization and restoration."[39]

Chapter Four

DAILY LIFE IN NORTH KOREA

What is essential "in heaven and earth" seems to be . . . that there should be *obedience* over a long period of time and in a *single* direction: given that, something always develops, and has developed, for whose sake it is worth while to live on earth, for example, virtue, art, music, dance, reason, spirituality— something transfiguring, subtle, mad, and divine.

Nietzsche, *Beyond Good and Evil*

NO SOCIETY CAN be understood without knowing where it came from. Modern Korea emerged from one of the most class-divided and stratified societies on the face of the earth, almost castelike in its hereditary hierarchy. At the top were the aristocrats, known as *yangban*, who combined landed wealth with government position and who showed an astonishing tenacity and adaptability in perpetuating their privileges for the better part of a millennium before the twentieth century: through the 1392 transition from the Koryŏ to the Chosŏn dynasty,[1] through the Chosŏn's half-millennial existence until 1910, then redoubling their efforts to retain control of their land and social position under Japanese imperialism. This ruling class won when times were good, and it won when times were bad; they were the only class to benefit from the Japanese takeover, as colonial officials rooted them to the land to keep the countryside stable and rice exports flowing to Japan.[2]

At their beck and call were huge numbers of slaves—Korea had one of the oldest and longest-standing systems of chattel slavery in the world. A great scholar, Yu Hyŏng-wŏn (1622–73), wrote that slavery ran so deep in his time that "80 or 90 per cent of the population are slaves"; this was certainly an exaggeration but indicative of the scope of the institution. Possessing slaves was a long-established custom, and he wrote that "all the scholar-officials rely on them." But if "a true moral king" were to come along, he would abolish the entire practice. After all, "They are human beings the same as we are. Under what principles can you treat a human being as chattel?" Another great scholar, James B. Palais, has demonstrated that hereditary slaves constituted around 30 percent of the population and were "crucial to the economy and lifestyle of the ruling class" from the inception of slavery in the tenth century, through its increase to about a third of the population from the twelfth through the seventeenth centuries. In Seoul where the elite gathered, the slave population often hovered around 60 percent.[3] Slavery was finally abolished in 1894. An observer penned a portrait of a *yangban* in 1911:

> The fact that he is a gentleman is sufficient ground for him to excuse himself from everything in the shape and form of common labor. He is born to rule—that is to hold office. . . . Our village gentleman is strictly opposed to undertaking anything that looks like manual labor. He may be ever so poor—yes, even dependent on others for his daily rice—but to get out and work is out of his line of business. It . . . would lower his standing as a gentleman and ruin his prospects for future promotion.[4]

At the same time, many Koreans were still noted in population registers as "Kim, slave" or "Pak, slave."

Ordinary people, however, had an old tradition of sharing and mutual aid of all kinds, from bringing in the harvest to putting a new roof on a neighbor's home. When the North knocked the slats out from under the landed class in 1946, through a relatively bloodless reform, it was a millennial change for the vast majority of the population (about 75 percent peasant at the time). They received titles to the land and the homes sitting on them; they were heritable within the family, but not alienable on a real estate market. Otherwise traditional family practices and customs continued and were never attacked by the regime (unlike China). When the land was collectivized in the 1950s, peasants moved from the long heritage of mutual aid groups (*p'umasi-ban*) to cooperative farms that pooled the work of an average of 275 households. Cooperatives encompassed the *ri* or "natural village" that had long been the lowest administrative unit of the state. The land was pooled, too, so that the patchwork of property lines and irrigation ridges could be smoothed over and worked with tractors and other machines.

Family homes remained heritable, as did family property; peasants could cultivate small gardens for themselves (which was the way many Korean families rode out the famine in the late 1990s). They worked on the land communally, however, and were compensated in "work days" that were accumulated over the year and then used to divide up the harvest.[5] Whatever produce came from their gardens or the animals they raised was their private property, and could either be consumed at home or sold in nearby farmer's markets that operated on a barter basis about three times a month (much as they always had). Cooperative farms were expected to handle and solve their own problems without government involvement, but the state sought to mechanize production with tractors, rice-transplant machines, and chemical fertilizers. There were few disruptions by ideological campaigns, unlike the incessant mobilizations carried out in Mao's China.

For those defined as poor and middle peasants, not only did their lives improve but they became the favored class. The "captured documents" in the U.S. archives contain well-nigh endless lists of the backgrounds of people working on farms and in factories, teaching in the schools, and serving in the party or government, all of them sorted by their class background. Internal evidence makes clear the extraordinary bulk of poor peasants in every walk of life. At the time of the Worker's Party founding in late 1946, laborers constituted 20 percent of the membership, poor peasants 50 percent, and *samuwŏn* 14 percent. (*Samuwŏn* connoted white-collar workers and was a highly elastic category within which many educated people hid their class background.) A year later, workers were still at 20 percent, peasants were at 53 percent, and *samuwŏn* at 13 percent (the latter probably reflected the movement southward of educated Koreans). From the fall of 1946 to the spring of 1948, the number of workers in the party doubled, but the number of poor peasants more than tripled. Figures for N. Ham'gyŏng Province, which had a significant proletariat, show that in 1946, 43 percent were workers and 26 percent poor peasants. A year later workers had dropped to 30 percent, poor peasants had gone up to 37 percent. At the end of 1947, only 10 percent of the party membership had schooling above the elementary level, with fully one-third illiterate—that is, a rather unenlightened vanguard.[6]

In a top secret compilation of data on some 1,881 "cultural cadres" in late 1949, 66 percent came from poor peasant background and 19 percent from proletarian background. Interestingly, 422 of these cadres had experience in Mao Zedong's Eighth Route Army, a different route to education and upward mobility.[7] By contrast, Soviet data from the decade of the 1920s showed the class composition of the Bolshevik Party ranging from 44 to 61 percent for workers and 19 to 29 percent for all peasants (i.e., not just poor peasants). Educational levels were much higher than in Korea, with only 3 percent illiterate and 63 percent having at least elementary schooling.[8] Here is the microcosmic evidence of a thorough social revolution, a class structure stood on its head. At any time before 1945, it was virtually inconceivable for uneducated poor peasants to become county-level officials or officers in the army. But in North Korea such careers became normal. Even something as fundamental as Korean marriage patterns began to change quickly. It became important to marry a woman with the proper class background, meaning poor peasant or worker, because this was a ticket to better life chances.[9]

If social and family traditions persisted, including specific regime strictures on preserving filial piety as a "cultural heritage," overnight the previously favored families—the rich, the aristocrats—became the ones other families no longer wanted for marriage alliances. Parents still decided who would marry whom, but "reactionaries" (defined as former landlords and their families, collaborators with the Japanese or with American forces when they occupied the North in 1950, and relatives of families who had fled to the South) were out. Hitching up with the son or daughter of a "socially unfavored family" was anathema, as it had been for centuries, but now the "socially favored" were the former have-nots.[10]

The majority of wealthy landlords took off for the South during the late 1940s; if they were willing to work the land, they were given the same size farm as everyone else, but in a county away from their home. This broke the back of landed power, but left many *yangban* families intact. Undoubtedly many of them suffered because they were now presumably at the bottom of the pecking order, but I would guess that when studies of contemporary North Korean society can be conducted with reliable information, we will find that many former aristocrats managed not only to persevere, but to move up the ladder again. (Certainly many of the North Korean diplomats one meets carry themselves like *yangban*.) The weight of their past activity unquestionably

fell on collaborators with the Japanese, however. "The single cri-
terion" distinguishing good and evil for the North Koreans "was
not class or ideology, but one's attitude toward Japanese imperialism."[11] Let me take two examples.

A textile worker named Pak got drafted into the army at the
age of 20, and after serving eight years as a private, he became
an officer. His new rank enabled him finally to make a home visit,
so in 1964 he went home to get married. His older brother, principal of a local middle school, had picked out a teacher in the
same school and recommended her to his younger brother. She,
however, had investigated the principal's family background, and
learned that his father-in-law had been a policeman during the
colonial period so she refused to marry the younger brother. The
principal located another teacher at a nearby school. When Officer Pak showed up and met her, they liked each other. The next
step was to get the marriage approved by the County Party Committee, but it disapproved of the marriage on the same grounds.
So the principal asked the chief of the County Bureau of Education to intervene with the Party Committee, and he did so,
saying, "Why should a man suffer because of his sister-in-law's
negative family background, since his blood has never mixed with
hers?" That argument prevailed, and the happy couple proceeded
to have a wedding ceremony with various customs and gift ex-
changes largely indistinguishable from rural marriages in South
Korea in the 1960s.[12]

A friend of mine who teaches theology in the United States
has six sisters in North Korea. After he was finally able to visit
them in the late 1980s, he has returned annually, bringing gifts
and money. His biggest gift, though, was for a sister who had
also been engaged to the son of a man who had served in the
colonial police force. They were deeply in love, and when the
Party Committee turned thumbs down on the union, she soon

became catatonic and remained that way for decades. Her brother brought psychotropic drugs from the United States for her, and she recovered enough to lead a normal life.

The best scholar of this agrarian transformation, a South Korean, offered this judgment in 1976 — which still strikes me as remarkable:

> What has happened in North Korea for the last quarter of a century may be summarized as a transformation into a new Confucian society or family-state that is well integrated as an extension of filial piety, expressed through strong loyalty to its leader. To some extent, then, it may be said that the society Chu Hsi had dreamed about has materialized in Communist North Korea.[13]

Chu Hsi, of course, was the founder of neo-Confucianism in the Song dynasty (960–1279). It can't possibly be true? Let's leave it as an expert judgment worth pondering.

THE PIVOTAL 1970s

The North Korea of today is still, fundamentally, the one that was formed in the 1940s. But time goes on, things change. In 1975 the first Swedish envoy to Pyongyang, Ambassador Erik Cornell, arrived just in time to witness the hubris and technological fetishism of a regime that had invested billions to bring its economy up to world standards. By 1975 huge amounts of foreign equipment, including entire factories, had been imported from Western Europe and Japan.[14] They had the finest Siemens medical equipment at the top hospitals, fleets of Mercedes and Volvos, an entire pantyhose factory for urban women, and very expensive monumental buildings and theaters in the capital, with the heat, air conditioning, and electricity of these vast emporiums computer monitored from elaborate central control rooms. North Korea's trading pattern had diverged remarkably from the Soviet bloc, bringing its trade with noncommunist countries up to the level of its bloc trade, from 1974 through 1979.[15]

Ambassador Cornell hailed from a democratic socialist country, and ably represents the achievements of the regime in rapid industrialization, building enormous complexes of housing from the ashes of the Korean War, providing free education and health care to everyone, achieving standards of living in the 1970s that he thought were higher and more equitably distributed than in the South, and certainly lacking in the widespread poverty and homelessness visible in the ROK at the time. No diplomats could go off to the countryside without permission from the Foreign Ministry, however, and then they were tailed; meeting Koreans in their homes was inconceivable. The country was so puritanical that walking through the streets holding hands with one's wife — one's Swedish wife — was frowned upon. All the diplomats complained of their isolation, and about the supercilious officials they often dealt with, convinced of Korean superiority in every field, yet woefully ignorant of the world beyond their borders. Their overweening pride knew no bounds and, of course, led to innumerable diplomatic scrapes where the foreign emissaries would point out gently that American capitalism was not necessarily on its last legs, South Koreans were not all starving to death, and Japan might have its good points. All would be met with indignant denials and condescending lectures. The diplomats were kept in such ignorance that they would speculate as to whether the DPRK had a court system. And they were *all* monitored, all the time. Once the ruffled skirts of a waitress gave off "a sudden crackling noise," and she rushed to the kitchen — her listening device had malfunctioned.

Ambassador Cornell found himself flabbergasted and unnerved by the endless displays of propaganda depicting the country as a paradise, one that seemed "altogether too perfect." After witnessing a nursery school where three year olds "with pointers in front of a miniature landscape" gave sing-song renditions of the Great Leader's life, "it was like coming across Kafka in a children's picture book." When he got to the adult musicals and operas, all said to be indigenous, various Western melodies wafted through the compositions. "The general impression was a mixture of Swan Lake and a romantic Viennese operetta.[16]" These were exactly my impressions during my first visit in 1981, when I watched a high school girl play what sounded to me like Bach on a Yamaha piano.

All this was nothing new. In 1947 the itinerant revolutionary Anna Louise Strong visited the North and didn't like a lot that she saw. The people were accustomed to "slave-teaching" and thought that "all government comes from above"; they hadn't fought enough for their freedom or reforms. "They have a land reform in twenty days. No, that's not life . . . there ain't no class struggle and no talk of one. . . . I have a feeling that people here live in a kind of fool's paradise, building industry, farming and schools and a 'People's Republic' with perhaps a civil war around the corner." (Not a bad judgment, the last one.) She was first but hardly the last Western leftist to run afoul of Korean isolationism and solipsism, complaining about being told that everything in the country was "100% successful."[17]

These accounts should disabuse anyone of the idea that it was only capitalists who were ensconced in phalanxes of "guides," with security people watching in the distance, their every movement choreographed in advance. The whole diplomatic community, communist and noncommunist alike, was inside a carefully monitored box. The regime enjoyed describing itself with words like "grandiose," "monolithic," "colossal," and a society "dyed in one color." Dogged insistence on always being right and ever self-sufficient led to enormously redundant manufacture of industrial goods, truly impressive when seen in an industrial exhibit, until one peered more closely and found numerous copies of well-known foreign brands—or the foreign brands themselves. The regime takes great pride in its truly awesome choreographed mass marches through the great central square in Pyongyang, with literally a million people marching in step in fifty parallel columns. Ambassador Cornell remarked that these extravaganzas and the enormous preparation they required "ignored all known principles for the allocation of resources," but for the participants it was also a welcome respite from the daily routine of work—and for their efforts they all took home presents from the Great Leader, such as watches, TVs, and washing machines.

Still, nearly all of the diplomats lack any facility in the Korean language and that adds to the stilted and artificial quality of what they see, as if the whole country were a Potemkin village. Ambassador Cornell visited a factory that seemed to have been emptied just before he arrived; the few people there seem to have been programmed in advance. In his two years in the North, he remembered but one truly spontaneous moment, when some Korean women grabbed him and began whirling him around a dance floor. But in several visits lasting only weeks at a time, I saw many such spontaneous moments—indeed, with a couple of our counterparts from the documentary film studio during a long visit in 1987, it was almost a laugh a minute. One of their cameramen, Mr. Shin, had filmed in New York City: He did a little short subject for Korean TV on Americans and their dogs, showing the folks back home the latest fashions for Fifth Avenue mutts, canine hospitals and grooming boutiques, doggy psychiatrists and plastic surgeons, and culinary delights from Madison Avenue pet stores. (I had wondered what the Koreans did for fun besides sit around their improbable Manhattan penthouse.)

In the South, Koreans have proved themselves to be stalwart and courageous advocates of liberal values, willing to sacrifice everything for the strong democracy and civil society now transforming the South. But the same Korean who leads a protest group into hailstorms of tear gas is also a loving and caring father or a son who solemnly performs *chesa* rituals (so-called "ancestor worship") to his forebears. Kim Il Sung was so deeply distressed at the drowning of his younger son in 1947 that he had a *mudang* (shaman) carry out rituals on the very spot a decade later; the "captured documents" in the U.S. archives contain long scrolls written by Buddhist monks, trying to assuage his loss and pain.

THE ROARING 1980s

When Ambassador Cornell returned in the late 1980s, like others he found a more relaxed scene, the population better and more colorfully dressed, people more relaxed around foreigners, and many new stores full of imported consumer goods — so-called Rakwon or "Paradise" stores — crowded with Koreans. Another visitor found hundreds of Koreans wandering the aisles of the Manyang store in downtown Pyongyang, "examining Gucci purses, gauzy Paris frocks, Savile Row suits, and Japanese frozen foods." The number of Nakwon stores had grown to thirty around the country by 1996.[18] Much of this was said to be Kim Jong Il's doing, but who knows, since obviously popular policies would always be ascribed to him or his father.

As a sign of the extraordinary changes of the 1980s, we can take the film called *Tenzan: Valley of Hell.* "The opening scene took place in a Hong Kong massage parlor. Mavi, a raven-haired Eurasian beauty, was recruiting mercenaries for the bad guys, a consortium of scientists who were seeking to develop a master race." Kim Jong Il took a personal interest in this film.[19] I learned about it during my stay at the Koryo Hotel in 1987, when I witnessed a four-door black Cadillac of mid-1970s vintage roaring through the streets, snow tires fixed to the front of this rear-drive vehicle, its top chopped off and inside a full Korean camera crew, filming in the streets and driven by a wild-eyed Korean who laughed hysterically. This surreal vision was topped by meeting the crew itself, one evening when they filmed a chase scene at the hotel. An Italian film company had come to Pyongyang because the *yen* had gone through the roof, making Japan prohibitive (they were going to say the film was done in Tokyo, anyway). The director was a seedy Englishman, the female lead a sultry brunette of indeterminate ethnicity (she, of course, played Mavi); until I heard her speak Italian I thought she might be a Portuguese-Chinese from Macao. She hung around the vast lobby of the hotel, usually leaning up against a pillar with a pouting, comely look on her face. The male lead was a well-muscled blond stallion from Hollywood whose career there, whatever it might once have been, was unavailing, so he took his slightly overripe but still passably pretty face to Italy, and wound up in the twin-tower Koryo Hotel.

An Englishman who lived in Pyongyang in the 1980s, Andrew Holloway, has produced a book on his year spent (or misspent) working on North Korean–English language publications. A first and lasting impression: Koreans were very clean. "The North Koreans have to be the cleanest and most orderly people in the world . . . cleanliness, tidiness and hygiene is an obsessive theme."[20] They are particularly keen on their hair. Hairdressers are everywhere, and the biggest shop is a downtown circular affair offering a choice of thirteen different male hairstyles. I once watched a Mercedes roar up, a cadre jump out leaving the door ajar; his driver slept in place until the coiffure was complete.

Until things fell apart in the 1990s, honesty was the rule: no one accepted tips, whether taxi drivers, waitresses, or hairdressers. Crime was nonexistent—"anyone, male or female, can walk the unlit streets at any hour of the day or night with as minimal fear of being robbed or molested as in a Shropshire village on a wet Thursday afternoon." There was no squalor, no begging, and extraordinary public civility. A foreigner encountering little kids on the street would get a quick and pleasant jackknife bow. The people were friendly, courteous, gentle, with "an air of unassuming dignity."[21] It's the latter that leaves the strongest impression, because in South Korea until the 1990s, the foreigner often felt besieged by cringing and obeisant hangers-on, looking for something or anything. The average North Korean lived "an incredibly simple and hardworking life but also has a secure and happy existence, and the comradeship between these highly collectivized people is moving to behold."[22] Collectivism, of course, strikes most Americans as odd, when it isn't an outrage. But Bernard Krisher, an American journalist, was also amazed at how successful the leadership had been in cultivating a spirit of communal effort; he likened the North to "one big kibbutz."[23]

Holloway's interpreters were overjoyed to go the Man'gyŏngdae "funfair," an amusement park—just as my taxi driver was in 1987. Their faces "were enraptured like small children" as they rode the roller-coaster. As for all females in their twenties, there was no question of seducing them. The moral code is chastity and virginity; no skirts above the knee, no premarital sex—and "sex with a foreigner is unspeakable."[24] But young people have plenty of (chaste) fun, dancing in the squares after big rallies, sports of all kinds, mastery of a musical instrument (required of all students), and what seems to be the national pastime, fresh-air picnics.

The overweening concern for "face" (another word for dignity) and proffering a perfect façade defines the street layout of Pyongyang: fronting on the boulevards are modern high-rise apartment buildings, many of them more pleasing than typical American high-rises; behind are older, less elegant buildings, which front for shabby old complexes thrown up quickly after the war ended. Sprinkled here and there are the oldest parts of the city, traditional Korean homes arrayed around a courtyard, always with tile roofs, but clearly awaiting the next available bulldozer. (Unfortunately the North's city planners think these beautiful homes are unsightly reminders of a poverty-stricken past.)

Like the ambassador, Andrew Holloway was appalled and mortified to find out about the depth, ubiquity, and never-ending self-parody of regime propaganda, but he got to know it better than most, because his job was to polish its English representation in various publications. Within just a week or two, he could barely stand his daily portion of hagiography, gross exaggeration, unseemly self-importance, ridiculous excess, profound solipsism, and all-around mind-numbing drivel that it was his lot to put into something resembling English and that is the butt of jokes around the world—when anyone is paying attention:

> Quarrymaster of the Gypsum Miracle, Kim Il Sung, price-loving people everywhere send greetings and link arms in solidarity to unanimously hail your Nuclear-ance Sale, forced by the insolent threats of the scalliwag 110 A.C. voltage camp of International-racketeer energy monopolists and their scapegrace buffoon hirelings, masked as the so-called "U.N. investigating team." . . . In the face of this provocation, we wholeheartedly support your recent call for Everything-Must-Go-ism as the only correct path.[25]

But if you repeat something often enough, soon the human mind succumbs: Holloway found to his amazement that "the sight of the old man on the television was arousing in me something akin" to the thrill he got when a star soccer player "ran onto the pitch at St. James's Park."[26]

I happened to be in Pyongyang on the eve of elections in 1987 for North Korea's people's committees, which exist at all levels of the political system. At dusk the city lit up with a thousand electric and neon signs—DPRK flags, paeans of praise and gratitude to "the Great Leader," slogans for the masses, patriotic axioms, and get-out-the-vote exhortations. The main railway station, one of the only big structures clearly influenced by Russian architecture, was a cornucopia of blinking bulbs and flashing neon; it had been dark the night before. Above the main square, I read this: "We have nothing to envy in the world." We descended into a subway station with shiny walls, spic-and-span floors, and extravagant chandeliers. I had the eerie feeling that I was in a cathedral. Each station-sanctuary played out a theme, in lavish marble and painstakingly done inlaid tile murals. The "harvest" station, for example, showed Kim Il Sung standing amid a big pile of corn. The shimmering porcelain was lit by chandeliers made of glass goblets done in lime green, hot pink, and bright orange, meant to represent bunches of fruit. Then I looked at the faces of the people on the subway, some of them friendly, some of them unmistakably scornful, most of them careworn and blank. Nothing to envy in the world?

North Korea prides itself on being a revolutionary society, and the "people's committees" were the first creation of that revolution back in the 1940s. When I watched the hoopla at each polling place during the 1987 elections, I was struck by the quaint simplicity of this ritual: a dubious yet effective brass band, old people bent over canes in the polling lines and accorded the greatest respect, young couples in their finest dress dancing in the chaste way I remember from "square dances" in the Midwest of the 1950s, and little kids fooling around while their parents waited to vote. Such child's play goes on in the middle of a great city of two million people; the streets are utterly safe for little kids, dawn to dusk, except for the speeding Mercedes sedans driven by officials. When a five year old happens upon a foreigner like me, he will give a bit of a start, with a mix of shyness and playfulness on his face, and then bow to the waist and say how-do-you-do. Old ladies awake at 5:00 A.M. to push street sweepers down the broad boulevards. Pyongyang mixes the bucolic pace of Alma Ata with the clean efficiency of Singapore.

Pyongyang is the regime's showplace model city, however, and errs on the Korean side of the formal. I was amazed when I first visited it by the crisp energy of city traffic, by its cleanliness, and by the absence of human-drawn and ox-drawn carts. On Chinese streets, elderly peasants dangle whips over donkeys pulling carts loaded with produce or carrying five or six dozing laborers. Phalanxes of bicycles serenely go forth into hailstorms of honking cabs and trucks. Traffic police make a pass at controlling all this, while trying not to offend anyone and thus touch off a row. Pyongyang, by contrast, is an exceedingly orderly, smoothly functioning, and sparsely populated city (in spite of its two million inhabitants). Electric buses, half-ton trucks, and European sedans (mainly Volvos and Mercedes) ply the streets, with hardly any bicycles. Smart traffic police, men and women in sparkling uniforms, control the flow with an iron hand and an electric baton, pirouetting this way and that with military precision in the middle of intersections.

With its broad avenues, green parks, willow-lined rivers, and omnipresent use of color, Pyongyang is anything but drab. It struck me that if the name of the game is effective urban management, the North Koreans had succeeded as well as anyone else, and far better than most Third World cities; the contrast with a teeming city like Manila or Mexico City is absolute. But at what cost, one can only guess. Here perhaps there is nothing to envy, even if the Koreans quite overdo it. Once I heard a deep male voice on the radio, intoning in a sonorous, hortatory voice, very slowly, and in total seriousness, "There are many fine cities in the world . . . but in all the world . . . there is no city so fine as Pyongyang." Above all, it is *clean*: "the cleanliness of the country can be hardly emphasized too much; all visitors are struck by it." (Most foreigners thought South Korea was irremediably filthy until the 1980s.) But then, everything good comes with a price. Every citizen "who travels, checks into a hotel, or dines at public restaurants is required to carry a sanitation pass," verifying that he or she has been to a public bathhouse within the past week.[27]

North Korea is a striking mix of the old and the new: elderly women in traditional dress dancing in a park; bustling bureaucrats in Western suits; flowing Korean roof lines fixed upon marble-pillared, grandiose government buildings; long-bearded grandfathers on bicycles and slick cadres in a Mercedes; modern conveyances amid an unexpectedly antiquarian atmosphere. What your Korean hosts most want you to say is this: how modern! Yet the maximum leader greets crowds from an open-air convertible of 1940s vintage. One hotel room I stayed in had a 1950s-style black-and-white TV of the Taedong River brand, the picture flipping vertically no matter what I did to the controls.

The architecture of Pyongyang expresses this contradiction between functionalism and modernism at all costs, between proletarian, plain utility, and world-class strivings. You get simplicity here and grandeur there, deprivation here and grandiosity there. The showplace Mansudae Theater is where most travelers are taken on the first night of their visit—usually to see *Song of Paradise* (about the DPRK, of course). It is a not a modern but a postmodern collage: mixed Korean themes with Romanesque and Beaux Arts pillars, streamline *moderne* with Stalinism thrown in, all lavished with marble. Inside are fountains with colored water and great chandeliers, gaudy paintings in hot-pink or lime-green, whirring neon creations, Versailles mixed with Disneyland (or merely with the Kennedy Center in Washington, which someone once likened to a Kleenex box lined with red velvet). Judging from many conversations, North Koreans take pride precisely in what is newest and biggest, above all the monstrous 105-story Ryugong Hotel, proudly claimed as the tallest building in Asia, shaped like a 1950s science-fiction spaceship (or like a pyramid, or like the TransAmerica Building in San Francisco), and reputed to be utterly empty.

Yet to the foreigner they seem to do much better at what they always have done with their long indigenous traditions — like the old homes I saw in Kaesong, the ancient urban home of Korea's landed elite. In 1987 I walked through this small city unhindered in the early morning hours, and was struck by the extraordinary care its citizens took with whatever they had, which often was not much. Old homes were crystal clean, the streets free of any litter, and family vegetable gardens were carefully extended to the very edge of the street. The villages we saw were plain, bucolic, and similar to South Korean villages in the 1970s, if not now, with the exception that there weren't many televisions. The homes had weathered tile roofs in various states of repair, electricity, and the usual barnyard animals running around. Mangy, skinny dogs scurried about, foraging what they could, trying to stay out of someone's cooking pot. Fetid streams in the villages suggested less than adequate sanitation.

I was surprised by the large numbers of people standing around in midday, gaping at us as if we were Martians, and the continued, inefficient use of massed human labor for construction in a country with a shortage of skilled labor. There were many tractors in the fields, however. Signs urged "self-reliance," using Maoist phraseology literally meaning "regeneration through your own efforts." I did not see this slogan in the cities, and assumed it was a way of saying, don't expect much investment from the center. There didn't seem to be much, either. As in Pyongyang, little old ladies got out with brooms to clean the public streets.

I was frequently astounded by the care people took to preserve what they had in North Korea, or just to provide a service.

Our documentary crew drove down to Sinch'ŏn, whose small city center was getting a new road. There were only one or two machines, supplemented by lots of kids scooping the ground or carrying rocks, who looked like local fifth and sixth graders. I strolled around and then stopped to chat with the driver of our older Mercedes, who was sitting on his haunches, drawing patterns in the dirt. Later we went on to P'anmunjŏm, the famous "truce village," entering a secured area several thousand yards north. We went by the Potemkin village that no one apparently lives in, a showplace put there to offset the Potemkin village on the southern side. Some people farmed inside the DMZ, including several well-tended crops of "Kaesŏng red ginseng," renowned for its tonic and restorative powers. We reconnoitered in the big building just above the quonset huts where military talks go on, bisected by the armistice demarcation line.

As our party moved out of the building and down to the line, an American soldier, standing about six feet six inches tall, wearing elevator boots and what looked like a pilot's broad-shouldered flight jacket, began huffing and puffing in his best imitation of a tough guy. Quick strides up to the line, big scowl, now a few paces back, arms folded, another scowl-skulk-glare, turn on the heel with hunched-over shoulder, as if to flex the biceps, back front again, more skulking and scowling. I stood there looking at this man from "enemy territory," who resembled a cross between Slim Pickens and Rambo, wondering how my compatriots could have become so deluded as to think this sort of posturing was worthwhile, or convincing, and not simply demeaning.

Everywhere there is the ubiquitous Leader and the rising Son above, and a huge flock below that projects an astonishing uniformity in the mass pageants that the regime favors, or the stadium card displays that it puts on with unparalleled skill. Kim is everywhere. He greets you from large murals in the foyers of government buildings and schools; buildings and rooms within them have plaques over the door showing the dates of his visits, and, lately, his son's. Quotations are everywhere, ranging from rip-offs of Marxist-Leninist slogans to quaint homilies, reminiscent of *Mr Rogers*. In a school, an intelligent young girl plays classical music on a Yamaha piano. Over her head Kim Il Sung writes, "It is important to play the piano well."

Family bedrooms have portraits of Father and Son on the wall, usually with a stolid, pensive look, sometimes with a smile. One story has it that a foreign cameraman, unhappy with his Polaroid take of the Great Leader, ripped it up and started to snap another. He was set upon by a phalanx of retainers: "[Y]ou *never* destroy a picture of the Leader." His photo is everywhere, and yet none can be ripped up: it is an extreme of Pierre Bourdieu's view that nothing is "more regulated and conventional than photographic practice . . . stilted, posed, rigid, contrived," and that every photograph connotes class ethos,[28] or, in this case, the maximum representative of a class state.

The largest Kim monument, a sixty-foot statue, towers over the entry plaza of the Museum of the Revolution. It is gargantuan, but there's a reason: it sits on the site of what was, at the end of the colonial period, the largest Shinto shrine in Pyongyang. I witnessed kindergartners assembling before it and bowing, chanting in unison "thank you father." If it is not Kim on display, it is his son, mother, father, grandparents, or his first wife (mother of Kim Jong Il) — but not, interestingly, his second wife. Even his great-grandfather gets into the act, helping to torch the unfortunate USS *General Sherman,* an American ship that ran aground just short of Pyongyang while trying to teach the Koreans a lesson about "free trade" in 1866. (The Americans arrived to chastise the Koreans in 1871, and got themselves into their biggest armed conflict "between the Mexican-American War of 1846–1848 and the Spanish-American War of 1898."[29]

In Pyongyang I saw a long film detailing the 1980 6th Party Congress, a typically elaborate extravaganza that served as Kim Jong Il's coming-out party. When Kim Il Sung mounted the podium in a cavernous assembly hall, the tightly packed delegates yelled themselves hoarse, tears streaming down their faces. Kim just stared back at them, deadpan, with a vague look of superiority. Like Mao, he had a feminine mouth and a curiously soft face. If you want to peg him exactly in that incarnation, giving a party speech at the age of 68, he was a cross between Marlon Brando playing a big oil mogul in a film called *The Formula*, walking with feet splayed to handle a potbelly and hands amidriff thus to pat the tummy, combined with the big head on narrow shoulders and the blank, guttural delivery of Henry Kissinger. Earlier in his life, when he worked crowds and pressed the flesh, he reminded me of Muhammad Ali doing the same thing, with the same broad no-flies-on-me smile, the same cheeky chutzpah, the same airy sense that everybody loves me, and why not? In pictures in the 1950s, he looked like Khrushchev, with a wide-brimmed hat and stuffed-shoulder overcoat. In the early 1960s, when he sided with China in the dispute with Moscow, he went round in Maocap and greatcoat, looking just like the helmsman. A few years ago, though, he materialized wearing a Western business suit and tie, and it seemed that North Korea was ready to do joint ventures (which they were).

The Leader, the Son, and the people are ever-heroic, says the daily paper, effortlessly accomplishing the next stage of the revolution. In between the leader and the seemingly uniform mass is a more recognizable and very numerous salariate, which departs unheroically at the crack of dawn from high-rise, three-room apartments, flooding into the buses and subways. They put in their day at the office and return in the early evening, the men hurrying home and the working women doing double-duty—carrying some fresh vegetables or fish for dinner or grasping the hand of a child brought home from day care. This could be Seoul, or Tokyo, or any other city where "modern" means being a cog in some bureaucratic wheel.

North Korea was supposed to have gone the way of the East European "satellite" regimes when the Berlin Wall fell in 1989, especially since it is widely said to be the worst of such totalitarian regimes, a wretched excess of communism. Yet today it perseveres as if nothing had happened with the same socialist slogans, billowing red flags, and communist formalism. Here are "the last communists," overcoming the feudal past in the socialist present, building toward the communist future. Taking off after those who proclaimed "the victory of the free world" and "the end of history," DPRK scribes instead project the inevitable doom of capitalism and imperialism. "History does not flow from socialism to capitalism but vice versa," they say, reversing the East European dictum that capitalism is the highest stage of communism. "A person with money enjoys the freedom of buying everything, unlimited freedom of buying not only things, but also human conscience and dignity." The moneyed imperialists are shameless enough to ask us to open our market, they write—but a door "flung open [will] allow the infiltration of corrupt imperialist ideology and culture." Instead North Korea will hew to its well-trod path, in a society where "[t]here is nobody who is exceptionally better off, nobody who goes ill-clad and hungry . . . no jobless people, no people who go bankrupt and wander around begging, no drug addicts, alcoholics and fin-de-siecle faggots [sic] who seek abnormal desires."[30]

The North Korea that Americans see is the one that correspondent Bob Faw of *CBS Evening News* chose to highlight after his visit there in 1989. Anchorman Dan Rather introduced Faw's report with these words: North Korea is "a society where individuality is the greatest crime"; "forty years of nationalism, state terror, and brainwashing" has turned the people into "thousands of cogs in an Orwellian wheel." Yet, says Faw, all the people seem to idolize Kim Il Sung, and all say they live in a utopia.[31] What if we were to take the North Koreans at their word and examine their claim to live in a utopia?

Thomas More's *Utopia* was literally "no place" (*outopos*). For most Westerners, the DPRK is "no place." The explorer whom More designated to take us to Utopia was *Hythloday*, a Greek compound meaning "expert in nonsense"—which, I think, is what neoconservative punditry would make of this book. More's odd commonwealth was fully egalitarian; except for a tiny elite, so is North Korea. No one went hungry in More's utopia, and no one was homeless. The same was true of Kimilsungland, until the 1990s famine. People in Utopia had to get permission to travel from place to place, and discussions of politics outside of the proper forums were punishable by death. Utopia was also autarchic, self-sufficient, and isolated:

> The island of Utopia is two hundred miles across . . . crescent-shaped, like a new moon . . . the coast is rugged by nature, and so well fortified that a few defenders could beat off the attack of a strong force . . . [the conqueror Utopus] cut a channel fifteen miles wide where their land joined the continent and thus caused the sea to flow around the country.[32]

Kim Il Sung is a modern Utopus, who cut his nation off from the world in search of an ancient Korean ideal, a self-sufficient Hermit Kingdom. Much like Thomas More, we observe the result with a mix of wonder, disgust, and sardonic discomfort. But it was our General MacArthur (another modern *Utopus,* not to

mention *Hythloday*) who wanted to blast out his own channel
along the Yalu River dividing Korea and China, using twenty-
four atomic bombs—some of them sheathed in the dirtiest cobalt—to make the area uninhabitable for a century.

Of course it is not possible to say that Bob Faw is wrong about
the "Orwellian cogs." In the night of our ignorance about this
country, all images have currency, from Joan Robinson's "miracle" to Che Guevara's ideal,[33] to the fascination in Japan with a
North Korea that seems to manage an organic politics that even
the Japanese cannot, and finally to Bob Faw's totalitarian nightmare. Does North Korea have political prisoners? Of course it
does—at least 100,000, according to Amnesty International. Is
there a gulag? Apparently even the highest officials and all their
families are in danger of shipment to hard labor in certain re-
stricted zones, should they transgress the Leader's will. Does this
system promote human freedom? Not from any liberal's standpoint. But from a Korean standpoint, where freedom is also
defined as an independent stance against foreign predators—
freedom for the Korean nation—here, the vitriolic judgments do
not flow so easily. This is a cardinal virtue among a people that
has preserved its integrity and continuity in the same place since
the early Christian era.

There is another way of thinking about this country: as a
small, Third World, postcolonial nation that has been gravely
wounded, first by forty years of Japanese colonialism and then
by another sixty years of national division and war, and that is
deeply insecure, threatened by the world around it. And so it
projects a fearsome image. This is the only postwar communist
state to have had its territory occupied by a foreign army, in the
fall and winter of 1950; the unrestrained bombing campaign remains a heavy memory, and its weight can still be felt in present-
day North Korea. From time to time one still senses the smell of

death and the nearness of evil. This feeling also issues forth merely from looking at the careworn, desolate faces of the older generation.

When I see these faces, I feel two sensations: The first is a sick feeling in the pit of my stomach because I am one of the few Americans in a position to know that they are right, they suffered one of the most appalling wars in an appallingly violent twentieth century. More daunting is the second sense that most Americans neither know nor care a thing about what was done in their name (actually in the name of the United Nations) back in the early 1950s. The Koreans are shouting themselves hoarse at a nation of amnesiacs, who aren't listening. But there is solace for the sad faces as well. One evening in the hotel I witnessed an entire extended family, some with the brown faces of peasants from the countryside, some with the light skin of urban life, get increasingly and more raucously drunk, with the older women in especially fine fettle. They were drinking P'yongyang boilermakers, Korean beer washed down with a ginseng whiskey chaser. One woman in her forties, with a lined, weathered face, was having a high old time; her typically Korean laughter, with a lot of wind forced through the jowls, was infectious. They had a plain-living, hardworking, Confucian-residue politeness about them at the start of the evening, and a flushed-face, fully satiated look of void immobility by the end. They were all, of course, wearing Kim Il Sung buttons. I remember staring at an aquarium in the same dining room, thinking that at least the goldfish don't have to wear those buttons.

The alien and unknown quality of North Korea is so deeply ingrained both as a fact and a metaphor, that South Koreans seem always to be surprised, even shocked, that North Koreans are "normal" or "regular" people who go about their daily lives much as any other person might. Roy Andrew Grinker's book is a strong argument for the quintessential characteristic of the two

Koreas *being* their separation, their division from each other, the "division systems" that have been built up over decades, and ideals of unification invoked by both sides in ways that are simultaneously utopian and unreachable. Thus, the half-century-old division and the impossible dream of unification are both constitutive of what it means to be Korean, and, more generally, "what it means to live in the modernist age of provisional truths and homelands."[34]

Defectors are the main sources of tales about the North, in the South. Grinker estimates defectors from the North to number a bit over 600 from the founding of the two Koreas through 1996, "very small" numbers indeed. The largest defector organization was first formed in 1965 under the name "Smash Communism Organization" (*Myŏlgong ŭi hoetang*).[35] They used to come around the school where I taught, to tell all the assembled students that everyone was starving in the North, and no one owned a watch or leather shoes. One famous defector, Kim Sinjo, was part of a guerrilla team dispatched to assassinate Park Chung Hee in 1968; they got all the way to the gates of the presidential compound before being stopped. Kim survived only because the regime wanted him to; nine other infiltrators were beheaded. For years Kim was an all-purpose source for exaggerated and inflamed propaganda about the North, as well as a well-known alcoholic. He later tried to re-defect back to the North.

A 1966 third-grade textbook, *Sŭnggong* (the title means "defeat communism"), devoted its first four chapters to the glories of the ROK military, the next chapter to the worst imaginable stories about North Korea told by alleged defectors, and the last two chapters to respect and worship of one's ancestors. This textbook related that during the war, South Korean forces "sank fleets of north [*sic*] Korean ships with only one shot," and included many other heroic, apocryphal tales. Until Kim Dae Jung became president in 1998, the North was always referred to as part of the

Republic of Korea, or the simply "the northern territory," or "territory beyond the military demarcation line."

The American assumption that only a fool or an idiot would think North Korea makes any claims worthy of respect is belied by the large (and growing) number of younger South Koreans who find appealing the doctrine of self-reliance and the North's strong anti-imperialism. The Korean Youth Federation (*Hanch'ŏngnyŏn*), the leading organization in student demonstrations in the past decade or more, subscribes to many central tenets of the North's ideology; the Kim Young Sam government cracked down on them in 1996, calling them "leftist revolutionary forces."[36] Meanwhile prominent novelists such as Hwang Sŏk-yŏng depict the North as unspoiled, unpolluted, plain, and bucolic, but all the more *pure* because of it, harking back to a lost Korean past. On his visits he believed that he witnessed the essential Koreanness of his northern counterparts.[37] After all, there is one undeniable freedom in North Korea, and that is the freedom to be Korean.

I don't know what the future holds for North Korea, but I doubt that it is a future that Kim Il Sung or his stolid prince/son would want. Shortly before his death in 1994 the elder Kim got the title "Generalissimo," but the generalissimos are all gone now, from Mussolini to Stalin to Franco to MacArthur to Chiang Kai-shek to Mao. Their politics is a politics of the 1930s, formed amid the Great Depression and the onset of World War II. And so, this has been a people that does well in crises and badly in the humdrum dailiness of competing with their neighbors. Their daily fate now is to be surrounded by former friends and relentless enemies that have prospered mightily in the commercial "dailiness" transforming East Asia in the past generation. It is an odd, exasperating, anachronistic, and faintly poignant nation.

Chapter Five

THE WORLD'S FIRST POSTMODERN
DICTATOR

Kim Jong Il is a pygmy.

George W. Bush, forty-third president

WHAT CAN HE possibly be thinking, standing there in his pear-shaped polyester pantsuit, pointy-toed elevator shoes, oversize sunglasses of malevolent tint, an arrogant curl to his feminine lips, an immodest potbelly, a perpetual bad hair day? He is thinking, *get me out of here.* It is a cruel fate to have but one country to give for your family; even crueler is to be born into that wrong family, in the wrong country, in the wrong century. "Live just like the anti-Japanese guerrillas!" the street slogans repeat endlessly, but why do that when the Internet is a keystroke away, your favorite "daughter" luxuriates in her Swiss chalet, your beloved son needs another Mercedes but wants a (sorry, still forbidden) Ferrari, and your country's irremediably low-tech hairdressers can't get a perm right? "Long live the Great Juche Idea!" the banners read, but what good are 1930s notions of autarky and self-reliance in the century of globalized cosmopolitanism, a borderless world where you can be on the Riviera at one minute, in Bali the next?

Kim Jong Il was born on February 16, 1942, in a guerrilla camp near Khabarovsk, just across the border from Manchukuo, to a father and mother who had been fighting Japanese suppression forces since 1932. If the father was tall, handsome, and charismatic, standing over six feet with a broad forehead prized by

Korean mothers and aestheticians, the son looks just like his mother—a formidable woman, nurturing, kind, and fun-loving, but less than five feet tall, standing pear-shaped in her guerrilla uniform. But where her face is round, wide, smiling, endearing, and optimistic, six decades later his is round, wide, frowning, off-putting, and cynical. And he sees himself as a pygmy: therefore the unkind cut from the forty-third president.

During her sojourn in the North, a South Korean movie actress found that Kim didn't like his body—he wasn't "comfortable in his own skin," to use the current cliché. Indeed, he asked her, "Well, Madame Choe, what do you think of my physique? Small as a midget's turd, aren't I?" Something was probably lost in the translation, though; my spouse thinks Kim referred to himself as a *nanjaengi ttongjib*, a mother's endearing phrase for an infant crawling around the house (it means the lower colon or "shithouse" of a dwarf).

Kim Il Sung and his allies chose to build their state by husbanding traditional virtues—loyalty, integrity, common sharing, and generosity, all based on the bedrock of Dan Quayle/George Bush "family values"—and with a fierce nationalism encompassing everything: politics, the economy, relations with enemies as well as friends, education, even the polyglot Korean language itself (in place of Chinese, Japanese, English, and other influences, they promoted the indigenous alphabet invented by King Sejong in the early fifteenth century). Any new spurts of cosmopolitanism met a quick death at the hands of two forces: the party of revolution in the name of the nation and the party of tradition in the name of an eternal Korean civilization. It never was clear which party informed Kim Il Sung's consciousness the more in creating his new Korean kingdom. One of the first films to appear in the North, *Nae Kohyang* (*My Native Town*, 1949) represented "a kind of socialist pastoralism," in Charles Armstrong's words, emphasizing "the pure, uncorrupted spirit of the peasants," and presenting Kim as the godlike figure who bestows goodies from on high; a nationalist ethos "suffuses the film from beginning to end."[1]

Very little is known about the mother, Kim Chŏng-suk. Her family was poor; her father was an agricultural laborer. She first joined a guerrilla unit in Manchuria at the age of 16. Russians who met her in the late 1940s recalled her as "a small, quiet woman, not particularly well educated, but friendly and life-loving." She died in childbirth in September 1949, a second terrible blow to her husband after the accidental drowning of Kim Jong Il's younger brother in the summer of 1947. "Throughout his life he retained warm memories of her," Lankov wrote, and was "badly affected by both bereavements."[2]

When the opposite sexes managed to find time together, a strict morality governed everything: no flirting, no holding hands, no dates, and parents arranged the marriages. If North Korea always far outpaced South Korea in gender equality, after passing a law on the equality of women in July 1946 to end the "triple subordination" of women to family, society, and politics and allowing free choice in marriage partners, it imposed a chaste modernity based on the nuclear family.[3]

So when he was seven years old, Jong Il marched off in his state-issued polyester summer uniform (students got another one for winter) and plastic shoes (one pair a year) to his gender-segregated elementary school. The whole society wears "Vynalon," the polyester that North Korean scientists claim to have invented out of limestone makings, because it is comfortable, cheap, launders easily, doesn't need much ironing, and is so clearly "modern" as compared with the old white cotton that Korean peasants always wore.

Jong Il read state-written textbooks informed by everything that made Korea great, from the past five millennia to a modern era that began on April 15, 1912: the day his father was born. Jong

Il read about the ancient virtues, founded on filial piety and the well-led family that was the essence of centuries of Confucian doctrine (the "Great Learning" is a primer for how the well-ordered family ordains the well-ordered state), and became the bedrock and singular social unit of the DPRK;[4] the struggles of his father and the Manchurian guerrillas who populated the commanding heights of the regime for fifty years, and who single-handedly liberated Korea in 1945 (American, Soviet, and Chinese contributions notwithstanding); the greatest of World War II battles at Poch'ŏnbo (where Kim and his friends knocked over a Japanese police station and briefly occupied the town); the great victory in the Korean War, where his father imposed the first humiliation on an American Army since the War of 1812; and the ever-widening influence of "the great Juche idea," his father's ideological substitute for Marxism-Leninism-Stalinism, taking North Korea back to the philosophical idealism, metaphysics, and family-based social order of neo-Confucianism and Korea's Hermit Kingdom past.

Juche (*chuch'e*) seems at first glance to be readily understandable. It means self-reliance and independence in politics, economics, defense, and ideology. It first emerged in 1955 as Pyongyang drew away from Moscow and then appeared full-blown in the mid-sixties as Kim sought a stance independent of both Moscow and Beijing. One can find uses of the term *chuch'e* before 1955 in North and South, but no one would notice were it not for its later prominence. But at that time Kim's rhetoric rang with synonymous language; a variety of terms translating roughly as self-reliance and independence structured Kim's ideology in the 1940s: *chajusŏng* (self-reliance), *minjok tongnip* (national or ethnic independence), and *charip kyŏngje* (independent economy). All these terms were antonyms of *sadaejuŭi*, serving and relying upon foreign power, which had been the scourge of a people whose natural inclination was toward things Korean.[5] Added up, these ideas were the common denominators of what all the colonized peoples sought at midcentury: their basic dignity as human beings. Han S. Park, a keen observer of the North, wrote that "the 'self' [in self-reliance] . . . is the nation as an indivisible and deified sacred entity. The notion that individuals are not worthy of living if they are deprived of their nation has been promoted so persuasively that complete loyalty to the nation is considered natural."[6]

On closer inspection, however, the term's meaning is less accessible. The North Koreans say things like "everyone must have *chuch'e* firm in mind and spirit"; "only when *chuch'e* is firmly implanted can we be happy"; "*chuch'e* must not only be firmly established in mind but perfectly realized in practice"; and so on. The second character, *ch'e* in the Korean pronunciation, is the *tai* of *kokutai*, a concept promoted in Japan in the 1930s that meant, in essence, what it means to be Japanese as opposed to everything else. *Kokutai* was deeply identified with the prewar emperor system and with ultranationalism. Japanese scribblers would write on and on about "getting *kokutai* firmly in mind," and once you have it firmly in your mind all else follows. In the postwar period, *shutaisei* (prounounced *chuch'esŏng* in Korean) has been a common theme among Japanese intellectuals, the central idea being how Japan can be modern and Japanese at the same time.[7] The Koreans use *chuch'e* in similar ways, in their case with the goal of creating a subjective, solipsistic state of mind, the correct thought that must precede and that will then determine correct action, but also as a means of defining what is simultaneously modern and Korean. The term is really untranslatable; the closer one gets to its meaning, the more the meaning slips away. For a foreigner its meaning is ever-receding, into a pool of everything that makes Koreans Korean, and therefore ultimately inaccessible to the non-Korean. *Chuch'e* is the opaque core of North Korean national solipsism.

A book appeared in Pyongyang entitled *The Great Teacher of Journalists*. It recounted a reporter's coverage of a performance at the Pyongyang Grand Theater in 1962. While watching the performance, "he kept trying to conceive the idea and form of his article, and as soon as the act came to an end, he opened his scribbling book." Just then "a functionary" hurried over to him, to say that he "was summoned by the Dear Leader" (then 20 years old). "He went with a throbbing heart." Kim Jong Il asked him "if he had any problems." The journalist replied that he was going to write about the program he had just witnessed. "The dear leader then told him that he . . . must emphasize the fact that our art was flowering and developing, in keeping with the great leader's juche-based idea [*sic*] on literature and art."[8] Just one idea on literature and art, we might ask? What might it be?

As Casey Stengel liked to observe, "You can't make this stuff up." This is one of innumerable examples of Pyongyang pablum, pouring forth in turgid, sentimental, far-fetched prose embarrassing to a 10 year old, as if irony, satire, self-parody, and wretched excess had yet to be invented. The best that can be said for Marxist elements in this doctrine is Marx's conception of man as *homo faber*, humans as makers—"I make therefore I am"—the human creatively interacting with and operating upon his environment, human and natural. Or as he expressed it in his early writings, "The confession of Prometheus: 'In one word, I hate all the gods,' is its very own confession, its own sentence against all heavenly and earthly gods who refuse to recognize human self-consciousness as the supreme divinity."[9] This phrase—human self-consciousness as the supreme divinity—might be taken as the apotheosis of North Korean ideology, in two senses: that humans differ from animals in their self-consciousness and creativity, and that the fount of human ideas, namely the Leader, is the supreme deity for the people. This is a perfect, and in a Weberian sense charismatic, meld of traditional ideas of the king and the people "united in one mind" and modern Promethean notions of man as the master (and the disturber) of the universe. The worst that can be said lies in Benjamin's metaphor of the automaton who always wins at chess; "the puppet called 'historical materialism' is to win all the time."[10] DPRK ideologues would embarrass even Stalin in their absurd presumptions that the Juche idea contains the solution to all problems, winning ever-greater victories, all the time—and for all time.

But that was then and this is now, in the world of what's-happening-now. In his many residences, Kim Jong Il created a perfect postmodern pastiche: Sony TVs in every room, with satellite dishes that bring in South Korean and Japanese stations, not to mention CNN and MTV; he has thousands of videos from around the world, but especially from Hollywood; he enjoys sitting on the floor playing "Super Mario" videogames with his son. His musical tastes run from a huge library of classical music to the Rolling Stones, Pink Floyd, the Beach Boys, and Paul Anka (to whose height and looks he bears a vague comparison). He likes *La Traviata* but also "Danny Boy." Kim pleased the masses by allowing Hollywood cartoons to be shown on TV—Donald Duck, Tom and Jerry, Bugs Bunny.

The daughter, soon to be famous,[11] is Li Nam Ok, adopted by Kim Jong Il to tutor and play with his beloved son Jong Nam. She was born into an aristocratic family from the South. Her grandfather was a landlord from the Southeast (the region whose elites ruled South Korea from 1961 to 1997) who grew up in material comfort, never worked with his hands, had every want taken care of by his tenants and household help (Nam Ok calls them "slaves"), but, like Kim Il Sung, was poised between an unknown modernity and a past suffused with venerable admonitions about how to live one's life. His son (Nam Ok's father) went to Posŏng School, founded by Korea's first great capitalist, Kim Sŏng-su, and now known as Korea University; her mother

went to Ewha School for Girls, established by American missionaries in 1886 and long Seoul's best women's university. She
remembers her grandfather as a *yangban* (aristocrat) of upright
morality and stern principle which—in her view—led to his fateful decision in 1947 to give over his landholdings to his peasants
and head north, to work with Kim's fledgling government in
spite of being a charter member of the "class enemy." But like so
many other wealthy Koreans, he had hedged his bets by giving
money to leftists in the South, ubiquitous in the 1940s, so he
was welcomed into the fold by Kim Il Sung.

Li Nam Ok's good fortune was really guaranteed, however,
by Kim Jong Il's mistress and great love of his life, Sung Hae
Rim, the most famous North Korean movie actress, who also
happened to be Nam Ok's aunt. She was not only a stunning
beauty, but also a *yangban* from the South; she fathered the Dear
Leader's first son, Kim Jong Nam, now heir-apparent—if father
and son can find some way to bring 23 million hidebound people
kicking and screaming into the twenty-first century. Because he
was an illegitimate son, he had to be hidden and secluded in the
royal palaces, themselves impenetrably remote and cloistered in
the most sequestered society on earth. Like the princes in the
imperial household in Tokyo, he had everything at his disposal
and whim except what he valued most: getting out into the city
and playing with kids his own age. So Nam Ok arrived as his
playmate, later his teacher, and finally his de facto sister.

The truth of the North Korean system is to come to understand, finally, that the isolated, cloistered royal family members
themselves were foreigners to their own society; they furtively
ventured out in one of Jong Il's twenty automobiles (including
Cadillacs and Lincolns), or on foot after dark or to uninhabited
parks while everyone else worked, and observed this society like
the aliens that they were. Compounding their isolation in Jong
Nam's childhood years was his father's desire that no one should

know about his illegimate son. Like everyone else, to travel out-side Pyongyang they needed a travel visa. Everyone is sheltered and compartmentalized so that most of the time, no one knows what's going on. (In recent years, errant glimpses of the life of common people with their emaciated bodies and tattered cloth-ing have brought central officials to tears.)

Kim Jong Il is not the playboy, womanizer, drunk, and men-tally deranged fanatic "Dr. Evil" of our press. He is a homebody who doesn't socialize much, doesn't drink much, and works at home in his pajamas, scribbling marginal comments on the end-less reams of documents brought to him in gray briefcases by his aides. He most enjoys tinkering with his many music boxes, sit-ting on the floor and opening them up with screwdrivers; at other times he would sit with Jong Nam and play Super Mario video games. He is prudish and shy, and like most Korean fa-thers, hopelessly devoted to his son and the other children in his household—vastly preferring to sequester himself with them, rather than preside over the public extravaganzas that amaze vis-itors to the DPRK. According to Nam Ok, he orchestrates them, but is bored to tears watching them. The Dear Leader has tired of all the absurd hero worship, too; he told a visitor, "All that is bogus. It's all just pretence."[12] But, like his father, he doesn't stop it from happening. He is a Stalinist, in that he keeps Stalin's hours, working into the early morning hours and then sleeping into the late morning—but these are the same hours his father kept, and that Bill Clinton kept. When the rest of us are sleeping, chief executives desperately husband their quiet time, Kim Jong Il more than most.

Jong Il likes parties, but relatively small ones of twenty or thirty people, lubricated by beer, Ginseng whiskey, and the French cognacs he imports by the case (not to drink, but to give away as gifts). He drinks sparingly, Nam Ok insists; he smoked like a chimney for years (mainly American and Japanese cigarettes), but recently gave it up under his doctors' prodding, and demanded that the entire general staff of the People's Army do so as well (undoubtedly among his most hated decrees). He is so discreet about his private life that Nam Ok can only relate rumors about the foreign women imported to sate his sexual appetites; she never saw any of them, and, after reading her account, one doubts that Jong Il has much of a libido.

The heir apparent, Jong Nam (*chŏng*, loyal; *nam*, man), is tall and handsome like his grandfather, but has the infernal pompadour of his father, hair that thins into middle age and that tends to stand straight up; thus he also putters around the palace in pajamas, perm, and rollers. (South Korean men do the same, and most dye their hair; both are accepted practices, like lavender hair for elderly ladies in the United States.) He grew up totally sheltered, piloting variously powered kiddy cars around the palace while a passel of hand-wringing servants waited on his every whim. Grand pianos, mainly Steinways and Yamahas, were in every palace, and after the piano teachers left, Jong Il would patiently sit and listen to his son play, just as my spouse does.

Like many boys, Jong Nam slept with his mother for years; unlike most, he remained in the maternal bed until he was an adolescent, whereupon he moved into his father's bedroom. If this sounds strange to Western readers, it is standard practice in Korean families (North and South): kids sleeping with their parents, which in my view promotes a remarkable individual security thereafter; parents doting in every way on their children, which would spoil them if it weren't so ubiquitous, and if the state and the schools were not so intent on imparting the opposite—regimentation and discipline. Fathers and mothers do seem to invest every ounce of their own vanity and hope into their childrens' upbringing.

Nothing is more important to the perpetuation and improvement of Korean family power than the proper rearing of the

young, especially the firstborn son. In South Korea the truly
powerful are the leaders of the giant conglomerates that dominate
the economy, and the familial succession principal means that
male descendants of the founding patriarch still run most of
them. If the "Great Leader" gave way to the "Dear Leader" after
many years of parental coaching (Kim Il Sung and Jong Il went
around together for decades, and talked on the phone for hours
when they were apart), Jong Nam is just a chip off the same
block. Increasingly North Koreans are willing to admit that they
live under a royal dynasty, as much or more than a communist
state. On Kim Jong Il's sixty-first birthday in 2003, a guide named
Li Ok Hwa told an American journalist that it's great that children all over the country get gifts on his birthday: "That way,
they learn who the Dear Leader is and that he is their king."[13]

Jong Nam's education came from tutors in the palace, befitting
the prince that he is; the tutors were demanding and he worked
hard to learn and please his father. Indeed his upbringing and
the interior life of the palace were modeled on traditional practice: a phalanx of decorators, seamstresses, cooks, and servants
re-created a modern version of Korean royal life. Servants old
enough to have been tutored in royal affairs a century ago passed
on their knowledge to succeeding generations of palace staff. This
traditional aura apparently extended to a bevy of female servants
on the old royal model; chosen from among "the pretty and
healthy virgins" from elite families, they were recruited to serve
the king. The ways in which they served him remain in dispute;
they were not a harem or even his concubines, although liaisons
certainly happened. The main idea, though, was to make the
king's life comfortable. Defectors often say Kim and his son continued this tradition, but they of course embellish this practice
with endless allegations of frolicking and womanizing.[14]

Koreans tend to gossip a lot, but nothing compares with the
gossip about families; it is their own Hollywood, informing every

drama and soap opera. Plus a few thousand years of history yields an endless repository of dynastic stories and a stunning example of the oedipal and Shakespearean ways in which primogeniture affects high politics and vice versa in the eighteenth epic of King Yŏngjo and his first son, Sado.[15] Yŏngjo was the longest reigning of Chosŏn dynasty kings (all the way from somnolent 1724 to providential 1776) and a prince who did precisely what the Confucian busybodies wanted him to do, by way of preparing himself for his august responsibilities. As a prince he did everything his royal tutors asked of him, and as king he returned to the classics time and again for guidance (in 1725 he spent four months on Confucius's *Analects*, and forty years later, four more months on them).

Yŏngjo was the ideal Confucian prince, and he turned into a formidable political leader whose daily problems and strategies would be familiar to any chief executive. His agony was that his son, Sado, was the worst prince in Korean history. Indeed, he had no idea what it meant to be a prince, or if he did, he did not like it. And so his regency ended in high tragedy, set out to die inside a sealed rice chest in the royal garden by his very own father, in the year 1766. It was, ironically, a gross transgression of kingly virtue done in the interest of effective kingly succession. Sado exemplified all the weaknesses of the Korean royal system, and hardly any of its strengths. Afforded every privilege, doted on by a hundred ladies-in-waiting, indulged by his father and worshipped by his people, he advanced not from playful childhood to Confucian adulthood, but from prolonged adolescence to palpable neurosis to a very well-documented schizophrenia. If he is an unquestioned special case, his lifelong trajectory makes a more general point: Korean kids are children well into their teens, and adolescents (*chŏngnyŏn*, youths) preparing for adulthood well into their thirties or even forties, and "adults" only when the father gives over the family responsibilities to the son and his wife, whereupon the father enters the hallowed (*hwan'gap*, 60th birthday) realm of revered elder—and relative freedom.

So far as one can tell, this tragedy did not befall either Jong Il or Jong Nam. As princes both did what they were told, more or less, and thus became the chosen successors to their father. But Jong Nam's youth was quite different, given his father's longing for things modern that were always superior elsewhere. So he grew up with every conceivable electronic gadget, most of them Japanese; with foreign clothes, most of them also Japanese—coats, shirts, slacks, shoes, and even underwear; later came sport jackets and even slippers by Dior and Cardin; Old London toiletries and blankets; French pillows; Noritake place settings; and meals of Swedish smoked salmon, mangoes from Indonesia, *paté de foie gras*, Japanese sushi and sashimi, Parma ham with melon, and Hungarian sausage. It was the postmodern, cosmopolitan hearth and home in the land of Juche, and the royal family was like a bunch of Christian Scientist hypochondriacs.

Nam Ok and Jong Nam were both educated in secondary schools in Geneva, Switzerland. It was both a Western haven for their adolescent dreams, and the death knell of her (and perhaps their) belief in the DRPK. North Korea now bores her. She hates the regimentation, even though she avoided much of it when growing up; she thinks the history she was taught is as pretentious and solipsistic as it is simple, a McGuffey Reader for rubes and simpletons. Above all she loathed the ubiquitous "meeting life," where hours every day are devoted to rote study of works by the two Kims and to grating criticism—self-criticism sessions. Nam Ok believes that even Kim Jong Il finds the DPRK's historical narrative absurd, collapsing everything modern into the history of his father from 1912 to 1994. She and Jong Nam loved shopping sprees in Geneva and Paris, buying whatever they wanted through cash handouts from the DPRK ambassador. They partied with the rich and famous of all sorts of countries, including prominent Americans. Nam Ok brought back Borsalino hats to both her father and grandfather, and suitcases full of designer sunglasses. She shared with O. J. Simpson a love for Bruno Magli shoes.

Kim Jong Il, according to Nam Ok, is highly intelligent and very sensitive—more than anyone she knows. He notices and comments on everything from a person's taste to their accent to their bad habits, of which he is an excellent mimic. At home he loves to laugh, especially about the foibles of the palace staff. He has advice for everyone, on everything. He believes every problem can be solved, and usually thinks he has the solution. The Dear Leader's problem, though, is to be surrounded by sycophants telling him what they think he wants to hear, officials desperate to hide bad news from him, hand servants catering to his every whim, and no one who will tell him the truth. Or hardly anyone. Thus, according to Nam Ok he prizes honesty above everything else and tries intently to ferret out people who will give him straight talk. He presides over a system consisting of boxes within boxes in descending order of importance, with each compartmentalized echelon seeking to maintain its relative privilege in a scarce economy in decline for the past two or three decades. At the same time he is short tempered and given to towering rages, which he can't contain; this puts the fear of God into anyone bringing him truthful bad news.

The ubiquity of "the American dream" and American mass culture is evident in its capacity to attract even (or perhaps above all?) its fervid enemies. Saddam Hussein and his entourage loved to watch Hollywood movies, just as Kim Jong Il does, but the latter's difference is visible in his frequent promises to send his eldest son and heir apparent—to Harvard! He longs to be free of his secluded existence. He drives himself and his family around the country (although usually just around Pyongyang for short trips) in a black, armored Mercedes S600 with tinted windows;

of course everyone knows who it is, and hides away from view. He likes to hunt in the mountains directly from his Mercedes Gelandewagen, the best off-road vehicle in the world. He loves all kinds of cinema, beginning with *Gone with the Wind* (ineluctably, ergo, it is the favorite Hollywood movie of all North Koreans) and ending with any James Bond film except the last one — *Die Another Day* — where Bond desecrates a Buddhist temple with his amorous adventures while caricaturing the North as a hellhole.[16] Kim's special train places Hollywood films at his immediate disposal, and here, too, huge flat-screen TV monitors on the walls put CNN and the World Wide Web never more than a moment away from this daily Internet surfer; a man who began to think about his body in middle age and thus gave up smoking; the proto-apostate heir to the wrong state at the wrong time who cruised across the vast Trans-Siberian railway in August 2001 and remarked to a Russian friend, "I can see that you've done well. Communism will never come back."

Kim Jong Il, like his father, truly trusts only his relatives when it comes to the top security organs. Several top commands responsible for the security of the capital are in the hands of a group of four brothers who are in-laws to Jong Il's sister, with the eldest brother responsible for the army corps that defends Pyongyang. Otherwise he is constantly at odds with the DPRK's sclerotic bureaucracy. In 1996 Kim directly admonished the highest officials for the nauseating street scenes of people starving, begging for grain, and boarding trains for the countryside in search of something to eat. "Heart-aching occurrences are happening everywhere, but the responsible [functionaries] . . . are simply telling the people to solve the problem on their own." Instead of trying to solve the problem, officials "clamp down" on the people. "No functionary assists me effectively," he complained; "I am working alone."[17]

Furthermore he still has the guerrilla elders to contend with.

When Kim Jong Il had his coming-out party at the 6th Party Congress in 1980, a new Central Committee and Politburo were also elected. Twenty-eight former Manchurian guerrillas were on that Central Committee, and twelve of them constituted the majority on the Politburo. There has not been a party congress since, but the leadership remained predictable and stable through the transition that followed Kim Il Sung's death in 1994, and indeed it had barely changed since the 5th Congress in 1970: thirteen of fifteen Politburo members served from 1970 through 1994. Change at the top has really only come through attrition, as the last of the anti-Japanese partisans die off; by and large the children of the guerrillas and the orphans sheltered by Kim Il Sung now are moving into the top elite, with an inner core composed of Kim Jong Il's own relatives. Still, of the top forty leaders in the DPRK in 1997, only one was under 60 years of age: none other than Kim Jong Il.[18]

The 6th party Congress, though, sounded more like a maternity ward when the succession to Jong Il was formally announced. In the aftermath of this congress, the party newspaper published editorials and articles chock full of organic metaphors and filial principles. For example, "Father of the People" in February 1981 read as follows:

> Kim Il Sung is . . . the great father of our people . . . possessed of greatest love for the people. Long is the history of the word father used as a word representing love and reverence . . . expressing the unbreakable blood ties between the people and the leader. Father. This familiar word represents our people's single heart of boundless respect and loyalty. . . . The love shown by the Great Leader for our people is love of kinship. . . . Our respected and beloved Leader is the tender-hearted father of all the people. . . . Love of paternity . . . is the noblest ideological sentiment pos-

sessed only by our people, which cannot be explained by any theory or principle or fathomed by anything.[19]

Another article argued that

> the blood ties between our Party and the people [mean that] . . . the Party and the people always breathe one breath and act as one. . . . The creed of the people [is] that they cannot live or enjoy happiness apart from the Party . . . today our party and people have become an integrity of ideology and purpose which no force can break. The Worker's Party of Korea . . . is the Mother Party bringing boundless honor and happiness to the people."[20]

The corporate state known as the Democratic People's Republic of Korea, in other words, was both the "fatherly" and the "motherly" source that had nurtured the Dear Leader, and of course everyone of his generation who climbed the greasy pole by clinging closely to his rise to power:

> O motherly Party, I will always remain true
> To you all my life.
> A baby gets to know its mother's face first
> It is most happy to see her. . . .
> The Party gives me a motherly image.
> I shall follow it all my life as a child longs for its
>   mother
> O whenever I am at its side
> I feel happy.[21]

The Worker's Party is mostly male, of course, like other communist parties, but no communist state ever depicted the vanguard of the proletariat in such womanly ways. Why? One of the more interesting and least penetrable aspects of East Asian parenting is the primordial relation between mothers and sons. The father leaves the "parenting" to the mother, and often spends most of the week working in an office in daytime and carousing late into the night, coming home only to pass out in bed, pending the return of the daily grind around sunup. Above all, though, what he wants is a son. An exuberant if anonymous observation from the 1920s makes the point:

> Theoretically he says, "Let me be married in the spring when the plum blossoms greet me, and when the peach flowers and apricots tint the hillside"; but he never thinks of his bride as his peach- or plum-blossom. Spring is the mating season and he would mate. He wants to be married, not for selfish pleasure, nor because a little sugar-coated heart longs to rest in his love and be looked after. Not a bit of it; he wants a son, a son of his very own. He wants him wildly, unreasonably; anything for a son.[22]

Sex is not the main point of Korean marriages, so you get lots of male philandering and lots of horny housewives. (Friends of mine in the Peace Corps found that living with Korean families offered an unexpected treat: sleeping with the mother of the house.) In a fascinating analysis, Charles Armstrong suggests that oedipal conflict, socked into the core of Western civilization and lately the unconquerable problem of the Mafia don in *The Sopranos*, is an uncomfortable fit with Korean and Japanese society. A Japanese psychoanalyst, Kosawa Heisaku, criticized Japan's ongoing "Westernization" for repressing "the primary fusion of son and mother in the Japanese character"; to avoid Western anomie ("the alienation from the oneness of subject and object") he sug-

gested a *return* — to "the pre-Oedipal state" that precedes alienation. Writing in the early 1930s, he interpreted the rampant
nationalism of the period to mean the individual's immersion
into the collective "we," led of course by the father-figure of the
emperor but analogous to "the oneness of mother and son."[23] It
is barely a stretch, then, from Mother Kang Ban Suk to Mother
Kim Jong Suk to her turdlike offspring to the unity of party,
family, and state.

   Another reason for close mother-son relations is that the
North continues to adhere to traditional social norms about
what's good for young people. They go to schools segregated by
sex, dating and holding hands were frowned upon until recently,
and thus out-of-wedlock pregnancies are very rare. If it nonetheless happens, the infant is given up to the state and treated like
other orphans — warmly. The result is that "most North Korean
males forego sex entirely until their late 20s or early 30s,"[24] and
so, presumably, do women. I once witnessed a group of Korean
adults dancing sedately in a park, accompanied by an accordion.
A few years later, I was strolling through Edinburgh and saw
exactly the same thing. But, of course, in twenty-first-century
America what North Koreans and Scots like to do for recreation
would seem hopelessly square and outdated. Maybe the Moral
Majority would still like it, though. Anthony Namkung, who
attended an evangelical Christian missionary school, said, "[I]t
helps in understanding North Korea if you have lived in a fundamental Christian community. . . . Just like the North Koreans,
we believed in the absolute purity of our doctrine. We focused
inward and didn't want to be tainted by the outside world."[25]
Perhaps this also explains Billy Graham's warm reception when
he has occasionally preached in Pyongyang; he seems to have
little difficulty understanding the country.

A GULAG THE SIZE OF GREENWICH

"Kim Jong Il's got a gulag the size of Houston!" George Bush exclaimed. I wonder if the forty-third president consulted an atlas before this particular outburst. Houston has about two million people, four million if you count its suburban sprawl. North Korea has about 23 million people, and its prison camps hold between 100,000 and 150,000, something over half of whom are political cases.[26] But Kim Jong Il does have a gulag. One of his favorite threats is to send his enemies off to it, according to Li Nam Ok, or to labor in the endless number of primitive mines in the country.

About three decades ago, Ali Lameda, a Venezuelan leftist, journeyed to Pyongyang to help the regime with its Spanish-language propaganda, which Lameda thought was unaccountably bad and counterproductive. After working for a while in their publishing houses, he realized that what you saw in Caracas was what you got in Pyongyang. He complained about this often enough—albeit in the quiet of his apartment, to his girlfriend. But his every word was monitored, and he got hauled up before a court for insulting the DPRK. The judge gave him two years in a prison camp, with Lameda's "defense lawyer" calling for three. They put him in the back of a truck with other miscreants and sent him off to the mountains; he could hear the wolves howling as he arrived at the remote labor camp. Returning to Pyongyang two years later, he again blasted the regime in private, again to his girlfriend. Off he went for several more years in the gulag. Finally they released him and let him go home to Venezuela, where he became the subject of Amnesty International's first report on human rights in North Korea.

Officially Kim Jong Il's gulag is made up of "educational institutions" that do not punish prisoners, but reeducate them. Common criminals who commit minor felonies and small fry with an incorrect grasp of their place in the family state who commit low-level political offenses go off to labor camps or mines for hard work and varying lengths of incarceration; murderers, repeat offenders, and big-time political criminals (particularly those who spy for the South) are incarcerated for good in some of the most godforsaken prisons in the world. Kang Chol-wan was held in the Yodok labor camp for ten years, and like most other prisoners, he went there with his family—a common practice and an odd aspect of the DPRK's belief in the family as the core unit of society. Mutual family support is also the reason that many survive the ordeal of prison.

This camp, like others, was in a valley enclosed by nature, that is, hills, mountains, rivers, and forests surrounded it and made escape impossible; barbed wire and booby traps were lying in wait for those who thought otherwise. The conditions were primitive and beatings were frequent, but the inmates also were able to improvise much of their upkeep on their own. The Kang family was allowed to bring with it a 125-pound bag of rice, which was made to last for many months. After that was exhausted, the food was monotonous; they had so much corn that pellagra (a disease prevalent among Native Americans who ate mostly corn) was a constant threat. The natural environs meant that small animals could surreptitiously be caught and cooked, however, and death from starvation was rare. Kang's uncle had worked in a brewery for many years, and soon had his own rudimentary still, churning out liquor—"after becoming lord of the alcohol bottles, my uncle wielded enormous power and prestige in the camp." Camp guards ranged from the most hated, known for their thuggery and brutality, to individuals who would find ways to help the inmates survive. But most inmates supervised themselves in work units that always had people willing to rat out another inmate in return for privileges.[27]

When they returned to society, the Kang family initially felt ostracized, but because "most North Koreans share an exceptional innocence and honesty," soon they were accepted back into the community. The family prospered mainly because of cash coming in from relatives in Japan; a color TV paid for a residence permit in a city near Pyongyang, and soon they were living in the capital, and living well—aided by bribes here and there. By that time, in the early 1990s, the state distribution and rationing system was fraying, and private markets spread rapidly in both villages and cities. Indeed Kang thought private farming was a contributing cause of the flooding that brought on famine, because peasants had "deforested slopes susceptible to soil erosion." Black markets were a major source of access to imported goods, which could be bought with the native currency. Kang succeeded in getting into college, but soon tired of it and made his way to China, where he defected.[28]

The Aquariums of Pyongyang is an interesting and believable story, precisely because it does not, on the whole, make for the ghastly tale of totalitarian repression that its original publishers in France meant it to be; instead it suggests that a decade's incarceration with one's immediate family was survivable and not necessarily an obstacle to entering the elite status of residence in Pyongyang and entrance to college. Meanwhile we have a long-standing, never-ending gulag full of black men in our prisons, incarcerating upward of 25 percent of all black youths. This doesn't excuse North Korea's police state, but perhaps it suggests that Americans should do something about the pathologies of our inner cities—say, in Houston—before pointing the finger.

Chapter Six

BEYOND GOOD AND EVIL

> The whole book represents an effort to rise "beyond" sim-
> pleminded disagreement, beyond the vulgar faith in anti-
> thetical values, "beyond good and evil." The point of the
> title is *not* that the author considers himself beyond good
> and evil in the crudest sense, but it is in part that he is
> beyond saying such silly things as "the Jews are good" or
> "the Jews are evil"; or "free spirits" or "scholars" or "virtues"
> or "honesty" or "humaneness" are "good" or "evil."
>
> Walter Kaufmann on Nietzsche[1]

SINCE THE DEATH of Kim Il Sung, the North has faced one terrible crisis after another. It has been visited with a near collapse of its energy system (which then caused many factories to close), two years of unprecedented floods (in 1995 and 1996), a summer of drought (1997), and a resulting famine that some say claimed the lives of two million people. This is a textbook example of the calamities that are supposed to mark the end of the Confucian dynastic cycle, and North Korean citizens must wonder how much more suffering they will endure before the economy returns to anything like the relatively stable situation that foreigners like myself observed in the 1980s. Kim Jong Il waited out the three-year traditional mourning period for the first son of the king before assuming his father's leadership of the ruling party. On the fiftieth anniversary of the regime's founding in September 1998, he became the maximum leader, but chose not to become head of state (i.e., president of the Democratic People's Republic of Korea)—probably because he appears to be uncomfortable in meeting foreign leaders.

Kim Jong Il assumed the mandate of heaven (a classical term that the North Koreans used repeatedly after Kim Il Sung died) with the regime's future shaky and with his people still starving. Confucian civilization put power in the hands of the morally superior man who would govern well; people were happy when a good king ruled, and nature was bountiful. Equality, too, is found in the emphasis on the capability of every person for education and moral refinement. In the past decade, the people of North Korea have been misled by Kim Jong Il, victimized by a cruel Mother Nature, with an equality that consists mostly of sharing their portion of stark misery.

No one knows how many people have died of starvation and disease since 1995. Andrew Natsios, the vice president of World Vision, told reporters in September 1997 that North Korea had lost 500,000 to one million of its citizens to famine, and if full information were at hand, the total might be closer to two million, that is, nearly 10 percent of the population.[2] Since that time newspapers reports simply assume that upward of two million have died. A survey in August 1997 conducted among some 400 Koreans living in China and crossing the border into North Korea frequently came up with an estimate that 15 percent of the population in towns along northern border had died. In orphanages, from which have come many of the televised images of this famine, the figure was 22 percent; in poor mining towns in the far north, about 9 percent.[3] The best scholarship on the North Korean famine, in my unbiased opinion, is to be found in my spouse's study done for the Asian Development Bank Institute; she estimates about half a million dead from the famine and its consequences.[4]

"On the sticky summer day of June 26, 1995," Don Oberdorfer wrote, "the skies over [North Korea] darkened. Rains began to pound the earth, rains that were heavy, steady, and unrelenting and that soon turned into a deluge of biblical proportions."[5] The DPRK Bureau of Hydro Meteorological Service recorded 23 inches of rain in ten days, and in some areas as much as 18 inches of rain fell in a single day, bringing floods considered to be "the worst in a century." Rain was three to five times the normal level. By the time the storms stopped in mid-August, the North Korean government said that some 5.4 million people had been displaced, 330,000 hectares of agricultural land destroyed, 1.9 million tons of grains lost, with the total cost of the flood damage pegged at $15 billion.[6] Torrential rains came again in 1996, doing less, but still very severe damage. A prolonged drought followed in 1997, accompanied by a large tidal wave crashing to the shore.

The extent of famine-related mortality in North Korea remains unclear. Estimates vary from 200,000 to 300,000 — thought to be the lower range by Peter Hayes, director of Nautilus Institute, to an uppermost figure of 3.5 million, based on interviews with refugees in China. A close study by American demographers put the figure between 600,000 and one million.[7] Such figures do not apply to the whole country, however. Regional differentiation is great in North Korea, with 10 percent of the population living in the highly centralized and much privileged capital. Foreign travelers have not witnessed starvation conditions in Pyongyang, and an international delegation that visited the upper east coast, to break ground for the light-water reactors envisioned in the October 1994 nuclear framework agreement, did not see much evidence of famine and malnutrition.[8] The DPRK is a class society, and those families with homes (as opposed to apartments) in villages and small cities have small plots of land at their disposal, every inch of which is under cultivation. A *Los Angeles Times* reporter visited several families with small gardens and found that such families did not need government rations and had enough to eat.[9]

Domestic sources of energy—coal and hydroelectric power—
were also severely impaired by the capricious weather. Energy
experts from the Nautilus Institute put it like this:

> Coalmines were flooded (some mines producing the
> best quality coal, near Anju, were on the coast below
> sea level to start with). Hydroelectric production was
> affected by floodwaters that damaged turbines and
> silted up reservoirs, then by drought that reduced
> water supplies below the levels needed to generate
> power. Electric transmission and distribution lines
> were damaged, as were roads and transportation
> equipment. Heavy erosion and scavenging for food
> denuded landscapes, reducing the availability of bio-
> mass for energy use.[10]

Professor Woo-Cumings linked North Korea's travails to os-
cillating weather patterns in Northeast Asia, particularly the El
Niño Southern Oscillation (ENSO) of 1997–98, one of the worst
in recorded history going back some 300 years. The floods in
1995 and 1996 were episodic events interrupting a long-term dry-
ing trend in northern China and North Korea from the 1950s to
the present:

> These may or may not be linked to El Nino, because
> North Korea is located at much higher latitudes (38
> degrees North to 45 N), far away from the main ef-
> fects of El Nino whose influence is mostly tropical
> and subtropical. Rather they may be related to global
> warming, and a natural phenomenon called the "Arc-
> tic Oscillations," which affects polar regions, includ-
> ing Eurasia and the North Pacific Ocean. It will
> require much more work on this recent period by me-

teorologists before weather anomalies of the mid-1990s can be sorted out.

On the other hand, the droughts of 1997 were profoundly affected by this huge ENSO. Nowhere, however, as she pointed out, was North Korea mentioned in connection to El Niño—the same country suffering one of the most publicized famines in recent history.

If Mother Nature shares blame for North Korea's recent travails, even in the best weather conditions the North's agricultural problems are irremediable short of major reform. The collapse of the Soviet bloc left the DPRK's export markets in a lurch, exports that had been exchanged at favorable rates for petroleum, coking coal, and other essential imports. A rapid decline in petroleum imports in the 1990s, in turn, hurt the national transportation network and the huge chemical industry, which provided so much fertilizer to the farms. For several years now, industry appears to have been running at less than 50 percent of capacity. North Korea must now find ways to export to the world market to earn the foreign exchange needed to import food, oil, and other essentials.

North Korea's economy dropped precipitously in the 1990s, with gross national income falling from $21.3 billion in 1994 to $12.6 billion in 1998, according to the Bank of Korea. Estimated per capita energy use in 1990 was 71 gigajoules per person, more than twice that of China in the same year, over half of Japan's, and similar to South Korea's.[11] But its energy supply dropped from 24 million tons of oil equivalent in 1990 to a nadir of 14 million tons in 1998. The vast majority of its energy comes from abundant coal reserves, but that, too, dropped from 16.6 million tons of oil equivalent in 1990 to 9.3 million tons in 1998. United Nations estimates of agricultural production stood at 4 million tons in 1995, dropping to 2.8 million tons for the each of the next two years; after another bad year in 2000 (2.6 million tons), it rose to 3.5 million in 2001.[12] Meanwhile throughout the 1980s Kim Il Sung called upon agricultural cooperatives to "scale the heights of 10 million tons of grain," and harvests annually brought in seven to eight million tons; the North exported large amounts of rice back then. (Estimates of how much the country needs for self-sufficiency vary, ranging from 4.5 to 6 million tons of grain.)

Various Non-Government Organizations (NGOs) eventually got far wider access to the North's interior than anyone did previously, including communist allies; some two-thirds of all counties have had aid and monitoring teams at the local level, with the remaining one-third divided between counties close to the DMZ and an interior belt of counties stretching from central counties northeast of Pyongyang running on a widening belt up to the Chinese border. These are closed to outsiders for alleged security considerations.[13] Unicef determined that malnutrition rates in 2003 had dropped considerably from their height in 1998: the proportion of underweight children had dropped from 61 percent in 1998 to 21 percent; wasting or acute malnutrition from 16 percent to 9 percent; and stunting or chronic malnutrition from 62 percent to 42 percent.[14] But an entire generation will grow to adulthood with infirmities like poor peasants had in the old days before 1945, when "spring hunger" (ch'un'gŭn) was endemic to the country, and people spread through the hills looking for tree bark, acorns, and roots to eat. Nor is the regime open to these NGOs; it is just doing what it has to do to get food aid. (Several NGOs have pulled out of the DPRK, saying it is impossible to do their work effectively; these include *Medecins Sans Frontiers*, Oxfam, and CARE.)

Washington likes to claim that it is the biggest aid donor to the North, but U.S. aid has not been nearly as substantial as it claims. Under the Framework agreement, the United States sent

$400 million in energy assistance, mainly heating oil, from 1995
to 2003; this was not aid, but compensation for the shutdown of
the North's nuclear facilities. Furthermore the oil that the United
States sent to the North, according to Peter Hayes of the Nautilus Institute, was a high-sulfur-content liquid coal, difficult to
use in Korean boilers and never amounting to more than 2 percent of its energy needs. The main American aid has come in the
form of food assistance, amounting to 1.953 metric tons valued
at $615 million from 1996 to 2003. The biggest bundle came in
1999, with 695,194 metric tons of food, and stood at 350,000 tons
when Bush took office. The Bush administration cut back to
207,000 tons in 2002, and drastically cut it to 40,000 tons
through the first half of 2003—while claiming it was not using
"food as a weapon."[15] Meanwhile China has provided from half
a million to a million tons of food aid annually since 1995, depending on the year.

On July 1, 2002, the North implemented a drastic set of economic reforms, trying to bring their currency in line with international exchange rates through a sudden, huge devaluation (the
wŏn cascaded from 2.2 to the dollar to 150–160), raising wages 20
to 25 times, greatly increasing the size of "private plots," allowing
farmers to keep or sell anything beyond their state quotas, and
beginning to phase out the national rationing system. The verdict
isn't in on whether this worked, but it predictably set off runaway
inflation.[16] In the fall of 2002, the North announced that it would
build a large free export zone on the Chinese border, called the
Sinŭiju Special Administrative Region, to be run on "capitalist"
principles. A great wall was to be built around it, to keep the
capitalists from contaminating the rest of the country. A Dutch-
Chinese named Yang Bin, who had made a fortune in raising and
selling tulips, was to run it. Somehow Kim Jong Il didn't bother
to consult the Chinese before putting another would-be Hong
Kong on their border, and in no time flat the Chinese had Yang

Bin in jail, charged with monumental corruption.[17] It's anybody's guess whether this zone will ever materialize, but it exemplifies the jerky, helter-skelter motion of North Korean "reform."

Any kind of coordinated reform seems difficult for the regime to accomplish. In the North Korean administrative system, bureaucratic lineages and hierarchies often exist as independent kingdoms, and have trouble communicating with each other. Hardliners in the military have clearly been at odds with those in the Foreign Ministry who want better relations with Washington and Tokyo (something that foreign diplomats have witnessed on occasion), but the problems go much beyond that. Relative bureaucratic autonomy, the practice of provincial self-reliance, a vast party apparatus organizing upward of one-third of the adult population, the privileged position of the military (gaining at minimum 25 percent of the annual budget), the death of the only leader the country ever had, intense generational conflict (between an increasingly small but still influential revolutionary old guard and people in their 40s–60s), and the piling on of externally generated crises have all resulted in a kind of paralysis and immobilism in the past decade. Decisions are pushed upward through the hierarchy, and at the top no one seems capable of making the hard choices necessary to push the country on a truly new course. North Korea is neither muddling through toward some sort of postcommunism, the way other socialist states did after 1989, nor is it seriously reforming like China and Vietnam. The leadership seems deeply frightened by the consequences of opening up the economy, preferring instead to open tiny coastal enclaves (like the Najin-Sonbong export zone in the Northeast). Still, for all the tribulations that have come in recent years, there are few signs that any of them have threatened the stability of the top leadership.

Probably the biggest obstacle to thoroughgoing reform is the relatively short time that has passed since the North thought it

was winning the race with the South, combined with the mind-
set of a septuagenarian old guard for whom the turn into the
1980s seems to have occurred just a sheer moment ago. That turn,
of course, heralded the neoliberal offensive that began with Mar-
garet Thatcher and Ronald Reagan and that, on a world scale,
was to be the beginning of the end for the social protections,
government regulations, and labor unions that were, everywhere
in the industrial world, the postwar heritage of the global depression in the 1930s. Here, the New Deal and the Democratic
Party coalition forged after 1932 came unstuck, and New Deal
Democrats became almost as scarce as Hoover Republicans after
the Depression. There, the shapers of Kim Il Sung's New Order
are still in power.

For decades the North far outstripped the South in economic
development. In the 1950s and 1960s, American officials in the
South never stopped talking about the ROK's basket-case economy and the huge challenge posed by a North whose heavy industry was growing rapidly. Scholars and pundits wrung their
hands over this challenging dilemma.[18] Inheriting heavy industry
from Japan and getting it renovated by Curtis LeMay's bombers
in the 1950s (after which Soviet bloc countries contributed a great
deal to rebuilding the flattened factories), North Korea was always the most industrialized and urbanized of the Asian communist countries. (Today agricultural pursuits encompass about
20 percent of the population, compared with 60 to 70 percent in
China and a higher percentage in Vietnam.)

Published data from the CIA indicated in 1978 that the ROK
had only just drawn even with the North in per capita gross
national product (GNP); the DPRK used as much electricity as
the South, with half the South's population; it produced more
crude steel and three times the number of machine tools (the
building blocks of industry) as the South. If industrial production
tripled in the South from 1971 to 1976 under Park Chung Hee's

"Big Push" in heavy industry, it more than doubled in the North, growing at an annual average rate of 14 percent between 1965 and 1976. Its agriculture was far ahead of the South's in productivity; it used miracle seedlings and its chemical fertilizer application was "probably among the highest in the world," while the South still ladled human waste on its rice fields.[19] (When I first visited the North in 1981, I was amazed to find that the rice paddies did not reek of this unforgettable manure.) North Korea's average food intake was higher than South Korea's in 1982, averaging 3,051 calories compared with 2,936; both were well over UN base levels for human sustenance. Life expectancy at birth in 1983, according to UN data, was essentially the same in North and South, at 65 and 67 years, respectively.[20] South Korea's rapid growth stalled in 1979, when it lost 6 percent of the GNP; it recovered by 1982, however, and began to grow by double digits annually, as its new heavy industrial products—steel, autos, ships, chemicals, machine tools—found many buyers at home and abroad. By the time the Berlin Wall collapsed, the ROK had opened a long, ever-lengthening, and soon insurmountable lead over the North.

The North responded dramatically to President Park's "Big Push" in heavy industry; it imported many entire factories and new technologies in the early 1970s, as we have seen, resulting in a CIA estimate of 35 percent growth in 1972, and around 20 percent per annum for the next three years. Much like the South, it financed these industrial and technological imports with loans; unlike the South, however, there was no big-power guarantor to bail them out when their calculations ran aground and the loans could not be repaid. (President Reagan and Prime Minister Nakasone arranged a $4 billion bailout for the Chun Doo Hwan regime in 1984, about 13 percent of the ROK's total outstanding debt, then ranked third in the world among developing countries.) North Korea defaulted on a number of expensive loans, totaling perhaps $2 billion. More difficult to understand, however, was the steady decline in capital imports that ensued for the next fifteen years, until the collapse of the Soviet Union sent the economy into a full tailspin. Just at the point where South Korea began to build one new factory after another using mostly imported technology, after the midseventies the North "locked itself into an aging industrial infrastructure that embodies generally obsolescent technologies."[21] The best explanation for this curious failure is the dogma of self-reliance, and the hidebound nature of an aging elite whose best days were disappearing in the rearview mirror. The more important point, though, is that the North's stagnation and the South's great leap forward began just twenty years ago, a wink of an eye to a people who calculate time by the century. That a South totally dependent on the United States in 1950, over which the North's tanks rolled with ease, could put the DPRK so clearly in the shade must be a terrible blow to the overweening pride that has always distinguished this leadership.

Instead of a steady reform program, the leadership lurches in one direction and then another, while the state system breaks down. Barter and regime-condoned black markets operate everywhere; there may be as many as 3,000. Hard currency, especially dollars, is in wide use and highly valued. The historically centralized, administratively planned delivery of goods and services by the state has almost completely broken down at the local levels, with many people lacking food rations for months at a time. Still, foreign relief experts say that food brought into the country is not diverted to the privileged military. It is more a matter of locally produced food stocks going to the elite in Pyongyang and to the vast military. Otherwise foreign observers speak of an egalitarian sharing of existing food stocks combined with a triage policy, whereby the young, the elderly, and the infirm are the first to suffer. The government is helping where it can, denying where it must, and keeping the essential pillar of its power—the military—sufficiently fed. Kim Jong Il approved a measure that would allow farmers to keep up to 30 percent of what they harvest, a truly major change if indeed it was implemented, but North Korean agricultural production remains mired in inefficiency. In recent years grain harvests have rarely gotten near four million tons, and the country remains dependent on foreign sources to feed its population.

This crisis has occasioned an unaccustomed candor on the part of the regime. Its official news agency said in 1998 that "the people are tapping all possibilities and reserves and eking out their living in reliance upon substitute food" but claimed that "the Korean people are moving ahead merrily in the teeth of the present difficulties." It acknowledged the large amounts of relief grain coming in from China—which had rendered "free assistance" to North Korea "on several occasions for years."[22] Unlike similar humanitarian emergencies around the world, however, this one has provided little evidence of a collapse of state power, except for the breakdowns at the local level. There have been few significant changes in the North Korean leadership since Kim died. There have been defections, many of them hyped in the South Korean press and the world media, but only one—that of Hwang Chang-yŏp in February 1997—was truly significant, and although the regime was embarrassed and demoralized by Hwang's departure, he had never been a central power-holder and the core leadership still appears to be unshaken. In August 2001, Kim Jong Il chose to spend three weeks on an armored train while traveling to Moscow and back, presumably a junket meant to indicate that his hold on power back home is firm and secure.

Another curiosity is that North Korea suffers as if it were Somalia or Ethiopia, but it has a much more developed and modern economy. The DPRK historically had a powerful industrial economy and remains relatively urbanized, and, as we have seen, until recent years international agencies found that life expectancy rates, child welfare, inoculation rates, and general public health conditions were all quite high in North Korea, comparatively speaking. Unlike other places afflicted by humanitarian disasters, this is not a peripheral, penetrated state with a weak government. North Korea has a notably strong central state, high state capacities, and the ability to reach its arms into the smallest communities.

Serious reform could happen in North Korea once the key decisions were taken, because this is a country that can mobilize everyone for centrally determined tasks. With its well-educated and disciplined workforce, North Korea could effectively exploit a comparative advantage in labor cost in world markets. Indeed, for years major South Korean firms have hoped to marry their skills with North Korean labor (and several have actually done so, like the Daewoo textile factory in Namp'o and the port of P'yongyang). In this sense the suffering of the North Korean population is truly inexcusable, because something could be done about famine conditions if there was truly a will to do so among the central authorities. Instead they seem morbidly insecure and determined therefore to give the armed forces what they need, to the detriment of every other institution in society. (Kim Jong Il has loudly talked about his "army first" policies since the mid-1990s, as if the Worker's Party no longer counts—an anomaly for a communist regime and a tragedy for the people.)

Kim Jong Il greeted the new millennium with a flurry of diplomatic activity, normalizing relations with thirteen West European and commonwealth countries, beginning with Italy. A year later in an explicit reference to his father's generation, he told the party newspaper that "[t]hings are not what they used to be in the 1960s. So no one should follow the way people used to do things in the past." He urged a bold "technical modernization" instead of being "shackled by ready-made ideas or hanging on to the old and outdated conceptions."[23] The United Nations Development Program (UNDP) has also found that the North's

unwillingness to divulge extensive statistical data and information
has given way to "unstinted cooperation" with a multibillion dollar UNDP program to help make the North once again self-
sufficient in agriculture. Kim Jong Il personally endorsed this,
which, among other things, expands double-cropping in rice and
brings under cultivation vast amounts of potatoes.[24]

The best signal the North Korean military has sent in recent
years is its development of powerful trading companies, just as
the Chinese military has done; soldiers getting rich are much less
interested in jacking up military tensions. These firms handle
commercial exports of the North's abundant minerals (gold, magnesite, tungsten, anthracite coal) and, press reports suggest, its
illegal trade in opium and methamphetamines. (The North's anthracite coal reserves exceed 10 billion tons, iron ore is around
three billion tons, and its magnesite reserves—a commodity used
for many things, but especially to line blast furnaces—run to six
billion tons.) Scattered searches for oil deposits along the North's
Yellow Sea coast suggest that the North may have nearly two
billion barrels of recoverable oil deposits.[25]

Gen. Cho Myŏng-nok, who it will be remembered visited Bill
Clinton in the Oval Office, controls the largest such firm, which
exports missiles to garner foreign exchange and presides over all
matters "related to the production, distribution, and consumption of goods utilized by the armed forces"—rice, uniforms, and
weapons.[26] This is the surest sign of the North's crablike movement toward reform along the lines of China and Vietnam and
the emergence of a wealthy class with a vested interest in continuing to open up the economy. Various kinds of smuggling net-
works have emerged along the Chinese border, moving people
and goods back and forth, and importing luxury items (including
cars) for those with foreign exchange. More than twenty-five "pa-
latial villas" on Mount Yaksan can now be seen from the highway
running from Pyongyang to the Yongbyon nuclear complex.[27]

Nor does Kim Jong Il hog the Internet only for his own pleasure. In 2001 the North joined Intelsat (the International Tele-
communications Satellite Program), and the state-run Chosun
Computer Center worked out an agreement with a leading South
Korean information technology firm, BIT Computer, to set up
satellite access in various places around the country. Access to the
Internet, of course, remains severely constrained by politics.[28] Private markets have now become a standard feature of the economy, where people barter goods and services for food and
consumer items. The largest private market is in Pyongyang, with
upward of 10,000 people trading there frequently. Small stalls
and shops are emerging along streets and highways, where people
sell fruit, home-baked goods, furniture, and the like.[29] Kim also
made a bold decision in June 2000 to let Hyundai set up a huge
investment zone in Kaesŏng, with some 700 factories; ground
was broken for this complex in 2002, and the railway ties through
the DMZ that had been severed since the Korean War were re-
opened in June 2003, linking Kaesŏng to Seoul and to the "hub"
of Inch'ŏn, where a huge new international airport anchors President Roh Moo Hyun's vision of Korea being the centerpiece of
a thriving Northeast Asian regional economy. Meanwhile various
joint ventures that got going in the late 1990s now produce cloth-
ing, televisions, and golf bags for export to the South and Japan,
and a branch of the best Korean restaurant in Pyongyang, the
Okryugwan, opened up in Seoul to a huge traffic in customers.

North Korean ideologues like to use the term "mosquito net"
as a metaphor for letting advanced technology come in, while
keeping capitalist ideas out: "It can let in breezes, and it also can
defend against mosquitoes." This is the same metaphor Deng
Xiaoping used when he began to open up China in 1978; the
North of course was much more shrill in denouncing the infiltration of liberal and capitalist ideas:

> It is the main strategy of the imperialists to dominate
> the world with corrupt ideas which they had failed to
> bring under their control with atomic bombs and dol-
> lars. This poisoning is aimed at doing harm to the
> excellent national character of each country and nation
> and making hundreds of millions of people across the
> world mentally deformed. . . . Corrupt ideas . . . are
> more dangerous than atomic bombs. . . . ideological
> education is our life line . . . to pay exclusive attention
> to economic construction and abandon ideological
> work is just a suicidal act of opening the door for
> imperialist ideology and culture to infiltrate. . . . It is
> imperative to set up a mosquito net in all realms of
> social life.

After flailing "vulgar" bourgeois society—"narcotics addicts, alcoholics and degenerates seeking to satisfy abnormal desires"—
the article said, "[T]he collapse of the erstwhile Soviet Union and
East European countries is entirely attributable to their flinging
the door open to imperialist ideological and cultural poisoning."[30] The overall burden of this missive, though, was to let in
joint ventures and keep out bad ideas.

AMERICAN FAILURES

Historians read secret documents after they are declassified, and
even though I learned a great deal from the thousands of pages
of intelligence reports I've read over the years, they were for the
most part appallingly bad at understanding and weighing the
most important questions: What kind of leaders run North Korea
or China or Vietnam? Where did they come from? What are their
goals? What is their standing with their own populations? What
kind of leaders have we sponsored in the same countries? Where

did they come from? What is *their* standing with their population? From 1945 down to the present, we have backed the wrong horses in these three countries (let's say, Syngman Rhee, Chiang Kai-shek, and Ngo Dinh Diem), wrong in the first instance because they couldn't *win*, but could cause big trouble for us. Or when democracy breaks out and we do get a good leader on our side, we don't like him (Kim Dae Jung, Roh Moo Hyun).

It is still unimaginable to me that in the summer of 1949, the United States allowed the border command along the 38th parallel to be run by the likes of Kim Sŏk-wŏn and several of his Manchukuo comrades, whom Tōjō had built up in the early 1940s as paragons of Korean service to the emperor, or who had been sent like the craven swine that they were to track down the Korean resistance at the behest of their Japanese masters. And we were surprised when a war broke out a year later? Yet when I had just begun to get into this subject—rank collaboration with the Japanese—during a recent public lecture (April 2003), an American in the audience could not stop laughing. After we exchanged a few comments back and forth, it became clear to me that he was incapable of taking North Koreans seriously, or perhaps any Koreans. It escaped him that principles of patriotism and treachery might have meaning for a people brutally colonized for forty years. To fail to understand such elemental things is not a "failure of intelligence;" instead it speaks volumes to the assumptions Americans bring to bear about the unknown countries we fight. (Two months after the end of the Iraq War, a *New York Times* reporter asked an Iraqi professor what was wrong with the postwar occupation: his first response: "You know nothing about this country.")

When I worked on the Thames Television documentary, *Korea: The Unknown War*, Thames researchers located Capt. James R. Graham, described as "Mr. Korea" in the CIA, where he had been reading the communist tea leaves in 1950 when the war began. I was interested in him both because he was reputed to have seen the North Korean attack coming, and because I had found in William "Wild Bill" Donovan's daily diary the notation "call Graham," just when the war broke out. Alas, Captain Graham was a disappointment. He was a retiring, mild-mannered pipe-smoker, wearing tweeds and looking a little depressed; he had the reserve of the professor, not the reticence of the spy. That is, he was just like my academic colleagues, or my aunt's CIA friends (my father's sister spent her whole career in the OSS and the CIA after getting a Ph.D. in French). Furthermore he had never had any contact with Donovan, or so he said; he had sensed that something might happen in Korea shortly before the war, but didn't push his views on his superiors. His pronunciation of Korean names was so execrable that he obviously had never attempted to learn the language. Captain Graham was a hard lesson for my delusion that there is in Washington someone, somewhere, who knows all there is to know about Korea.

My spirits brightened, however, when former Congressman Stephen Solarz, long interested in Korean affairs, found a "brilliant and breathtaking" study by a CIA analyst and concluded that it was for North Korea "what the Rosetta stone was to ancient Egypt." So rare and privileged was the author's knowledge that it took him a decade to get the CIA to declassify the book. Helen-Louise Hunter was for two decades "a Far East Specialist" in the CIA, which is where her book first appeared (if that is the right word) as a long internal memorandum. Here was the solution to another problem we hear a lot about from Beltway pundits: this is "a country about which we knew virtually nothing" (in Solarz's words). That is, we have trouble penetrating and surveilling them: how scary!

Hunter's work has some excellent information on arcane and difficult to research subjects like North Korean wage and price structures, the self-sufficient and decentralized neighborhood liv-

ing practices that mostly eliminated the long lines for goods that
characterized Soviet-style communism, and the decade of one's
young life that almost every North Korean male is required to
devote to military service in this garrison state. She points out
many achievements of the North Korean system, in ways that
would get anyone outside the CIA labeled a sympathizer — compassionate care for war orphans in particular and children in general, "radical change" in the position of women ("there are now
more college-educated woman than college-educated men"), genuinely free housing, preventive medicine on a national scale accomplished to a comparatively high standard, infant mortality
and life expectancy rates comparable to the most advanced countries until the recent famine, "no organized prostitution," and
"the police are difficult, if not impossible, to bribe." The author
frequently acknowledges that the vast majority of Koreans do in
fact revere Kim Il Sung, even the defectors from the system
whose information forms the core evidence for her book. According to Prince Norodom Sihanouk, a close friend of Kim's
who frequently stayed for months at a time in the North, "Kim
ha[d] a relationship with his people that every other leader in the
world would envy"; he described it as "much closer" than his
own with the Cambodian people (where he is both venerated
and highly popular).[31]

American cheerleaders for the South never tire of saying that
its GNP is ten times larger than North Korea's; certainly it is
much larger, but if, say, the World Bank were to value goods
and services in the North in terms of what the equivalents would
cost in the United States, as it did for China after it opened up,
the North's GNP would mushroom overnight. In Hunter's account of the DPRK when its economy was still reasonably good,
about twenty years ago, she found that daily necessities were very
low priced, luxuries vastly overpriced. Rents were so nominal that
most housing was effectively free, as was health care, and "the

government subsidizes the low prices of rice, sugar, and other food necessities, as well as student uniforms and work clothes." All homes in the country had electricity by 1968, far ahead of where the South was at the time. To take a measure close to home, she estimates that a husband and wife who were both university professors would be able to save about 50 percent of their monthly salaries. Rice and corn, the major staples, were rationed by the state, as were cooking oils, meat, soy sauce, bean curd, and *kimch'i*. Other things—fruits, vegetables, nuts, noodles, beer—could be purchased at low prices, with meats and luxury foods overvalued. The general egalitarianism of the society was remarkable, in her view, even if the elite lived much better than the mass.[32]

One of Ms. Hunter's big themes is that North Korea is a "cult society" akin to the folks trundling along behind Jim Jones or Charles Manson.[33] But this analogy merely betrays her lack of knowledge about the society she spent so many years studying, presumably with the best intelligence materials that the U.S. government can muster at her fingertips. She ought to know just how extensive kingly worship, paeans of praise to the king's fount-of-knowledge wisdom and metaphysical idealism, abject obeisance to authority, the people being "of one mind and one body" with the king, and veneration of leaders and elders to seemingly absurd lengths was (and is) in Korean patriarchal society. A knowledgeable scholar put it this way: "The religion-like cult surrounding Kim Il-sung . . . appears to be in large part an unplanned outgrowth of Confucian values placed in a new context"; more broadly, it is "a new and well-integrated family-state that, in certain respects, resembles Confucian society."[34]

A few years ago I was standing in front of the original Rosetta stone at the British Museum. Behind me two Koreans were chatting, with one of them pointing out that all three archaic languages depicted on this stone were in fact derivatives of the

original mother tongue of humanity—Korean. There is more in-
sight in this anecdote about the absurd and grandiose claims
made about all kinds of things in both Koreas than there is in
Hunter's "cult society" thesis.

What truly characterizes her book, though, is nothing that
would suggest a superior fount of wisdom on North Korea hiding in the bowels of the CIA, compared with what can be found
in the existing scholarship. I was surprised to find little on the
social organization of work in North Korea's industrial structure,
and particularly in the vast chemical sector—an industry always
central to the DPRK's attempts at a self-reliant economy, which
Hunter acknowledges to be highly developed. She appears to believe that all North Koreans are ignorant of the outside world,
never mentioning the "reference news" that carries articles from
American and other papers of record and that circulates widely
among the party, government, and military elite. Surely some of
that news trickles down to the mass of the population?

The leading inside-the-Beltway pundit is Nicholas Eberstadt,
who has been with the American Enterprise Institute for fifteen
years, and initially distinguished himself by using demographic
data to pinpoint the wretched health care system and dramatic
declines in life expectancy of the Soviet Union, several years before it fizzled. Since 1990 he has been predicting the impending
collapse of North Korea,[35] as he again did in his 1999 book, *The
End of North Korea*. Eberstadt understands North Korea to be an
industrialized economy in an urban society, unlike the frequently
quoted ignoramuses who compare it to Albania or Cambodia or
Somalia. Although routinely denounced as "Stalinist," North Korea, he says, "has too few farmers to permit a policy of 'squeezing
the countryside' any realistic chance of success." Eberstadt is particularly good at depicting a systematic decline in either importing or investing in capital goods after 1975, an odd thing given
the regime's previous heavy-industry-first strategy and its desire

to keep up with a rapidly industrializing South. In the past decade, the DPRK's deepest economic problems have arisen because of its obsolescent industrial structure and the collapse of its
energy regime, which left the chemical sector unable to supply
the massive doses of fertilizer that used to be laid on the fields,
resulting in declining food production that became catastrophic
when the flooding hit in 1995 and 1996. Eberstadt does not pre-
tend to know how many North Koreans died as a result of food
shortages, citing claims of two to three million but suggesting
that it might be closer to the DPRK's official figure of 200,000.
He does not point out, though, that in its worse phase the famine
only began to approach India's year-in, year-out toll (in propor-
tionate terms) of infant mortality and deaths from malnutrition
or starvation, which I only mention because of the media's recent
habit of depicting Kim Jong Il frolicking amid a heap of starved
cadavers.

Eberstadt's "end-of-North-Korea" theme is fundamentally
flawed, for reasons that can help us understand the DPRK's post–
Cold War endurance. He enjoys arguing throughout the book
that North Korea has been *wrong-wrong-wrong* in all of its strategies from the word go, but he does not tell the reader that he
brings purely liberal and capitalist assumptions to bear on a society that constituted for most of its existence the self-conscious
antiliberal, somewhat as if Milton Friedman were to describe how
stupid the Ayatollahs have been for not charging interest on
loans. Thus we hear about how the "amazingly naïve" North
Koreans just couldn't understand what a World Bank official
meant when he used such terms as "macroeconomics" and "mi-
croeconomics." But Eberstadt has also been *wrong-wrong-wrong*
throughout the past fifteen years in his prognostications of North
Korean collapse. Why? Because he sees the DPRK entirely
through the lens of Soviet and East European communism and
therefore cannot grasp the pragmatic shrewdness of the regime's

post-Cold War foreign policy, the desperate survival strategies it is willing to undertake, let alone the anticolonial and revolutionary nationalist origins of this regime and those in Vietnam and China, yielding no significant break in Asian communism since 1989.

Repeating the Cold War mantra that Moscow saw everything in the world through the Marxist-Leninist doctrine of "the correlation for forces" (*"sootnoshenie sil"*), Eberstadt argues that this is also the basis of North Korea's global strategy. If so, Pyongyang should have folded its hand and cashed in its chips in 1989; no other state faced such an incredible array of enemy "forces" and seemingly insurmountable crises since then, with little help from anyone and universal hopes that it simply erase itself and disappear. Eberstadt said it first in 1990, and Deputy Secretary of Defense Paul Wolfowitz said it again in June 2003—"North Korea is teetering on the brink of collapse."[36] In between we heard Gen. Gary Luck, commander of U.S. forces in Korea, say in 1997 that "North Korea will disintegrate, possibly in very short order"; the only question was whether it would implode or explode.[37] In this he was plagiarizing another of our commanders in Korea, Gen. Robert Riscassi, who never tired of saying Pyongyang would soon "implode or explode." (Riscassi retired in 1992.) When does the statute of limitations run out on being systematically wrong?

Those in South Korea who funded Eberstadt's study knew what they were getting (at the time the Korea Foundation was led by the former number two man in Seoul's intelligence agency), but American taxpayers often wonder what they get for the $28 to $30 billion they annually pour into various governmental intelligence groups—and so did I when I had to read to page 68 of Hunter's book before I learned anything new, which is that Kim Il Sung University has a baseball team. (The Japanese introduced this venerable American game to Korea, and given its popularity in the South, I had wondered if any remnant interest survived in the North; it must be a good sign that it does.) My long-standing impression that "intelligence" inside the Beltway is a euphemism for the halt leading the blind was reinforced by Hunter's painfully obvious lack of language facility in Korean, leading her twice to misspell a word as significant as "*sasang*" (*thought*, as in "Kim Il-song thought"), which is rendered as *sangsa* in its only two appearances in the book.[38] But then, when we invaded Afghanistan the CIA lacked a single employee fluent in the language of the majority, Pashto.

That war brought American power for the first time into Central Asia, where the interests of China, Russia, India, and Pakistan collide—all of them nuclear powers. We now occupy former Soviet military bases in Afghanistan, Kyrgyztan, and Uzbekistan, with various clandestine bases in Pakistan. For more than a decade, Americans have watched as the Pentagon and its many garrisons abroad continue to soak up one-third of the national budget, and spend more than all our conceivable enemies combined; here is a perpetual motion machine of ravenous appetite. Any administration would have responded forcefully to the tragic attacks on September 11, but Bush and his allies have vastly expanded the Pentagon budget, added another zone of containment (Central Asia), put yet more billions into "Homeland Defense," and shown a callous disregard for civil liberties, the rights of the accused, and the views of our traditional allies. The news media and Hollywood fawn on the American military and take jingoism to an embarrassing extreme. Major outlets like Fox News cater exclusively to an imagined audience from the "red" states of the 2000 election (or the 70 percent of the armed forces who voted for Bush).

Have we also become a "garrison state"? We are well advanced on that path today, yet this is hardly a country with a strong military tradition; you can count on the figures of one hand the decades since 1789 when the U.S. military has been a powerful and respected factor in national life. Nor is the military the basic source of American power and influence in the world. There is a stronger countervailing tendency, hard to define but deeply influential in American history. The first thought that struck me after witnessing (on television) thousands of casualties resulting from an attack on the American mainland, for the first time since 1812, was that over the long haul the American people may exercise their long-standing tendency to withdraw from a world deemed recalcitrant to their ministering, and present Washington with a much different and eminently more difficult dilemma than the here-today, gone-tomorrow "axis of evil": how to rally the citizens for a long twilight struggle to maintain an ill-understood American hegemony in a vastly changed world.

Our failure is manifest in our inability to extract our troops from the Korean political thicket that we barged into in 1945, a commitment now caught in a profound time warp, but still one in which American GIs denigrate Koreans as "gooks" and "helmet-heads."[39] In December 2000 I visited P'anmunjŏm once again, this time courtesy of the U.S. Army. Our hosts gave us the army's construction of the history of the Korean War (a version that could not have changed since 1953) and a luncheon of rib-eye steak and french-fried potatoes of similar vintage, offered in a café that had a country music poster on the wall advertising Hank Williams' tour of Atlanta in 1952. The waitresses wore miniskirts and bright red lipstick that might have been enticing around the same time. An obsequious Korean man offered various trinkets and mementos for tourists. The army loves its bases and its multitude of operations in Korea (now approaching the status of venerable institutions), because it is one of the last places in the world where the army can flex its muscles against a real, live enemy just across a heavily fortified border—train and mobilize troops, hold war games, gain field experience for officers, and plan incessantly about how to fight the next war. Find the highest-ranking generals in the U.S. Army over the past fifty years, and you will find that nearly all of them commanded troops in Korea as an important way station in their career advancement. Likewise the Marines love Okinawa, the only place in the world where they permanently station a large expeditionary force. And in both places established institutional practice assures a steady supply of thousands of poor young women to sate the sexual appetites of the troops, as a new book by Northwestern University scholar Ji-yeon Yuh demonstrates.[40]

Six decades after we first occupied their country, many Koreans still believe that racism pervades American attitudes toward, and coverage of, Korea and Koreans. This is our greatest failure. Mostly unbeknown to our mainstream media, time and again they have protested biased treatment of Koreans (including North Koreans), whether it is the latest James Bond film, *Die Another Day*, where Bond defiles a Buddhist temple; the presumed "black-Korean" conflict in the 1992 Los Angeles disturbances;[41] American coverage of the 1988 Olympics, which ranged from the blatant racism of P. J. O'Rourke in *Rolling Stone* to the aversions and aspersions of Ian Buruma in the *New York Review of Books* (he compared it with Hitler's 1936 Olympics);[42] or the ease with which Americans blamed Koreans for the Koreagate scandals in the 1970s, instead of the congressmen happy to pocket the Korean ambassador's wads of hundred dollar bills.

What is racism? Consider these statements:

- From the American Commander in Korea in 1980, John Wickham: "Lemming-like, the people are kind of lining up behind [Chun Doo Hwan] in all walks of life."
- A sentiment deemed "characteristic of many near the top of [the U.S.] government": "These [North] Koreans are wild people."[43]

- Korean authoritarianism goes back to the Confucian tradition.
- Koreans are "the Irish of the Orient—highly emotional, very nationalistic."
- Koreans are "about as subtle as *kimchi* . . . and as timid as a *tae kwon do* chop."
- "Koreans could not strike the first blow in their own defense."
- "Koreans are not ready for self-government."
- "Unlike the Philippines, Koreans are not yet ready for democracy."[44]

None of these statements are overtly racist; they do not call names or use what the Supreme Court calls "hate speech." Yet if we substitute "Americans" or "blacks" or "Jews" for Koreans, and we imagine foreigners of great influence giving voice to these views, we sense that these are biased judgments. Every statement beginning "Koreans are . . ." violates the extraordinary diversity found in Korea, or among Koreans abroad.

Americans of Korean descent now inhabit all professional walks of life and contribute in a wide variety of ways to American culture, and their growing prominence negates any holistic construction that begins, "Koreans are. . . ." To take just one example, a hugely talented artist who was murdered on the streets of New York at the age of 29, Theresa Hak Kyung Cha: her most famous painting is an American flag marked only with the word *"AMER"*—meaning "bitter" in French. Her various works of art dwelt on Korea's twentieth-century history of colonization, war, and division, yet without "falling prey to the lure of racial exceptionalism," and thus

> exceed[ing] their own specificity to situate themselves
> within the global conflict of North and South, of the
> West and the Rest, or of darker and lighter races. No
> history (of any single nation) without (the) histories
> (of other nations). Each society has its own politics

of truth; each oppressed people, their own story of
special horrors and inflicted sufferings.[45]

David Theo Goldberg locates contemporary racism, after the
end of formal racist institutions such as slavery or Jim Crow seg-
regation, in an Anglo-Saxon liberalism that is "self-conscious in
its idealization of acceptable social conditions" (truths that are
self-evident, norms of democracy, rule of law, neoliberalism),
leading to a denial of the possibility of "Otherness"—who can
possibly disagree with these ideals, or reject democracy and the
market—or, at best, a mere tolerance of the Other (who has yet
to learn the self-evident truths). Accusations of racism by people
of color are thus seen as "irrational appeals to irrelevant categories," because they implicitly delimit liberal universalism, and in-
validate its claims of plurality and openness. Power shows itself
in the dual liberal practice of *naming* (all Koreans are. . . .) and
evaluating (the degree to which Koreans fall short of idealized
liberal categories). Liberalism will then "furnish the grounds of
the Other's modification and modernization, establishing what
will launch the Other from the long dark night of its prehistory
into civilized time."[46]

When Attorney General John Ashcroft spoke at the annual
gathering of global elites in Davos, Switzerland, he reacted to
accusations of racial profiling of Muslims in his Justice Department by saying that he does not distinguish people according to
their race, but according to their values.[47] It is a perfect illustra-
tion of Goldberg's point: I am not a racist, I accept all people
who value the same things I do. I am incapable of discrimination
unless we are talking about people who do not value modern liberalism.
Martin Luther King wanted blacks to be judged by the content
of their character, not the color of their skin, but character, for
him, did not originate from a single mold.

BEYOND GOOD AND EVIL

In a recent book, Susan Nieman distinguishes between the En-
lightenment conception of evil, focused on natural disasters (like
drought and floods) that led people to question how God could
"create a world full of innocent suffering," and the modern, post-
Auschwitz idea that evil is "absolute wrongdoing that leaves no
room for account or expiation." Nieman rightly argues that the
September 11 attacks "embodied a form of evil so old-fashioned
that its reappearance is part of our shock;" it combined a modern
nihilism with Old Testament fire and brimstone, and left us with
a "sense of conceptual helplessness." But true evil is not the opposite of good, as President Bush seems to believe; rather it "aims
at destroying moral distinctions themselves."[48] In this sense Saddam Hussein's Iraq represented less something "evil" than a banal
example of a police state, a replica of any number of regimes in
the past century. The other two charter members of "the axis of
evil," Iran and North Korea, are founded on principles that they
quite sincerely believe to distinguish them morally and ethically
from American imperialism. The North Korean case is com-
pounded, though, by what Koreans think about evil.

"The West divides, chopping things—and people—up. The
East creates relationships modeled on the family." So writes so-
ciologist Fred Alford, in a fascinating account of Korean conceptions of evil.[49] Evil comes from the creation of dualisms and
oppositions. a Buddhist told him, "You Americans destroyed the
Indians because of dualism. . . . You are always fighting and finding an enemy." South Korea has plenty of Christians, but on this
particular Old Testament question, "they sounded like Bud-
dhists," too. Koreans do not construct an "Other"—their fear is
rather "becoming other to oneself," a stranger to one's proper
self. You do that not by straying from your true self, through

what we would call alienation; you do it by cutting your family ties. The highest value in Korea is *chŏng*: belonging and affection. Alford says it is for Koreans what honor and shame are for the Japanese. Belonging and affection begin in the family, with a strict father and a loving mother (*ŏmbu chamo*). Without this core element, a Korean told him, there can be "no discipline in society." The Korean family system produces "respect for authority combined with tenderness." A society like this has no place for evil; in fact Koreans don't *have* a conception of evil: "Evil couldn't exist because Koreans have created a universe in which there is no place for it."[50] Alford is talking about South Korea, not the North, but he helps us to understand that vexing family state. After sixty years, it's high time for Americans to find out if Koreans don't have a lot to teach us.

On a sparkling Indian summer day in 1987, I was waiting in front of the Pyongyang Hotel with a British documentary producer. Our North Korean "counterparts" were picking us up for another round of "discussions" over when, where, and what our film crew would be allowed to shoot. "They're all a bunch of liars," we both agreed, after days of bluff, prevarication, dissembling, and bait-and-switch games using even their own people, I was convinced that one of the men we dealt with the week before had appeared with a different name card that morning. We had run afoul of the most popular sport in North Korea, rubbing foreign noses in the bloody-minded subjectivity of a regime that answers to no one. Then our eyes were caught by a tall monument across the street, an inlaid tile mural of a willowy, soft-featured woman leaping forward in flowing, brilliantly colored traditional dress—the heroine of *Sea of Blood*. Koreans hold that women of the north country are more beautiful; she matched the myth. In her right hand was a military-issue revolver. A different version of that same female image is the "George Washington" of their one-dollar (or *wŏn*) bill. North Koreans live every day amid violence—at home from an abhorrent family dictatorship, and abroad from our half-century-long failure to engage in serious diplomacy to end the Korean War and normalize relations with the DPRK.

After all, they aren't going away. As a North Korean spokesman put it at the height of the nuclear crisis, "We have so far lived on our own without any relations with the United States, we can live on our own in the future, too. We have become constitutionally adapted to such life."[51] In an indication that some learning might actually be seeping into the American media, Eason Jordon, the president of CNN International, who had made nine visits to Pyongyang, told a Harvard audience this in 1999: "When you hear about starvation in North Korea, a lot of very level-headed people think, 'There is no way a country like that can survive.' Well, I can guarantee you this: I'm here to tell you with absolute certainty those guys will tough it out for centuries just the way they are. Neither the United States nor any other country is going to be able to force a collapse of that government."[52] That's exactly what I think, when I reflect back on people like Chu To-il, who lost three brothers to the Manchurian battlefield and his mother to starvation, or Yi O-song, whose father and two sisters starved to death. Yet both continued their bitter struggle against General Tōjō and his ilk—fascists who truly would stop at nothing, and define the face of evil.

RECOMMENDED READING

Alford, C. Fred. *Think No Evil: Korean Values in the Age of Globalization*. Ithaca: Cornell University Press, 1999.

Armstrong, Charles K. *The North Korean Revolution, 1945–1950*. Ithaca: Cornell University Press, 2003.

Balazs, Salontai. "The Failure of De-Stalinization in North Korea: The DPRK in a Comparative Perspective, 1953–1964." Unpublished Ph.D. dissertation. Central European University, Budapest, 2003.

Buzo, Adrian. *The Making of Modern Korea*. London: Routledge, 2002.

Cornell, Eric. *North Korea Under Communism: Report of an Envoy to Paradise*. Translated by Rodney Bradbury. London: RoutledgeCurzon, 2002.

Grinker, Roy Andrew. *Korea and Its Futures: Unification and the Unfinished War*. New York: St. Martin's Press, 1998.

Han, Hong-Koo. "Wounded Nationalism: The Minsaengdan Incident and Kim Il Sung in Eastern Manchuria. Unpublished Ph.D. dissertation. Seattle: University of Washington, 1999.

Harrison, Selig S. *Korean Endgame: A Strategy for Reunification and U.S. Disengagement*. Princeton, N.J.: Princeton University Press, 2002.

Holloway, Andrew. *A Year in Pyongyang*. London: 2003. www.aidanfc.net/a_year_in_pyongyang_1.htm.

Hunter, Helen-Louise. *Kim Il-song's North Korea*. New York: Praeger, 1999.

Kang, Chol-hwan, and Pierre Rigoulot. *The Aquariums of Pyong-yang: Ten Years in a North Korean Gulag*. Translated by Yair Reiner. New York: Basic Books, 2001.

Lankov, Andrei. *From Stalin to Kim Il Sung: The Formation of North Korea, 1945–1960*. London: Hurst, 2002.

Lee, Chong-sik. *Counter-Insurgency in Manchuria: The Japanese Experience, 1931–1940*. Santa Monica, Calif: RAND Corporation, 1967.

Lee, Moon Woong. *Rural North Korea Under Communism*. Rice University Special Studies, 1976.

Li, Nam Ok. *Breaking North Korean Silence: Kim Jong Il's Daughter, A Memoir*. Written by Imogen O'Neill. Forthcoming.

Oberdorfer, Don. *The Two Koreas: A Contemporary History*. New York: Addison-Wesley, 1997.

Park, Han S., ed. *North Korea: Ideology, Politics, Economy*. Englewood Cliffs, N.J.: Prentice-Hall, 1996.

Rosegrant, Susan, in collaboration with Michael D. Watkins. "Carrots, Sticks, and Question Marks: Negotiating the North Korean Nuclear Crisis." Harvard University, John F. Kennedy School of Government, 1995.

Sigal, Leon V. *Disarming Strangers: Nuclear Diplomacy with North Korea*. Princeton, N.J.: Princeton University Press, 1998.

Suh, Dae-sook. *Kim Il Sung: The North Korean Leader*. New York: Columbia University Press, 1988.

Thompson, Reginald. *Cry Korea*. London: MacDonald & Co., 1951.

Wada, Haruki. *Kim Il Sŏng kwa Manju Hang-Il Chŏnjaeng* (Kim Il Sung and the Anti-Japanese War in Manchuria). Translated from the Japanese by Yi Chong-sŏk. Seoul: Ch'angbi-sa, 1992; published also in Japanese as *Kin Nichi-sei to Manshu konichi senso*. Tokyo: Heibonsha, 1992.

Yang, Sung Chul. *The North and South Korean Political Systems: A Comparative Analysis*. Seoul: Hollym, 1999.

NOTES

PREFACE

1. The "goose-step" long predated Hitler's Nazis; the Bolsheviks used it, and virtually every postwar communist country did so as well. Less well known is that our fledgling army in postwar Afghanistan now can be seen goose-stepping around the capital.

2. Hunter (1999).

3. Edward Neilan, "Soviets Demand Look at Reactors in North Korea," *Washington Times* (April 16, 1991), p. A1. Soviet–DPRK trade was cut in half from 1988 to 1992, and shipments of oil dropped by three-quarters in one year alone (from 440,000 tons in 1990 to 100,000 tons in 1991).

4. Of course, South Korean intelligence also has disparaged the son for decades. This often takes the form of "mysterious absences" in which Kim Jong Il drops from view, whereupon they speculate on what caused it (other than a vacation). After his father died in 1994, Kim wasn't seen for a while, so they speculated that the reason must be "diabetes, cirrhosis of the liver, a brain disorder, paralysis, or a combination of these diseases." Suddenly he reappeared on TV looking "unbelievably vigorous," so the South Koreans thought that "possibilities are high that Pyongyang doctored the TV screens involving the junior Kim." Naewoe Press, *North Korea: The Land That Never Changes* (Seoul:

ROK Government, 1995), p. 33. (Naewoe Press is the official North Korea–watching arm of the government, drawing on reports prepared by ROK intelligence agencies.)

CHAPTER ONE

1. National Foreign Assessment Center, "Korea: the Economic Race between the North and the South," U.S. Central Intelligence Agency (January 1978), ii.
2. Yang (1999), 729–31, 907–8. The South's expenditures went from $5 billion to nearly $8 billion in 1990; today the ROK spends an amount on defense much greater than the DPRK's gross national product.
3. Robert Marquand, "Bleak Tales of Army Life in N. Korea," *Christian Science Monitor* (May 13, 2003), 1.
4. Public Record Office, London, Foreign Office file 317, piece no. 83008, Stokes to Bevin, December 2, 1950.
5. Schnabel and Watson, *The Korean War*, part I, 178–81; "Memo for General Bolte," July 17, 1950, giving MacArthur's remarks on July 13 in Tokyo.
6. Roy Appleman, *South to the Naktong, North to the Yalu* (Washington, D.C.: Office of the Chief of Military History, 1961), 70; Arthur Krock Papers, box 1, notebooks, vol. 2, 222, entry for July 1950.
7. *Foreign Relations of the U.S.* (1950), 6: 128–30, Dulles to Acheson, August 4, 1950; FO317, piece no. 83014, notes on talk between Dening and Rusk, July 22, 1950.
8. Col. Donald Nichols, *How Many Times Can I Die?* (Brooksville, Fla.: Brownsville Printing, 1981), cited in Korea Web Weekly, www.kimsoft.com.
9. Thomas McPhail, KMAG adviser who finished his career as head of the U.S. Military Advisory group to Nicaragua under Somoza, wrote to Ridgway in 1965, "[T]he old Guardia

[National Guard] members who fought with the Marines against Sandino still talk about General Ridgway" (Ridgway Papers, box 19, Thomas D. McPhail to Ridgway, April 15, 1965).

10. Ridgway Papers, oral interview, August 29, 1969. His interviewer, a Vietnam veteran, told him the North Koreans sounded "about the same" as the Vietcong.

11. *New York Times* (September 1, 3, 1950).

12. *New York Times* editorial (July 5, 1950); *New York Times* (July 27, 1950). The CIA at this time also listed Kim as an imposter, who stole the name of an heroic guerrilla who died in Manchuria about 1940. See "National Intelligence Survey, Korea," (Washington: CIA, 1950).

13. *New York Times* (July 14, 1950).

14. Ibid. (July 19, 1950).

15. Letter to the *New York Times* (July 16, 1950). Taylor noted that these precepts have not always been followed even by Western armies.

16. Ridgway Papers, box 16, notes on conference with MacArthur, August 8, 1950.

17. Public Record Office, FO317, piece no. 84130, enclosing Johnson's address of August 20, 1950, in Lenox, Massachusetts. See also *Far Eastern Economic Review* (August 31, 1950). Also FO317, piece no. 84070, Adams to FO, October 5, 1950.

18. Anderson, *Imagined Communities*, 135–6.

19. See P. C. Tullier, "The Oriental Mind," *New Yorker* (July 15, 1950).

20. *Nation* (August 26, 1950).

21. See, for example, *Haebang ilbo* (July 24, 1950).

22. Conrad C. Crane, *American Airpower Strategy in Korea, 1950–1953* (Lawrence: University Press of Kansas, 2000), 66. A

tram driver got "drenched from head to foot with the burning fluid. His whole body was covered with a hard, black crust sprinkled with yellow pus, and he could not sit down."

23. Quoted in Blair, *Forgotten War*, 515.

24. National Archives, 995.00 file, box 6175, George Barrett dispatch of February 8, 1951; Acheson to Pusan Embassy, February 17, 1951.

25. National Archives, RG338, KMAG file, box 5418, KMAG journal, entries for August 6, 16, 20, 26, 1950.

26. *New York Times* (July 31, August 11, September 1, 1950).

27. See "Air War in Korea," *Air University Quarterly Review* 4 no. 2 (fall 1950): 19–40; "Precision Bombing," *Air University Quarterly Review* 4 no. 4 (summer 1951): 58–65; and other articles on the air war in Korea in the 1951 volume.

28. MacArthur Archives, RG6, box 1, Stratemeyer to MacArthur, November 8, 1950; Public Record Office, FO 317, piece no. 84072, Bouchier to Chiefs of Staff, November 6, 1950; piece no. 84073, November 25, 1959 sitrep.

29. Cumings, *The Origins of the Korean War*, vol. 2 (Princeton, N.J.: Princeton University Press, 1990), 753–4; *New York Times* (December 13, 1950, and January 3, 1951).

30. Cover story, "Why America Scares the World," *Newsweek* (March 24, 2003).

31. Truman Presidential Library, PSF, CIA file, box 248, report of December 15, 1950; FO317, piece no. 84074 and no. 84075, Bouchier situation reports, December 5, 17, 1950; *New York Times*, December 13, 1950, and January 3, 1951; Blair, *Forgotten War*, 603. Crane wrote that twenty-eight Tarzon bombs were dropped before the AF suspended their use; "twelve had been controllable" by radio, and, of those, six had destroyed their targets (*American Airpower Strategy in Korea, 1950–1953*, 133).

32. On the hurricanelike firestorms that atomic bombs produced in Hiroshima and Nagasaki, see my *Parallax Visions*, ch. 2.

33. For a fuller account with documentation in formerly classified archives, see Cumings, *Origins of the Korean War*, vol. 2, 747–53.

34. *New York Times* (November 30 and December 1, 1950).

35. Hoyt Vandenberg Papers, box 86, Stratemeyer to Vandenberg, November 30, 1950; LeMay to Vandenberg, December 2, 1950. Also Richard Rhodes, *Dark Sun: The Making of the Hydrogen Bomb* (1995), 444–6.

36. Cumings (1990), 750; Charles Willoughby Papers, box 8, interviews by Bob Considine and Jim Lucas in 1954, printed in *New York Times* (April 9, 1964).

37. Carroll Quigley, *Tragedy and Hope: A History of the World in Our Time* (New York: MacMillan, 1966), 875; Quigley was President Bill Clinton's favorite teacher at Georgetown University. See also Cumings (1990), 750.

38. Documents released after the Soviet Union collapsed apparently do not bear this out; scholars who have seen these documents say there was no such major deployment of Soviet air power at the time. However, it is clear that U.S. intelligence reports believed the deployment to have occurred—perhaps based on effective disinformation by the Chinese.

39. Referred to variously as the "capsule," "core," or "softball," this is the fissionable center around which the rest of an atomic bomb is built.

40. Thomas B. Cochran, William M. Arkin, Robert S. Norris, and Milton M. Hoenig, *Nuclear Weapons Databook*, vol. 1 (Cambridge, Mass.: Ballinger, 1987), 26; same authors, *Nuclear Weapons Databook,* vol. 2, *United States Nuclear Warhead Production*, 10; also Charles Hansen, *United States*

Nuclear Weapons: The Secret History (Arlington, Texas: Aerofax, 1988), 125–33.

41. Cumings (1990), 750–1; Rhodes (1995), 448–51.

42. This does not mean the use of so-called tactical nuclear weapons, which were not available in 1951, but the use of the 11,000-pound Mark IVs in battlefield tactical strategy, much as heavy conventional bombs dropped by B-29 bombers had been used in battlefield fighting since late August 1950.

43. Samuel Cohen was a childhood friend of Herman Kahn. See Fred Kaplan, *The Wizards of Armageddon* (New York: Simon & Schuster, 1983), 220. On Oppenheimer and Project Vista, see Cumings (1990), 751–2; also David C. Elliot, "Project Vista and Nuclear Weapons in Europe," *International Security* 2 no. 1 (summer l986), 163–83.

44. Cumings (1990), 752.

45. Friedrich Nietzsche, *On the Geneaology of Morals*, trans. Walter Kaufmann and R. J. Hollingdale (New York: Vintage Books, 1969), 61.

46. Crane, *American Airpower Strategy in Korea* (Lawrence, KS: University Press of Kansas, 2000).

47. Matthew Ridgway Papers, box 20, MacArthur to Ridgway, January 7, 1951; memo of Ridgway's conference with Almond and others, January 8, 1951.

48. *Memoirs of a Chinese Marshal: The Autobiographical Notes of Peng Dehuai (1898–1974)* (Beijing: Foreign Languages Press, 1984), 479; also Mark A. Ryan, "Nuclear Threat and the Korean Armistice: Historiographical Perspectives and Battlefield Realities," paper prepared for the annual meeting of the Association for Asian Studies, March 1989.

49. Matthew Connelly Papers, "Notes on Cabinet Meetings," September 12, 1952. I am indebted to Barton Bernstein for calling this reference to my attention.

50. Hermann Lautensach, *Korea: A Geography Based on the Author's Travels and Literature,* trans. Katherine Dege and Eckart Dege (Berlin: Springer-Verlag, 1945, 1988), 202.

51. "The Attack on the Irrigation Dams in North Korea," *Air University Quarterly* 6 no. 4 (winter 1953–54): 40–51.

52. Thames Television, London, transcript from the fifth seminar for the documentary entitled "Korea: The Unknown War" (November 1986); Thames interview with Tibor Meray (also 1986).

53. Crane, *American Airpower Strategy in Korea,* 168–9.

54. Jon Halliday and Bruce Cumings, *Korea: The Unknown War* (New York: Pantheon Books, 1988), 166.

55. J. F. Dulles Papers, Curtis LeMay oral history, April 28, 1966.

56. Here I draw on my 1990 book, *Origins of the Korean War,* vol. 2, and on Callum MacDonald, " 'So Terrible a Liberation'—The UN Occupation of North Korea," *Bulletin of Concerned Asian Scholars* 23, no. 2 (April–June 1991): 3–19. MacDonald cited NSC 81/1 in ibid., 6.

57. Max Hastings, *The Korean War* (London: Michael Joseph, 1987), 105, quoted in Macdonald (1991), 3.

58. Roy Appleman, *South to the Naktong, North to the Yalu* (Washington, D.C.: Office of the Chief of Military History, 1961), 587–8, 599.

59. London, *Daily Worker,* August 9, 1950.

60. National Records Center, RG242, SA2009, item 6/70, KPA HQ, *Chosŏn inmin ŭn tosalja Mije wa Yi Sŭng-man yŏkdodŭl ŭi yasujŏn manhaeng e pukssu harira* (The Korean people will avenge the beastly atrocities of the American imperialist butchers and the Syngman Rhee traitors), no date, but late 1950, 40–1. The *Haebang ilbo* (Liberation Daily) of August 10, 1950, put the figure at 4,000.

61. Callum MacDonald, *Korea: The War before Vietnam* (New York: The Free Press, 1987), 41.

62. Harry S. Truman Presidential Library (HST), Presidential Secretary's File (PSF), "Army Intelligence—Korea," box 262, joint daily sitrep no. 6, July 2–3, 1950; National Security Council (NSC) file, box 3, CIA report of July 3, 1950.

63. August 11, 1950; Public Record Office, London Foreign Office records, FO317, piece no. 84178, Tokyo Chancery to FO, August 15, 1950; Gascoigne to FO, August. 15, 1950; Chancery to FO, August 17, 1950. (J. Underwood may have been from the well-established Underwood missionary family in Korea.) Another British report said that when reporters photographed brutal beatings of prisoners by ROK police, American and ROK authorities prohibited publication of the photos (Chancery to FO, September 13, 1950).

64. Do-young Lee, *Ch'ukumŭiyebi kŏmsŏk* (Seoul, 2000).

65. Col. Donald Nichols, *How Many Times Can I Die?* (Brooksville, Fla.: Brownsville Printing, 1981), cited in Korea Web Weekly, www.kimsoft.com.

66. Donald Knox, *The Korean War: An Oral History, Pusan to Chosin* (New York: Harcourt, Brace, Jovanovich, 1985), 295.

67. MacDonald, (1987), 9.

68. RG242, SA2012, item 5/18, *Sŏul Si wa kŭ chubyŏn chidae esŏ ŭi chŏkdŭl ŭi manhaeng* (Enemy atrocities in Seoul city and its vicinity), are two secret reports compiled by the Seoul branch of the KWP after the second recapture of Seoul; no date but early 1951.

69. National Archives, 795.00 file, box 4268, Durward V. Sandifer to John Hickerson, August 31, 1950, top secret.

70. PRO handwritten FO notes on FK1015/303, U.S. Embassy press translations for November 1, 1950; piece no. 84125, FO memo by R. Murray, October 26, 1950; piece no. 84102, Franks memo of discussion with Rusk, October 30, 1950; Heron in *London Times*, October 25, 1950.

71. RG338, KMAG file, box 5418, KMAG journal, entries for November 5, November 24, November 25, November 30, 1950.

72. 795.00 file, box 4270, carrying UPI and AP dispatches dated December 16, 17, 18, 1950; FO317, piece no. 92847, original letter from Private Duncan, January 4, 1951; Adams to FO, January 8, 1951; UNCURK reports cited in HST, PSF, CIA file, box 248, daily summary, December 19, 1950. See also *London Times*, December 18, 21, 22, 1950.

73. Almond Papers, General Files, X Corps, "Appendix 3 Counterintelligence," November 25, 1950; William V. Quinn Papers, box 3, X Corps periodic intelligence report dated November 11, 1950. Quinn was the X Corps G-2 chief. (Emphasis added.)

74. FO317, piece no. 84073, Tokyo to FO, November 21, 1950.

75. MacDonald, *Korea: The War before Vietnam*, 13.

76. FO317, piece no. 92847, containing a TASS report of December 29, 1950.

77. MacDonald, *Korea: The War before Vietnam*, 15.

78. Ibid., 11.

79. Department of State documents, cited in ibid., p. 17, n. 136, and other information cited on 18–9.

80. National Archives, 895.00 file, Bix 5693, Embassy to State, November 11, 195, giving official ROK figures; Ridgway Papers, box 16, memo on official Department of Defense count of American casualties, October 5, 1950.

81. Rapoport, "Editor's Introduction," Carl von Clausewitz, *On War* (New York: Penguin Books, 1968), 62–3.

82. Michael Walzer, *Just and Unjust Wars: A Moral Argument with Historical Illustrations* (New York: Basic Books, 1977), 117–23.

83. See David E. James. "Documenting the Vietnam War," in *From Hanoi to Hollywood: The Vietnam War in American*

Film, eds. Linda Dittmar and Gene Michaud, (New Brunswick. N.J.: Rutgers University Press, 1990), 245.

CHAPTER TWO

1. Charles Krauthammer, "North Korea: The World's Real Time Bomb," *Washington Post*, November 6, 1993.
2. David E. Sanger, *New York Times* (December 16, 1992), A6.
3. Ibid. (May 5, 1993).
4. *Newsweek* (November 15, 1993), 41.
5. Nearly all of these references can be found in the best book on the first nuclear crisis, *Disarming Strangers* by Leon V. Sigal (1998), 33–7, 53–4, 56–7, 66–7, with slightly different wording (e.g., "you cannot sell that horse twice," 37). "Skirting the red line" can be found in Michael R. Gordon, "U.S. Plans North Korean Talks, Citing Progress on Nuclear Plant," *New York Times* (May 21, 1994), A7. "Catch a rerun" comes from an unnamed Defense Department official, quoted in the *Chicago Tribune*, November 26, 1991. A preemptive strike was widely discussed from 1991 to 1994. Perhaps the South Korean reaction would be different today, but the ROK defense minister endorsed such a strike in a meeting with Defense Secretary Dick Cheney in November 1991 (Sigal, 37.)
6. When I wrote to *Newsweek* about these falsehoods and pointed them to thirty-year-old books based on Japanese military and police records that documented Kim's guerrilla war, they defended their information, saying it came from Korean exiles in the former Soviet Union. These same people had formed a "Down with Kim Il Sung" group.
7. Doug Struck and Steven Mufson, "North Korea's Kim Sheds Image of 'Madman,'" *Washington Post* (October 26, 2001), A-1.

8. Sigal (1998), 95; Harrison (2002), 263. Albright thought 8.5 kilograms might be "just enough" for a single bomb.

9. Sanger, "News of the Week in Review," *New York Times* (March 20, 1994).

10. Fox News (January 15, 2003), 10:08 P.M.

11. It is rare to find a public statement about this, but in June 1994 a map in *Time Magazine* showed 90 percent of the ROK Army concentrated between Seoul and the DMZ.

12. Gen. John R. Hodge, commander of U.S. forces in Korea, first warned of a North Korean attack in March 1946. See Cumings, *Origins*, vol. I, 236.

13. James Wade, *One Man's Korea* (Seoul: Hollym Publishers, 1967), 23.

14. *ABC Nightline* (November 16, 1993), transcript #3257.

15. Leslie Gelb, "The Next Renegade State," Op-Ed Page, *New York Times* (April 10, 1991).

16. I sought to do so in Cumings, "Spring Thaw for Korea's Cold War?" *Bulletin of the Atomic Scientists* 48 no. 3 (April 1992): 14–23; and "It's Time to End the Forty-Year War," *Nation* 257 no. 6 (August 23–30, 1993), 206–8.

17. For a fuller discussion of this episode, on which I draw here, see Cumings, *Parallax Visions: Making Sense of American–East Asian Relations* (Durham, N.C.: Duke University Press, 1997), ch. 5.

18. Peter Hayes, *Pacific Powderkeg: American Nuclear Dilemmas in Korea* (Lexington, Mass.: Lexington Books, 1991), 35.

19. Ibid., 47–8.

20. Quoted in ibid., 49.

21. Ibid., 50, 58.

22. Sigal (1998), 29–30. The reference to nuclear-armed subs is in David E. Sanger, "Seoul Looks North, Balancing Hope and Anxiety," *New York Times* (December 16, 1992).

23. Harrison (2002), 119.

24. Janne E. Nolan, *Trappings of Power: Ballistic Missiles in the Third World* (Washington: Brookings Institution, 1991), 48–52.

25. Donald MacIntyre, "Korea's Dirty Dozen," *Time Asia Magazine* (May 20, 2002).

26. Report on an interview with Kim Il Sung, December 22, 1978, in *Tokyo Shakaito* (March 1979), 162–8 (U.S. Joint Publications Research Service translation #073363).

27. Information from Energy Data Associates, cited in Economist Intelligence Unit, *China, North Korea Country Profile 1992–93* (London, 1993).

28. Ed Paisley, "Prepared for the Worst," *Far Eastern Economic Review*, February 10, 1994.

29. The North had a 50MWe reactor under construction at Yŏngbyŏn, due to be completed in 1995; and a 200MWe reactor under construction in Taech'ŏn, due in 1996. "North Korea's Nuclear Programme Revealed," *Nuclear News* (July 1992).

30. This information is culled mostly from Richard Rhodes's two books on the atomic and the hydrogen bombs: *The Making of the Atomic Bomb* (New York: Simon & Schuster, 1986), and *Dark Sun: The Making of the Hydrogen Bomb* (New York: Simon & Schuster, 1995), and from Peter Hayes, Nautilus Research Center, "Should the United States Supply Light Water Reactors to Pyongyang?" Carnegie Endowment, November 16, 1993.

31. Peter Hayes, Nautilus Research Center, "Should the United States Supply Light Water Reactors to Pyongyang?" Carnegie Endowment, November 16, 1993.

32. *New York Times* (November 10, 1991).

33. Quoted in *Newsweek* (April 22, 1991).

34. Rosegrant and Watkins (1995), 11.

35. Harrison (2002), 33. Sigal, however, cites U.S. government officials who believe the nuclear talks were always supervised by Kim Jong Il and that there wasn't much dissent or debate behind the scenes—"we have never seen clear or even unclear signs of a debate on nuclear issues" (Sigal [1998], 173).
36. Segal (1998), 138–9.
37. "Nuclear Site in North Korea Provides Clues on Weapons," *New York Times* (May 17, 1992).
38. Quoted in *New York Times* (January 6, 1992). Such demands enter the realm of the unnegotiable, of course, since the North Koreans will not allow this, nor would any sovereign state. These officials were also quoted as saying "what we don't know about the North is still terrifying."
39. Rosegrant and Watkins (1995), 13; Nuclear Safety Campaign, *Beyond the Bomb* (San Francisco: Tides Foundation, 1994), 22.
40. For example, Tim Weiner found these words in CIA Director R. James Woolsey's testimony before the Senate Select Committee on Intelligence, *New York Times* (January 26, 1994).
41. Nayan Chanda, "Bomb and Bombast," *Far Eastern Economic Review* (February 10, 1994).
42. *Vantage Point*, 17, no. 1 (Seoul, January 1994): 19.
43. Ibid.
44. One source reported that a senior member of the IAEA had said that the IAEA shipped plutonium samples from North Korea to the United States, "where they were tested for their isotopic content." See Kenneth R. Timmerman, "Going Ballistic," *New Republic* (January 24, 1994), 14.
45. Tim Weiner, *New York Times* (November 13, 1993).
46. Oberdorfer (1997), 103.
47. Kent Wiedemann, who was on Clinton's National Security Council as a senior director for Asia, said in 1995 that "[w]e

finally came to recognize that from the North Korean perspective, it's in their interest to maintain an ambiguity about this whole thing"—that is, the purpose of their Yŏngbyŏn program (Rosegrant and Watkins, 29). That recognition came about four years late by my reckoning.

48. *New York Times*, Op-Ed page (March 21, 1993).

49. *Chicago Tribune* (March 18, 1993).

50. See, for example, Fred C. Ikle, "Response," *National Interest* 34 (winter 1993–94): 39.

51. *New York Times* (February 24, 25, 1993).

52. Hayes, *Pacific Powderkeg*, 214.

53. The IAEA did conduct two special inspections in the past, in Rumania and Sweden. But they were not at the behest of U.S. intelligence, and the one-month deadline to comply issued on February 25, 1993, certainly had no precedent.

54. Several public sources pointed this out, but the best information was in Chanda, "Bomb and Bombast," *Far Eastern Economic Review* (February 10, 1994).

55. Korean Central News Agency, Pyongyang (February 22, 1993).

56. Bruce D. Blair (a senior fellow at the Brookings Institution), "Russia's Doomsday Machine," *New York Times* (October 8, 1993). See another article on the front page of the *Times* on December 6, 1993, saying that American officials were retargeting strategic weapons onto "rogue" Third World states, with Russian targets now relegated to "secondary" status.

57. The Korean Central News Agency referred in September 1993 to a "regular missile launching exercise in the DPRK," which Japanese authorities were "making quite a noise about," wishing to add "a 'missile problem' to the 'nuclear problem,'" thus to block normalization of relations. It justified the missile test as a necessary measure of self-defense,

given that Japan is dotted with American military bases of all kinds. See KCNA, DPRK Foreign Ministry statement issued September 24, 1993. (It is highly unusual for KCNA to report any DPRK military exercise.)

58. *New York Times* (November 8, 1993).
59. Michael R. Gordon, *New York Times* (March 20, 1994).
60. The best source that I have found on the LWR issue is Peter Hayes, Nautilus Research Center, "Should the United States Supply Light Water Reactors to Pyongyang?" Carnegie Endowment, November 16, 1993. North Korean negotiators raised the issue of LWRs at the second round of high-level talks in June 1993; the United States at this time said North Korea should discuss LWRs with South Korea and Russia (the latter had already agreed to supply four such reactors when the North complied fully with its NPT obligations). LWRs again came up in high-level talks in Geneva in July 1993, when Kang Sŏk-ju offered to give up the Yŏngbyŏn facility in return for U.S. provision of LWRs. On July 16, the United States agreed that LWRs would be a good idea, but said that LWRs could only work after the NPT safeguards were implemented fully (Rosegrant and Watkins [1995], 20–1). Robert Carlin, one of the negotiators, expressed his "total shock" in Rosegrant and Watkins (1995), 20. The North Koreans first proposed to substitute LWRs for their own reactors when Hans Blix visited in May 1992; this got so little attention that when they revived the idea in negotiations with Americans in 1994, it "came as a complete surprise" to U.S. negotiators who served in both the Bush and Clinton administrations. See Sigal (1998), 40.
61. Selig Harrison, "Breaking the Nuclear Impasse: The United States and North Korea," testimony to the Subcommittee on Asian and Pacific Affairs, U.S. House of Representatives, November 3, 1993.

62. There was next to no information about this package deal in the American press in the winter of 1993–94. The Korean press in both Seoul and P'yŏngyang was better. See the summary in *Vantage Point* 17, no. 1 (Seoul, January 1994): 16–17; on the DPRK's "package solution," see also the pro-P'yŏngyang *Korean Report*, no. 280 (Tokyo, November 1993), and KCNA, reporting a Foreign Ministry statement of February 1, 1994.

63. Rosegrant and Watkins (1995), 25.

64. Press Release, November 30, 1993, DPRK Mission to the UN, New York.

65. Rosegrant and Watkins (1995), 1–2; "Public Enemy Number One," *Newsweek* (November 29, 1993).

66. Patrick E. Tyler, *New York Times* (April 3, 1994).

67. Thomas Flanagan, the JCS's representative on Clinton's interagency working group on Korea, believes this act was the key element that got everyone to focus on resolving the nuclear crisis. See Rosegrant and Watkins (1995), B-9.

68. Sigal (1998), 115–9.

69. Quoted in *Chicago Tribune* (April 4, 1994). In a memorandum to the UN dated April 10, 1996, the DPRK stated that "a second Korean War would have broken out had the United Nations chosen to repeat its past by unilaterally imposing 'sanctions' against the DPRK." Press Release, April 10, 1996, DPRK Mission to the UN, New York.

70. Rosegrant and Watkins (1995), 2, 33–5.

71. Ibid., 34–5. Although this study discounts Pentagon desires to remove Yŏngbyŏn entirely with a "surgical strike" (15, 32–4), State Department negotiators with North Korea told me they were constantly confronted with Pentagon and CIA officers who would say, "Why negotiate with these people? We can handle the Yŏngbyŏn problem overnight." Another informant told me that Gen. Colin Powell played a critical

role in pointing out the costs of a new Korean War to Clinton. See also Oberdorfer's harrowing account of how close Washington and P'yongyang were to going to war in *The Two Koreas*, 305–36.

72. The full text of the 1994 agreement is in Rosegrant and Watkins (1995), Exhibit I1.

73. Sigal (1998), 9; Harrison (2002), 184.

74. Rosegrant and Watkins (1995), B-11.

75. Selig Harrison interviewed a North Korean general who told him that whereas the North may call publicly for the withdrawal of American troops, in reality the troops should stay—to help deal with a strong Japan, among other things. See Harrison, "Promoting a Soft Landing in Korea," *Foreign Policy* 106 (spring 1997).

76. David E. Sanger, "North Korea Site an A-Bomb Plant, U.S. Agencies Say," *New York Times* (August 17, 1998), A1, A4; Lt. Gen. Charles R. Heflebower, the top USAF commander in Korea, cited in Bill Geertz and Rowan Scarborough, "Inside the Ring," *Washington Times* (June 9, 2000).

77. Quoted in Geoffrey Klingsporn, "The Sovereignty of Space, The Space of Sovereignty," an excellent paper done for one of my graduate seminars in 1993.

78. David Wright and Timur Kadyshev, "An Analysis of the North Korean Nodong Missile," *Science and Global Security* 4 (1994): 129–60.

79. David C. Wright, "Will North Korea Negotiate Away Its Missiles?" privately circulated paper, 1998.

80. Selig Harrison, "The Missiles of North Korea: How Real a Threat?" *World Policy Journal* 17, no. 3 (fall 2000): 13–24.

81. Harrison (2002), 227.

82. Editorial, "New Deal for Pyongyang," *Wall Street Journal* (October 21, 1994), A14.

83. Howard French, "Work Starts on North Korea's U.S.-Backed Nuclear Plant," *New York Times* (August 8, 2002), A9.

84. Hans M. Kristensen, "Preemptive Posturing," *Bulletin of the Atomic Scientists* 58, no. 5 (September/October 2002): 54–59.

85. Richard Halloran, a veteran correspondent, was in this audience and reported Ayres's statements on the Internet on November 14, 1998. When I asked him to identify the source by name, he declined; however, Selig Harrison identified the source as General Ayres. Harrison (2002), 119–20.

86. Quoted in Harrison (2002), 122.

87. Richard Halloran, *Far Eastern Economic Review* (December 3, 1998). Halloran quoted the second statement in his November 14, 1998, story put out on the "Global Beat" Internet site. Lee Sung-yul, "U.S. Prepared to Send 640,000 Troops If North Korea Invades South," *Korea Herald* (September 28, 1998).

88. "Talks between Kang Sok Ju and William Perry," KCNA (May 28, 1999).

89. See Michael R. Gordon's investigative report, "How Politics Sank Accord on Missiles with North Korea," *New York Times* (March 6, 2001), A1, A8. I also confirmed the details of his report during a meeting with Ambassador Perry at Stanford University in March 2001.

90. Gordon (2001).

91. An unnamed adviser said it was "embarrassing" in *Korea Herald* (March 13, 2001). I spoke with a Korean member of the National Assembly at a conference on Korea on March 13, who talked about Kim's advisers cursing Bush for his ham-handed tactics.

92. The DPRK ambassador to the UN, Pak Gil Yon, said this in his news conference at the UN on January 10, 2003.

93. Kang Jung-min, a South Korean nuclear analyst, said, "It's a sheer lie. There is no sign whatsoever that North Korea has restarted its reprocessing facility." Quoted in Sang-Hun Choe, "Experts Doubt North Korean Nuclear Claim," Associated Press (Seoul, April 25, 2003). American experts had yet to detect the telltale krypton gas that reprocessing would give off. *New York Times* (July 1, 2003), A1.

94. I draw on *New York Times* and *Wall Street Journal* articles on this issue, October 18–22, 2002.

95. DPRK Foreign Ministry statement, carried by KCNA (October 25, 2002). See also Byung Chul Koh, "Is North Korea Changing?" Institute for Far Eastern Studies, Kyongnam University (March 5, 2003).

96. David Albright, "Finding Our Way Anew to a Denuclearized Korean Peninsula," Working Paper, Task Force on U.S. Korea Policy (Washington: Center for International Policy and Chicago: Center for East Asian Studies, University of Chicago), November 19, 2002, 2–3. See also the diagram on extracting U238 via centrifuges from *Scientific American*, pictured in *New York Times* (January 15, 1992), A7.

97. Among many well-informed news articles on these internal splits and their effects in causing frequent reversals of policy, see David Sanger, "U.S. Sees Quick Start of North Korea Nuclear Site," *New York Times* (March 1, 2003), A1; and James Dao, "Criticism of Bush's Policy on Korea Sharpens," *New York Times* (March 6, 2003), A16. Bush's pique at Armitage is reported in Sanger's article.

98. Biden quoted in *USA Today* (April 25–26, 2003).

99. Doug Struck cited these talking points in his article in the *Washington Post* on April 20, 2003.

100. Paul Eckert and Brian Rhoads, "Talks End after North Korea Claims to Have Nuclear Bomb," Reuters (April 25, 2003); BBC News, "North Korea Blames US in Nuclear

Row" (April 25, 2003); Joseph Kahn, "China Seeks to Put a Positive Spin on Talks with North Korea," *New York Times* (April 25, 2003).

101. South Korean newspapers suggested that the North had offered "to verifiably scrap or suspend its nuclear programs," in exchange for U.S. steps to recognize the DPRK and promise not to invade or attack it. "S. Korea Seeking Unity with the U.S. on N.K. Nukes," *Korea Herald* (April 28, 2003).

102. A State Department official told me this on April 25, 2003, and the North Koreans also have said that in 1993 they told the Clinton people the same thing they said to Kelly in Beijing.

103. *New Yorker* (October 8, 2002).

104. Bob Woodward, *Bush at War* (New York: Simon & Schuster, 2002), 340. In typically convoluted syntax, Bush referred to what would happen "if we try to—if this guy were to topple." Some people thought the "financial burdens" of such an outcome would be too onerous, but not the president: "I just don't buy that. Either you believe in freedom, and want to—and worry about the human condition, or you don't."

105. William Perry and Ashton Carter, Op-Ed article, *New York Times* (January 19, 2003).

106. I was told this on a not-for-attribution basis by two former Clinton administration officials at a conference in Washington in January 2002.

107. Sanger, *New York Times* (September 28, 1902), A17.

108. See the excellent discussion in David Sanger, "A Decision Made, and Its Consequences," *New York Times* (March 17, 2003).

109. Graham Greene, *The Quiet American* (New York: Modern Library, 1955), 213.

110. A former American general who ran Army intelligence in Korea told me this on a not-for-attribution basis at a conference in Chicago on December 5, 2002.

111. Quoted in Peter Hayes, *Pacific Powderkeg*, 214.

112. *New York Times* (July 9, 1996).

113. This was the main thrust of Ambassador Pak Gil Yon's news conference on January 10, 2003.

CHAPTER THREE

1. Grinker (1998), 128.

2. Han Hong-koo's brilliant historical exegesis, based on rare materials in Korean, Chinese, and Japanese, is the best English-language source on the origins of the North Korean leadership. See his discussion of the *Ma'an-shan* events in Han (1999), 330–46. See also Wada (1992), another pioneering effort.

3. This dramatic change was codified at the 15th Plenum of the Korean Worker's Party, May 1967.

4. Han (1999), 360–8.

5. Armstrong (1993), 9.

6. See Michael Shin's unpublished Ph.D. dissertation (University of Chicago, 2002).

7. James Scarth Gale, *History of the Korean People*, annotated and introduced by Richard Rutt (Seoul: Royal Asiatic Society, 1972), 319–20: "Why not go whirling off for joy-rides, boys and girls? Why not be divorced at pleasure? Why not be up-to-date as the west is up-to-date? This wild dream . . . well expresses the mind of the advanced youth of the city of Seoul in these days of confusion."

8. Han (1999), 31.

9. Japanese official sources estimated that among Koreans arrested for communist activities, 82 percent were leftist or

revolutionary nationalists, 15 percent were pure communists, and the rest were anarchists or bandits. Han (1999), 62.

10. Han (1999), 8, 13,

11. Han (1999), 162.

12. Han (1999), 158, 179–80. Other sources suggest that upward of one to two thousand ethnic Koreans may have been executed. See Armstrong (2003), 30 n.

13. Kim's arrest by Chinese comrades was long shrouded in mystery, but various sources now attest to it. See Han (1999), 185–6.

14. Professor Chong-sik Lee of the University of Pennsylvania completed a massive study of Japanese counterinsurgency in Manchuria for the RAND Corporation in 1967 to gauge its lessons for the Vietnam War; it remains the best source in English on this suppression campaign. See Lee (1967).

15. Kang Man'gil, "Hwajŏnmin ŭi saengwhal" (The life of the slash-and-burn farmers), in Kang, ed., *Ilchesidae Pinmin Saengwhalsa Yŏn'gu* (Studies of the life of the poor in the Japanese colonial period) (Seoul: Ch'angjak kwa pip'yŏngsa, 1987), 117–234.

16. Owen Lattimore, *Manchuria: Cradle of Conflict* (New York: MacMillan, 1932), cited in Armstrong (2003), 19; I also draw here on Armstrong, 18–23.

17. Kim Pong-sik, "Kapsan — My Birthplace," www.kimsoft. com/korea/eyewito4.htm.

18. Armstrong (2003), 33–6.

19. Han (1999), 324–6.

20. Kim Se-jin, *The Politics of Military Revolution in Korea* (Chapel Hill: University of North Carolina Press, 1973), 48–57. Syngman Rhee came to rely on a small core of Manchurian officers after coming to power in 1948, mainly those with experience in counterinsurgency, and continued to do so well into the late 1950s — "so that they could best be util-

ized in suppressing the roaming bandits and remnants of guerrilla units" still in the South, in Professor Kim's words.

21. Cumings, *The Origins of the Korean War*, vol. 1 (Princeton, N.J.: Princeton University Press, 1981), 37.

22. National Archives, Army Chief of Military History manuscripts, box 601, "Military Studies on Manchuria," book IV, ch. 9, "Bandits and Inhabitants" (Tokyo: Far East Command, 1952).

23. Suh (1988), 37–8.

24. Armstrong (2003), R 31.

25. Han (1999), 355.

26. Kwŏn Rip, "Kim San," in Pak Ch'ang-uk, ed., *Chosŏnjŏk hyŏngmyŏng yŏlsa chŏn* (Biographies of Korean revolutionaries) (Yŏnbyŏn: Yŏnbyŏn ch'ulp'ansa, 1983), vol. 2, 66, cited in Han (1986), 339.

27. Saburo Iyenaga, *The Pacific War*, trans. Frank Baldwin (New York: Pantheon Books, 1976).

28. National Archives, Intelligence Summaries — North Korea, no. 37, May 31, 1947.

29. Yukiko Koshiro, "Eurasian Eclipse: Japan's End Game in World War II," forthcoming.

30. National Archives, "Military Studies on Manchuria, 1952."

31. Pioneering research in Korean, Chinese, and Russian documentation on Kim's real background was done by Wada Haruki in the 1980s, but unfortunately his work is available only in Japanese and Korean. See Wada (1992), 41–2, 136–48, 245–54, 271–7. In English, see Armstrong (2003), 26–37; and Lankov (2002), 52–5.

32. As do ideologues here: thus Nicholas Eberstadt introduces Kim Il Sung as "this former Soviet Red Army officer" on page 1 of his book, *The End of North Korea* (American Enterprise Institute, 1999).

33. See the sources cited in Armstrong (2003), 39.

34. Lankov (2002), 57–8.

35. Ibid., 7–8, 59.

36. Kim's speech on February 8, 1948, is in *Choguk ŭi t'ongil tongnip kwa minjuhwa rŭl wihayŏ* (For the unification, independence, and democratization of the homeland) (P'yŏngyang: August 1949), 73–87.

37. See Kim Il's articles in *Nodong Sinmun* (Workers' Daily, NDSM), January 12 and January 19, 1950.

38. Kang Kŏn's article on the KPA is in *NDSM* (February 6, 1950); Ch'oe Yong-gŏn's was in ibid. (February 8, 1950); Ch'oe Hyŏn's, ibid. (January 20, 1950); Mu Chŏng's appeared on February 5, 1950. Other articles cited in the text came from *NDSM* in January and early February 1950. Kang Kŏn died in the Korean War fighting in September 1950. His obituary is in *NDSM* (September 11, 1950). His son was then reared in the Man'gyŏngdae School for Orphans of Patriots, and reportedly directed the 1983 terrorist attack on South Korean leaders in Rangoon, Burma.

39. Armstrong (2003), 228.

CHAPTER FOUR

1. Duncan, John, *The Origins of the Chosŏn Dynasty* (Seattle: University of Washington Press, 1998).

2. For a fuller discussion, see my *Korea's Place in the Sun: A Modern History* (New York: W. W. Norton, 1997), chs. 1, 3.

3. Yongho Ch'oe, Peter H. Lee, and William Theodore DeBary, eds., *Sources of Korean Tradition*, Volume II, *From the Sixteenth to the Twentieth Centuries* (New York: Columbia University Press, 2000), 157–61; also James B. Palais,

Confucian Statecraft and Korean Institutions: Yu Hyŏngwŏn and the Late Chosŏn Dynasty (Seattle: University of Washington Press, 1996), 208–73.

4. An American missionary quoted in Lee (1976), 15.
5. The best study in English on agrarian life in the DPRK is Lee (1976); for a full account of the land reform and cooperativization, see 17–48.
6. MacArthur Archives, Record Group 6, ATIS Issue no. 31, April 3, 1951, based on captured KWP records; National Archives, Record Group 242, SA2005, item 4/45, party identification sheets from Yŏngbyŏn County.
7. Data from RG242, courtesy Pang Sun-joo.
8. Merle Fainsod, *How Russia Is Ruled*, 211–3, 221.
9. See some handwritten personal statements from Ch'ŏlsan County in RG242, SA2006, item 6/20. One respondent says he "forgot to be politically conscious" and allowed his parents to arrange a marriage for him, "according to village custom" and without proper checking on the bride's "*sŏngbun*." Thus he ended up with Kim Suk-hyŏng of an unfortunate (i.e., high) class background.
10. Lee (1976), 72–3, 81.
11. Han (1999), 24.
12. See the account in Lee (1976), 133–5.
13. Lee (1976), 120.
14. Cornell (2002), 5.
15. Yang (1999), 657.
16. Cornell (2002), 13–4.
17. MacArthur Archives, RG6, box 17, "Communist Far Eastern Ring," February 6, 1948, enclosing an intercepted letter from Ms. Strong to Hugh Deane, August 15, 1947. Sad to say, she left out these criticisms in her pamphlet, *North Korea* (New York: 1947)
18. Harrison (2002), 30, 34.

19. Ibid., 31.

20. Holloway (2003), ch. 1, 3.

21. Ibid., ch. 2, 8.

22. Ibid., ch. 3, 6.

23. Quoted in Harrison (2002), 16.

24. Holloway (2003), ch. 5, 4.

25. Bruce McCall, "Wisest Owl of the Electronics Retailing Forest Tells More of the Nuclear-ance Sale," *New Yorker*.

26. Holloway (2003), ch. 14, 4.

27. Hunter (1999), 236.

28. Pierre Bourdieu, *Photography: A Middle-Brow Art*, trans. by Shaun Whiteside (Stanford: Stanford University Press, 1990) 7–8.

29. Gordon Chang, "Race and Civilization in the U.S.-Korean War of 1871," *Journal of American History* 89 no. 4 (March 2003): 1331–65.

30. This comes from *Nodong sinmun*, December 22, 1989, as translated by Korean Central News Agency, dispatch #7711 of the same date. Part of this discussion draws on my *War and Television* (New York and London: Verso and Visal Routledge, 1983).

31. Faw's report was on *CBS Nightly News*, July 24, 1989, and again the next day on *CBS This Morning*.

32. Thomas More, *Utopia*, ed. George M. Logan and Robert M. Adams (New York: Cambridge University Press, 1989), xii, 42–3.

33. Joan Robinson, "The North Korean Miracle," *Monthly Review* (May 1965). Che Guevara declared after his 1968 visit that the DPRK was precisely the model Cuba should follow.

34. Grinker (1998), 271.

35. Grinker (1998), 229–39. The numbers ran higher in the 1990s than before, but not by much: 64 from 1981 to 1990,

134 from 1991 to August 1996. On the comparatively small number of defectors over the years, see also Lankov (2002), viii.

36. Grinker (1998), 184–5.
37. Hwang (1989).

CHAPTER FIVE

1. Armstrong (2003), 145 n, 186–7.
2. Lankov (2002), 54–9.
3. Armstrong (2003), 93–5.
4. Lee (1976), 80–1. Instead of communist cells, the family was the basic "cell" (*sep'o*) or building block for society.
5. Michael Robinson, "National Identity and the Thought of Shin Ch'ae-ho: *Sadaejuŭi* and *Chuch'e* in History and Politics," *Journal of Korean Studies* 5 (1984).
6. Han S. Park, "The Nature and Evolution of Juche Ideology," in Park (1996), 12.
7. Victor Koschmann, *Revolution and Subjectivity in Postwar Japan* (Chicago: University of Chicago Press, 1996).
8. *The Great Teacher of Journalists* (Pyongyang: Foreign Languages Publishing House, 1983), 113.
9. Quoted in Nieman, *Evil in Modern Thought* (Princeton: Princeton University Press, 2002) 14; on *homo faber*, see Shlomo Avineri's excellent account in *The Political and Social Thought of Karl Marx*.
10. Walter Benjamin, *Illuminations*, ed. Hannah Arendt (New York: Schocken Books, 1969), 253.
11. My account is based on Li Nam Ok's memoir, *Breaking the Silence,* edited and introduced by Imogen O'Neill (forthcoming from Duke University Press); Harrison (2002), 39–40, 54–8; and various South Korean press accounts.

12. Harrison (2002), 57.
13. James Brooke, "North Koreans Celebrate Birthday of 'Dear Leader,' " *New York Times* (February 17, 2003), A7.
14. Lankov (2002), 72 n.
15. For a more detailed presentation, see Cumings, *Korea's Place in the Sun: A Modern History* (New York: W. W. Norton, 1997).
16. "Koreans United in Hatred of New Bond Flick," Reuters News Service (January 7, 2003).
17. These quotes were related by the highest defector ever to leave the North, Hwang Jang Yop, as cited in the *Chosun ilbo* (October 10, 1997).
18. "Aged Leaders around Kim," in Naewoe Press, *North Korea: Uneasy, Shaky Kim Jong-il Regime* (Seoul: ROK Government, 1997), 96–7. In 1997 the average age of the ten Politburo members besides Kim Jong Il was 74, and included octogenarian Manchurian guerrillas Pak Sŏng'ch'ŏl and Yi Chŏng-ok in the number two and three slots. The average age of eight Associate Members of the Politburo was 72, and the five top military leaders averaged 75 years of age. See also Buzo (2002), 126, 146.
19. *Nodong sinmun* (February 13, 1981); KCNA (February 16, 1981).
20. *Nodong sinmun* (February 4, 1981); KCNA (February 7, 1981).
21. "Party of the Motherly Image," *Korea Today* (P'yŏngyang, February 1987).
22. Quoted in Gale, *Korea: A History*, 109–10.
23. Armstrong (2003), 227. Kosawa's ideas are discussed in Peter N. Dale, *The Myth of Japanese Uniqueness* (New York: St. Martin's, 1986), 215.
24. Hunter (1999), 74–5.
25. Quoted in Harrison (2002), 18.

26. One hundred thousand is a figure that has been cited for decades; the presumable worst case would be put out by South Korean intelligence, which in 1995 found ten camps holding 150,000 people. Naewoe Press, *North Korea: The Land That Never Changes* (Seoul: ROK Government, 1995), 93.

27. Kang Chol-hwan and Pierre Rigoulot, *The Aquariums of Pyongyang: Ten Years in a North Korean Gulag*, trans. Yair Reiner (New York: Basic Books, 2001).

28. Kang (2001), 175–6.

CHAPTER SIX

1. *Beyond Good and Evil*, 185–86 n.

2. *Chicago Tribune* (September 17, 1997).

3. Korean Buddhist Savior Movement; the figures provided to me in September 1997.

4. Meredith Woo-Cumings, *The Political Ecology of Famine: The North Korean Catastrophe and Its Lessons* (Tokyo: Asian Development Bank Institute, 2001).

5. Oberdorfer (1997), 370.

6. Woo-Cumings (2001).

7. Ibid.

8. Nicholas Kristof, "A Ceremony in North Korea Breaks More Than Ground," *New York Times* (August 20, 1997).

9. Teresa Watanabe, "In North Korea, Resilience in the Face of Famine," *Los Angeles Times* (June 8, 1997).

10. Meredith Woo-Cumings (2001).

11. Ibid.

12. Bradley Babson, "Economic Cooperation on the Korean Peninsula," Working Paper, Task Force on U.S. Korea Policy (Washington, D.C.: Center for International Policy, and Chicago: Center for East Asian Studies, University of Chicago), January 9, 2003, 6–7.

13. See the map in Mark E. Manyin and Ryun Jun, "U.S. Assistance to North Korea," Congressional Research Service, Washington, D.C. (March 17, 2003), 13.

14. Unicef, "Child Nutrition Survey Shows Improvements in DPRK," Geneva (February 20, 2003).

15. Data from Mark E. Manyin and Ryun Jun (2003), 8–10.

16. Byung Chul Koh, "Is North Korea Changing?" Institute for Far Eastern Studies, Kyognam University, March 5, 2003.

17. "Don't Get Too Capitalist, Comrade," *Economist* (October 12, 2002).

18. See, for example, James William Morley, *Japan and Korea: America's Allies in the Pacific* (1965), 39–40, 52.

19. National Foreign Assessment Center, "Korea: The Economic Race between the North and the South," U.S. Central Intelligence Agency, January 1978.

20. Yang (1999), 337.

21. Eberstadt, *The End of North Korea* (Washington: American Enterprise Institute, 1999), 102–5.

22. Korean Central News Agency (July 9, 1998).

23. Kim Jong Il, "The 21st Century Is the Century of Great Change and Creation," *Nodong sinmun* (January 4, 2001). (The North calculated the new millennium to start in 2001, not 2000).

24. Harrison (2002), 36–7. The North pledged $2 billion in local currency to go with $300 million in foreign exchange needed for the project.

25. Ibid., 50–1.

26. Ibid., 38.

27. Ibid., 42.

28. Ibid., 39.

29. Ibid., 40, citing observations by a top Chinese expert on the North, and Erich Weingartner, who has been to the North many times on humanitarian missions.

30. "Combating Imperialist Ideology and Cultural Poisoning Called For," KCNA (June 1, 1999), reporting a joint article in the *Nodong Sinmun* (Worker's Daily) and *Kulloja* (The Worker), the two leading ideological organs.

31. Hunter (1999), 26–7.

32. Ibid., 146–51. She has a full price list of daily necessities on 147.

33. Ibid., 34.

34. Lee (1976), 130–1.

35. See his "The Coming Collapse of North Korea," *Wall Street Journal* (June 25, 1990).

36. Wolfowitz's statement came during his June 2003 visit to Seoul.

37. Naewoe Press, *North Korea: Uneasy, Shaky Kim Jong-il Regime* (Seoul: ROK Government, 1997), 143.

38. Hunter (1999), 3, 14.

39. According to a former student of mine, now serving in the military in Korea.

40. *Beyond the Shadow of Camptown* (New York: New York University Press, 2002).

41. A careful, sensitive treatment of this episode is available in Nancy Ablemann and John Lie, *Blue Dreams: Korean Americans and the Los Angeles Riots* (Cambridge, Mass.: Harvard University Press, 1995).

42. O'Rourke did a sort of racist potpourri/travelogue in *Rolling Stone* (October 1988), dwelling (for example) on Korean facial features that he found outlandish. After Buruma visited Korea's Independence Hall (which commemorates the resistance to Japanese imperialism in 1919), he asked if his "revulsion" against Korean nationalism was "a sign of decadence," or is there something "to the idea of the rise and fall of national, even racial vigor?" See Ian Buruma, "Jingo Olympics," *New York Review of Books* (November 10, 1988).

43. Wickham's comment and the widespread "sentiment" are both found in Oberdorfer (1997), 79, 132.

44. These last three statements encapsulate American diplomacy at the time of the Japanese annexation in 1910 (the United States was the first major power to remove its legation from Seoul), at the end of the colonial period in 1945 (when this idea was reflected in Roosevelt's trusteeship policy), and in 1995 (when Secretary of State George Shultz infuriated Koreans with words to this effect). The other statements I have heard many times; they often appear in the American press, and, to my chagrin, are things I have sometimes said myself over the years.

45. Trinh T. Minh-Ha, "White Spring," in *The Dream of the Audience: Theresa Hak Kyung Cha (1951–1982)*, ed. Constance M. Llewallen (Berkeley: University of California Press, 2001), 38, 105.

46. David Theo Goldberg, *Racist Culture: Philosophy and the Politics of Meaning* (Cambridge, Mass.: Blackwell, 1993), 6–7, 150–1.

47. Alan Cowell, "Ashcroft Soaks Up a World of Complaints," *New York Times* (January 25, 2003), A8.

48. Susan Nieman, *Evil in Modern Thought* (Princeton, N.J.: Princeton University Press, 2002), 3–4, 281–8.

49. Alford (1999), 1.

50. Ibid., 89.

51. Press Release, DPRK Mission to the UN (February 1, 1994), no. 4.

52. Quoted in Harrison (2002), 3.